GROUND ZERO

BEHIND THE SCENES

10-YEAR ANNIVERSARY EDITION

World Trade Center September 11, 2001
A Collection of Personal Accounts

God Bless You

Michael Bellone

:: Never Forget

GROUND ZERO

BEHIND THE SCENES

10-YEAR ANNIVERSARY EDITION

World Trade Center September 11, 2001
A Collection of Personal Accounts

By

Michael Bellone and Robert Barrett

With

Kelly A. Cox, FF Kenny Escoffey, FF George Kozlowski, FF Bob Humphrey, Capt. John Viola, FF Tom Fenech, PD Lt. Cluadio Fernandez, FF Lou Chinel, FF Jim Cody, FF Nick DeMasi, Deputy Chief Jim Riches, FF Tim Lapinski, FF Mike LaRosa, Chief Dave Dean, Ralph Shakarian, Eric Joyner, Julie Bellone, Pepper Burruss, Dennis Fisin, Vincent LaVien, The Rev. Mitties DeChamplain Ph.d., Jiri Boudnik, Solange (Hollywood) Schwalbe, Debbie Zimm, Nicholas Gallo, Jan Snyder, Frank Silecchia, Noah Silecchia, Justine Schiano-Romano, Stephen P. Porter, Sam Elijah, Kathy Barrett, Rob Miller.

Ground Zero September 11, 2001

Co-contributors: Doug Ewell and Gail Swanson

Edited by: Robert S. Nahas and Helyn Dunn of Writer Services, LLC

Cover Design and Book Layout by: Writer Services, LLC (www.WriterServices.net)

ISBN: 978-0-9800705-4-5

Published by
Prominent Books, LLC
Clearwater, FL USA
www.ProminentBooks.com

Printed and bound in the United States of America.

Office papers from the twin towers strewn on the streets

FACT SHEET

U.S. Department of State
Washington, DC
August 15, 2002

September 11, 2001 Chronology

Victims came from more than 90 countries around the world.

Within 45 minutes before the north and south towers collapsed, approximately 35,000 people were evacuated, had escaped, or were rescued.

The following members of the government/municipal services were killed:

343 Firefighters

37 Port Authority Police Officers

23 NYPD Officers

6 EMS

3 Court Officers

1 Secret Service Agent

1 FBI Agent

The following are the number of people who died at each site:

World Trade Center 2,823 (includes airline passengers)

Pentagon   125 (not including plane victims)

Flight 11	92 people on board
FLight 175	64 people on board
Flight 77	64 people on board
Flight 93	44 people on board

8:46 AM   Plane crashes into the north tower of the World Trade Center.

9:03 AM   Plane crashes into the south tower of the World Trade Center.

9:17 AM   The Federal Aviation Administration (FAA) shuts down all New York City area airports.

9:21 AM	The Federal Aviation Administration (FAA) halts all flights at U.S. airports. It is the first time in history that air traffic has been halted nationwide.
9:38 AM	Plane crashes into the Pentagon. Evacuation begins immediately.
9:45 AM	The White House evacuates.
10:05 AM	The south tower of the World Trade Center collapses.
10:10 AM	A portion of the Pentagon collapses.
10:10 AM	Plane crashes in Somerset County, Pennsylvania.
10:22 AM	The State and Justice Departments, as well as the World Bank are evacuated.
10:28 AM	The World Trade Center's north tower collapses.
10:45 AM	All federal office buildings in Washington, D.C. are evacuated.
1:44 PM	Five warships and two aircraft carriers are ordered to leave the U.S. Naval Station in Norfolk, Virginia to protect the East Coast.
4:10 PM	Building 7 of the World Trade Center collapses.

Source: Web Site, U.S. Department of State, Washington, DC, August 15, 2002

Mike Bellone
Honorary Firefighter, Ladder Co. 20
Fire Department City of New York

While watching the motion picture movie , The Blind Side, the main characters talk about a poem written by Albert Lord Tennison, "Charge of the Light Brigade". They changed the text of this poem to describe the LSU college football team in comparison to the soldiers of war, the playing field to the battlefield, and so on.

As my mind and imagination started to shift into overtime, with pen in hand, we now have another comparison born. The soldiers to the responders, the battlefield to the World Trade Center, and so on.

This is how I have lived my life for the last ten years. Associating every book, movie, event and anything and everything I do to Ground Zero.

Charge of the Fire Brigade

Half a league half a league,
Half a league onward,
All in the tower of Death
Ran the six hundred:
'Forward, the Fire Brigade!
Charge for the fire he said:
Into the Tower of Death
Ran the six hundred.

'Forward , the Fire Brigade!'
Was there a man dismay'd ?
Not tho' the Responder knew
Some one had blunder'd:
Theirs not to make reply,
Theirs not to reason why,
Theirs but to do & die,
Into the Tower of Death
Ran the six hundred.

Fire to the right of them,
Fire to the left of them,
Fire in front of them
Volley'd & thunder'd;
Storm'd at with heat and
Boldly they protect and serve
Into the Tower of Death,
Into the Mouth of Hell
Ran the six hundred.

Flash'd all their tools bare,
Flash'd as they turn'd in air
Sabring the collapsing there,
Charging a hell while
All the world wonder'd:
Plunged in the debris & smoke
Right thro' the line they broke;
Fire and Heat
Reel'd from the battered tower
Shatter'd & sunder'd
Then they ran back, but not
Not the six hundred.

When can their glory fade?
O the wild charge they made!
All the world wonder'd
Honour the charge they made!
Hounour the Fire Brigade,
Noble six hundred!

TABLE OF CONTENTS

ACKNOWLEDGEMENTS

FF Jimmy Cody, FF John Masera, FF Michael LaRosa, FF Bob Barrett, Rev Mitties DeChamplain, Chaplain Chris Keenan, The Firefighters and officers of Ladder Co. 20 F.D.N.Y., Robert Crawford, Vincent LaVien, Joy Carol, Carmine Gallo, Nicholas Gallo, Forte Pizzimenti, Kathy Sheley, The Family of Brian and Jodi Sheley, Linda and Weldon Lawrence, Nicholas Bellone, Joseph Bellone, Gary Suson and the Ground Zero Mueseum Workshop, Camile Basil, Chief Dave Dean, Solange of Hollywood, Frank and Noah Siliccia, Wendi Keenan, John Keenan, Wendi and the staff of Staples in Geneva N.Y., Doug Ewell Jr.

St. Paul's Chapel – May 30, 2002, 7 a.m ... Last Truck Day... A Man on His Knees
Honoring the Sacrifice

May 30, 2002, St. Paul's Chapel—John Masera preying for hope. This painting was done by artist, Janet A. Stevens

DEDICATION

In loving memory of the 343 firefighters who perished that day and all those who died on September 11, 2001.

Michael Bellone

I dedicate this book to my mother and father, Christina Bellone and Alfonso Bellone who were always there for me no matter what the circumstances, and taught me the meaning of love and respect. To my children Meaghan, Maura, and Patrick Bellone, who have given me a whole new outlook on what life is really about and I wish to spend every moment with them. To my wife, Julie, my soulmate, who after all this time taught me the meaning of unconditional love and support. To all the children in the world who leave small footprints with their huge hearts who place their trust in us. God bless them.

Bob Barrett

This book is dedicated to those people most important in my life, Mom and Dad, Mary Barrett and Thomas Barrett, who instilled in me everything good that I have learned in life. To Kathy Barrett my devoted wife for over 30 years. I was half until she completed me. To my children, Tommy, Simone, and Kari who gave me a purpose for being. To Dave LaForge, John Burnside, John Fischer, Jimmy Gray, Sean Hanley, Bob Linnane, and Bobby McMahon. To their loving wives, parents, and children. To all the children, whose support, prayers, and innocence motivated me after 9/11, and will continue to do so for the rest of my life. God Bless them all.

Note to Readers

The contents of this book may be disturbing.
Parental Guidance is <u>strongly</u> suggested, please.

Cutting a steel beam

FOREWORD

Captain John Viola
Ladder 15 FDNY

It is my pleasure to introduce these profound stories of the men and women who were at Ground Zero in the moments and months following the devastation that occurred on September 11, 2001. Their personal accounts of this event are the most intimate, detailed experiences of 9/11 ever revealed.

In this book, Honorary Firefighter Mike Bellone and Firefighter Bob Barrett share not only their own moving experiences, but the experiences of so many others who were on the scene—the volunteers, the firefighters, emergency personnel and the friends and families of those we lost . . . to all of them we owe this poignant tribute.

In the unreserved pages that follow you will hear, firsthand, how these courageous individuals committed themselves in a selfless endeavor to assist those less fortunate. The outpouring of empathy and help received from people around the world who came together in this difficult time is a testimony to the human condition and an inspiration to myself and my brother firefighters. Amidst the stories in this book is also the most comprehensive collection of photographs of this attack—and its aftermath—ever compiled into one publication.

The 9/11 attacks had obvious, immediate and overwhelming effects upon Americans. Hundreds of police officers and rescue workers across the country took leaves of absence to travel to Manhattan in order to assist in the process of recovering bodies from the twisted remnants of the Twin Towers. Over 3,000 children were left without one or more of their parents. And for the first time in history, an "Air Traffic Control Zero" condition was invoked, closing all airspace and thereby forcing all non-emergency civilian aircraft in the United States, and several other countries, to be immediately grounded, stranding tens of thousands of passengers worldwide.

The thousands of tons of toxic debris resulting from the collapse of the Twin Towers contained more than 2,500 contaminants, including several known cancer-causing agents. This has led to many debilitating illnesses and deaths among rescue and recovery workers. Mike Bellone tells of his own exposure to many of these chemicals and how he took measures to detoxify his body.

We were all subjected to the rampant and ruthless news reports, overlapping and repeating for days and weeks on end; the gruesome images, the resulting fear and panic of the masses . . . But what many of us didn't get to see were the acts of courage that were taking place behind the scenes, twenty-four hours a day, seven days a week—the men and women who were there with relief efforts, the "ordinary heroes" as this book depicts them.

Mike and Bob put their own lives on the line, along with the many other volunteers who cared enough to want to help. They lived and breathed Ground Zero for nine months. Now you can be there with them—until the cutting of "the last beam"—the chapter in which these extraordinary individuals try to come to terms with the last day of their relief efforts . . . the last day to find some remnant to return to a family member . . . the last day to share a world with their "Ground Zero family"—a world that no one else could possibly understand. It is to these people, and all who dedicated their lives to the recovery efforts at Ground Zero, that my hat is off. The emptiness of the lower Manhattan skyline will always be sadly evident, but your dedication fills that void for all of us and replaces the emptiness with encouragement and hope for the future.

I invite you now to cross the threshold with Mike and Bob into the heart of Ground Zero, for this truly is a behind the scenes account that will reveal the courage, the resolve and the humanity of the story behind the story.

Captain John Viola, Ladder Company 15

John Viola is a retired F.D.N.Y. Captain. He served for 28 years. On Sept 11, 2001, he was serving as Company Commander for Ladder 15 in lower Manhattan. On that day, 14 brave young men from his firehouse lost their lives. Since his retirement he has served with H.E.A.R.T. 9/11 as a member of the Executive Board and has been Project Manager on all of their responses throughout the United States and Haiti.

INTRODUCTION

Michael Bellone
Honorary Firefighter, Ladder Co. 20
Fire Department City of New York

I wanted to let people know that you don't have to be a "somebody" in order to make a difference. There are so many ordinary people in this world who go unnoticed every day. Maybe once in a while we should learn that there's a "somebody" in everyone. I stayed down at Ground Zero for 257 straight days during some of the darkest times in my personal life, because it was something that affected me. I felt the need to help those who needed my help. It became infectious for me to be there for anyone and to respond to any call of duty. I was honored for being accepted into the tight brotherhood of FDNY firefighters as "one of their own" and work side-by-side with them through their most difficult times. These stories are not just about individual achievements; it's about stepping up to the plate as a team. It's only because of each other that it was possible to do what needed to be done in order to recover so many who died that day and return them to their families.

Robert Barrett
Retired Firefighter, Ladder Co. 20
Fire Department City of New York

I wonder just how much of what happened that day might be remembered in the future. I know my father told me stories about the depression and World War II. I don't believe I ever totally grasped what he was saying until now. I am most curious if what happened on 9/11 will have an effect on anyone except those who were actually there? Will all the rest simply pay a brief homage to this event or will this experience actually stand as a glowing example of how precious we are to one another? For myself, life can never be the same. There is no going backward for me. I can only hope that I can translate what I feel and express it to those around me. I only wish I could find the words that would make the reader stop and say, "I know exactly what he's saying." If that is not to be, nevertheless, I must try to express what I feel, that which is covered in the vague images in my mind.

Gail Swanson

I met Mike Bellone and Bob Barrett March 2003 in Naples, Florida. They were giving an educational presentation about Ground Zero. Because of what they experienced during Ground Zero, Mike Bellone founded TRAC Team, Trauma Response Assistance for Children. All across the country Mike and Bob give educational presentations to schools, organizations, firehouses, hospitals, emergency services, and more.

I went to Mike and Bob's presentation to learn, not to write. In addition to the educational aspect, the reaction to those around me was really indescribable. How do you describe families, people, and children who can actually talk to someone who worked at Ground Zero, who searched for their loved ones, and probably found them?

343 firefighters lost on September 11, 2001

Throughout their week in Florida, Mike and Bob told me about the recovery operation and how they helped recover hundreds of the victims.

I told Mike and Bob, "People need to know this. We all need to know what happened inside Ground Zero."

I had never been to New York, and all I knew about Ground Zero was what I saw on television or read in the newspapers. I did not jump at the chance to do this book. I thought long and hard about it and prayed about it.

I felt compelled to help Mike and Bob document what they had experienced. But was I the one to do it? The first thing I asked God was, "Are you sure you know what you're doing?" I told him I know nothing about New York, firemen, or recovery operations.

The last thing I wanted to do was to hurt anybody by writing down the stories. I thought of the victims and their families. But it was when Mike put a small piece of steel in my hand, cut from a beam from Ground Zero, that I crumbled.

I told Mike and Bob, "It feels like I'm holding something Holy."

I was.

I told God, "Okay, I'll do it, but I'm not doing this without you."

Not wanting to hurt people continually weighed heavily on me throughout the book. Most of the time when something devastating happens, the public isn't really told exactly what happened.

It was one o'clock in the morning when I finished interviewing Frank Silecchia at the TRAC Team office. I was alone in a side office, and Frank's 12-year-old son Noah came in.

I asked Noah, "Aren't you tired?"

He said, "No. Can I talk to you?

I said, "Sure, come on in.

He asked, "Do you think it'd be all right if I talked to you like my dad talked to you? But I don't want to hurt you by telling you… you know… exactly what I saw."

I said, "Noah, it's okay. I'll be all right. I want to hear what you have to say."

World Trade Center

After a few minutes, I said, "I'm just going to start typing while we talk, and you and your dad can decide afterwards if you want other people to know."

Noah talked, and I typed.

He stopped in the middle of a sentence and said, "I can't believe you're listening to me talk about this. People don't want me talk to about it except my dad."

I said, "Noah, what you're telling me is important. It can help teach others."

Noah was very intense, looked me straight in the eye and said, "People need to know what happened at Ground Zero. We can't let them forget."

We're all listening now, Noah.

The only way to do the book was to follow the truth. To let the people I interviewed say what they wanted to without my digging inside of them and creating more pain. The reason they decided to share their experiences is because of the bond of friendship they have with Mike and Bob. They also wanted to document what happened during the recoveries for the sake of history, themselves, and their families.

Something happened at Ground Zero. If we weren't there, we cannot know. This is a glimpse into what occurred. It was almost as though those who were at Ground Zero experienced a battle of hell and heaven at the same time, and went through it with each other. If they meet on the street and identify themselves as "I was at Ground Zero," they give a nod, and nothing else needs to be said. These people held onto each other, depended upon each other, and "love overcame evil," as Chaplain Mitties describes.

World Trade Center at dusk

Many of the events happened simultaneously. The book is written through personal interviews and is told first-person. The person speaking is identified by the appearance of their name. The style is casual, as though you were sitting across the kitchen table with them.

The information in this book was obtained 23 months after September 11, 2001 from individuals who to the best of their knowledge have given an eyewitness account.

Please be respectful of those who have given these interviews and realize that these are very private moments for them. Those wishing to contact anyone in this book please do so through TRAC Team.

My dedication to this book is to the September 11th victims, their families, and friends. To Mike and Bob and everyone who helped at Ground Zero, especially the members of the Fire Department City of New York. To Dennis Fisin who fed 5,000. To those who allowed us to use their photographs in the book, it is greatly appreciated. While Mike did bring photographers into the site in order to be able to have copies and be able to use the photographs later, as of going to press, agreements have not been reached. To Daryl, thank you for your support and understanding why I had to do this. And to my darling daughter Jessica, who was away at college at the time, I told her, "I am so very, very sorry that you had to see this happen in our country. You're safer where you are, than where we are. If they strike again, we will drive north to you." May you and all of our children and their children never experience this again. May God Bless America.

World Trade Center

This book was written while listening to Mass in B Minor, Martin Pearlman, Boston Baroque. It is my honor and privilege to have been given the opportunity to record just a few of the stories, out of the so many, from those involved in 9/11, who helped keep our country together during our time of need.

Contributions to this book go toward helping to fund TRAC Team's ongoing efforts to help educate the public about 9/11.

A view from front door, straight up

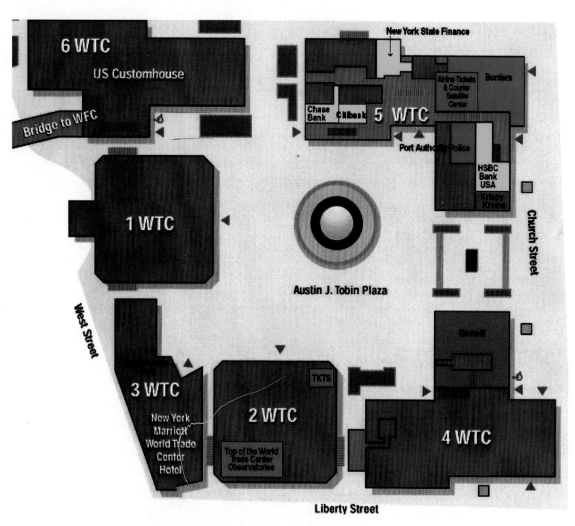

World Trade Center Map

WTC Site
Emergency Evacuation Route

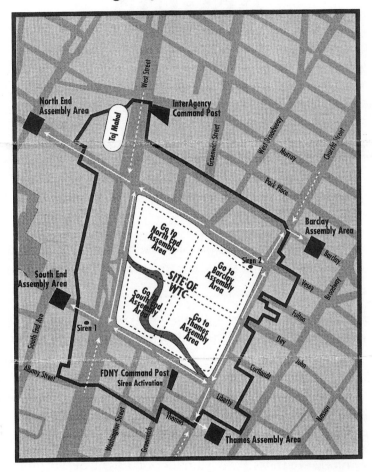

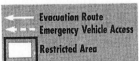

- Personnel should proceed to the closest Assembly Area following the routes marked on the map.
- Personnel shall remain at Assembly Areas until further instructions are received from the Incident Commander.
- Emergency vehicles will be coming in via Church and West—Keep these roads clear.

CHAPTER 1
TAKEOFF: THE TIMELINE BEGINS

Kelly A. Cox
Base Manager Flight Service
Logan Airport
Boston, Massachusetts

September 11, 2001 – One individual's story

How this terrible tragedy brought two people together in the crossroads and intersection of human connection, which helped shape and share the common threads and the amazing ability to help each other heal.

When Mike called me a few months ago and asked me if I would consider writing a piece for his new book about 9/11 and how we met and what has happened over the last 10 years – I was taken back. It was a surprise and my initial thought and feeling was how the heck he could even be thinking about me when he himself has so much to share beyond anyone else. What he went through and what he deals with day to day is more than anyone I know could endure, and yet, his outlook, attitude and incredible determination outweigh all the tough physical, emotional and spiritual pain that he and so many others deal with.

Here is my story on 9/11. I was Base Manager of Flight Service for American Airlines in Boston, a position that I held since late Fall 1995. I've since shared with many, that even though I was in this job the longest than any other in my 24 years at American, it was like working 3 different positions: (1) pre-9/11, with lots to learn starting in a new department as complex and dynamic as Flight Service; (2) 9/11, with a myriad of never before historical crisis response handling; (3) post-9/11, with the fallout of a changed business world and acceptance of trying to "move on" and to balance the personal and professional opposing forces.

It was a beautiful Fall day, sun shining, and I awoke with eager anticipation for a lovely day. I had spent the evening before with Susan, who was dealing with her own family situation with her mother's health issues that had caused her great concern. We hadn't known each other that long, but I wanted to be supportive. So I had her over for dinner and we had a really nice evening together. I felt good being there and she appreciated it, too.

As I was leaving to head out to work, my phone started to ring and the beeper was going off. I picked up the phone and it was Jim (a special assignment flight attendant who was working as my staff assistant). He was telling me that something bad was going wrong on our flight (AA#11) to L.A. He told me one of the flight attendants (learned it was Amy Sweeney) called into the Flight Service office and said there was a stabbing onboard and that he turned the phone call over to one of the Flight Service Managers that was in the office, all the while talking with me. My immediate thought was some crazy air rage guy went off his rocker and I already knew that a stabbing onboard was going to be a very involved situation and that I hoped whoever was stabbed was going to make it. I remember pounding my first into the

Take-off from Boeing 757

kitchen counter saying something like, "How the hell did he bring a knife onboard??" Susan looked at me and knew something was very wrong. I immediately said I have to go quickly to the airport. Jim also mentioned that other flight attendants were injured, too. I told him to "page" all the managers as this was an emergency. I also remembered that half of them were in Dallas for training. I told him to call every one of the staff that was local and to get into the office/airport as quickly as possible. He sensed from my tone that this was serious. I don't think at this point he even processed what information was being shared with him. But I knew from my crisis response experience that this would be big. However, it wasn't until I got into my car and called SOC that I knew the gravity of the situation.

I lived just a short distance to the airport (a few miles) and there was no traffic, but the ride there took forever. I called SOC from my cell phone and told them who I was (a lot of new people since my CARE days) and that there had been a stabbing. They said they knew. Another flight attendant, Betty Ong, I later learned had called into the reservation line for onboard situations and the call got transferred to SOC. They got a lot of details from Betty and also what our Boston Flight Service office had provided from their conversations with Amy Sweeney.

In the short ride to the airport, this went from what I thought was an air rage stabbing to a highjacking, to the plane hitting the World Trade Center. It was surreal. I couldn't absorb it. Especially since I drove fast into the airport, bypassing the employee lot – right into the curbside parking telling the attendant I had an emergency and showed my AA ID. He let me in, not knowing anything about what had just happened. I ran into the terminal and people were not informed at that point. They were walking about like everything was ok. I ran downstairs to my office area where Flight Service is located. Flight attendants were gathered around our office area – they knew. Unlike all the passengers upstairs in the Terminal – our people knew. I told employees to call their families to let them know they were okay and then I sent one of the managers to get Father Rich. I realized that half my staff was in Dallas and so were some of the union reps. Our General Manager (GM) of the station was out of town. I went back upstairs to see what was going on and went into the GM's conference room where several of the local managers were already listening in on the system-wide SOC conference call.

We knew at that point that #11 had hit and then we could hear people at SOC talking about other missing flights and another one "hitting". Our Flight #77 was thought to be the second plane into the World Trade Center, but later learned it hit the Pentagon. It was surreal and felt like Armageddon. All these planes from all different airlines missing, hitting and not knowing exactly what was happening. I took only a brief second to absorb the information shed a tear and realized I needed to "kick into gear" and start helping the flight attendants' families. That was my responsibility – I was in charge of Flight Service and the flight attendants on #11 were my crew.

When the FAA shut down the air traffic control system, they wanted to divert a lot of the European flights to Boston, as we were the closet point, but I strongly urged them to go elsewhere, knowing we would have a full plate of activities with the Flight #11 response. Things pretty much took care of themselves on this as the whole U.S. shut down and our planes were diverted to Canada and elsewhere. Sadly, our own Boston crew members were stuck elsewhere and called despite being able to get home to their families. Since half our office staff was in Dallas, I asked our VP of Flight Service, Jane Allen, to do everything possible to get our managers and union reps home. She worked all day to get clearances and we were able to bring them home around midnight on a special charter. It was the only plane to land at Logan that day.

Once I made sure our employees at base were safe and secure, I started the process of calling the flight attendants' families. In my mind, it was not to give death notification, but rather "notification" that their loved one was in fact part of the crew and that once we knew more I'd be in touch and also provided them my contact info should they want to call me. I knew from other aviation accidents, that there is always a chance of survivors. While I didn't verbalize that to the family members, I did in fact think it. I hadn't seen any of the coverage on TV, so I thought all day and into the night that it was possible. I needed to believe. Half of the families that I called already knew their loved one was onboard and the other half did not. Each and every call was incredibly emotional and difficult. I had to take a few minutes between each one to muster enough strength to continue.

Somewhere in the earlier hours that morning, one of my managers was sent to get Father Rich. This was before we knew of the United planes and the overall situation. He was there right away providing comfort to our crew members in the office and lounge area. Not long after, the FBI labeled the airport as a crime scene and everyone, including passengers and non-essential employees, had to leave the terminal. In a strange way, this actually helped us in Flight Service, as we had no other distraction from responding to and assisting the flight attendants and their families.

We created a hotline, recorded message with updates, and as the days followed, the crew members at the base needed a place to gather to obtain information and be with each other. The Hilton Hotel at the airport became that place. We had the United employees gathering as well. Since the airport was a crime scene and there were no flights, we would do the family assistance and operations tasks while at the airport and then I'd go over to the hotel and provide updates as best I could. By the second and third day, we also had our CARE team members in place and they, too, set up a Command Center at the Hilton. Of course, my focus was on the crew members' families and the local flight attendants – but we also had out of

Logan Airport—Boston, Massachusetts

town crew members "stuck in" Boston at three different area crew layover hotels. So I went with our Domestic APFA Chair to each of these hotels to provide an update on the situation. It was ever-changing and it was extremely difficult, as you might imagine.

There are so many more details that I will ultimately outline in another publication, but the scope and magnitude of what we were dealing with in the hours, days and weeks into the tragedy were monumental to say the least. Handling the families, loved ones, co-workers, friends and the operation proved to be quite challenging. Many of the managers and I attended the individual funeral services as they were planned. Our lives, our jobs, our profession, our industry and our world had completely changed. It would never be the same.

We held a private Boston employee remembrance in the aircraft hangar a few months later and invited the families. We presented an Alabaster Eagle with their wings and names engraved and it was the highest honor we could bestow on these heroes' families. It was their brave, calm handling of the crisis that provided key pieces of information to us and the authorities. Without their help and info we never would have known what they did and would not have been able to respond to the other flights as quickly.

There are other details and pieces of this unprecedented event that I can honestly say that no preparation or procedure would have covered it adequately. However, the CARE training and my accident response experience uniquely positioned me to be able to respond in a way that no other person would have been able to do. To me that was the fateful interaction of what was meant to be. I was placed in the unique position to be able to respond to this catastrophic event. I say this in the most spiritual way possible. No matter if you believe in God, a Higher Power, or something else great than ourselves, it wasn't "me" responding, but a higher being that allowed me to be the vehicle to respond. I truly and absolutely believe this. That's why I outlined all the previous reasons as to why I was where I was that day.

I will always be grateful for the crew's collective response during this historic tragedy. My heartfelt gratitude, appreciation and admiration to: Captain John Ogonowski, First Officer Thomas McGuinness, Flight Attendants – Bobbi Arestegui, Jeff Collman, Sara Low, Karen Martin, Kathy Nicosia, Betty Ong, Jean Roger´, Dianne Snyder and Amy Sweeney. You were and are our heroes. You will never be forgotten, nor will your colleagues from AA#77, UA#175 and UA#93 and all those that perished that tragic day.

So as I review the path that lead me to Mike and 9/11 – I can only conclude that I was meant to be exactly where I was that fateful day – just like Mike. We are two individuals that were placed in the roles we were in and then later to meet and become friends. Whether you are religious, spiritual or somewhere in between – this was meant to be our connection. We saw the worst in humanity that day and also since, but the overwhelming message I'd like to share is that I also saw the very best in humanity and that was, and is, more powerful than what some people tried to take from us that day. We are resilient people and always rise above tough and difficult circumstances and that's what we must remember. Our collective strength and spirit is what represents those we lost that day and since. To honor and remember those lost souls is what we are to do and must do.

CHAPTER 2
TOTAL RECALL

Mike Bellone
Honorary Firefighter, Ladder Co. 20
Fire Department City of New York

I was home sleeping after working a night shift. I had just fallen asleep when the phone rang. A friend asked, "Do you know what's going on?"

I said, "No, I just fell asleep."

They said, "There's just been an accident at the World Trade Center, and they're looking for help."

I turned on the TV and on the bottom of the screen I saw a Total Recall, a notice that said, "Anyone with medical experience report to the World Trade Center area."

I'm Red Cross Certified in First Aid, CPR, with some medical background from college. Not to waste any time, I put on the same clothes I had just taken off and headed down. On the way I encountered heavy standstill traffic and noticed a fire truck from my neighborhood in my rear view mirror. I knew some of the men, and said, "I'm headed down there, too."

They said, "Hop on."

From the FDR Drive (Franklin D. Roosevelt East River Drive) southbound

40

7th Ave South, Southbound

While we were driving down the Gowanus Expressway toward the Brooklyn Battery Tunnel we could see the two towers with heavy smoke rising from the upper floors. It was a beautiful, sunny, clear, warm morning as we approached the entrance to the Brooklyn Battery Tunnel. The traffic was unbearable but the chauffer, the driver of the fire truck, made his way to the Manhattan side of the tunnel. We then encountered a landscape of what was an unimaginable disaster.

It was dark, extremely hot, papers flying, and debris everywhere. I immediately smelled different toxins in the air. As I looked for those two burning towers, I realized they no longer stood there. I had used the towers as a guide to let me know where I was standing in the city and now my guide was lost. I felt like a blind person whose furniture had just been rearranged.

As I made my way down Trinity Street, I heard a paramedic say that as he got closer to the site he heard car alarms going off. I knew they weren't car alarms. They sounded more like Scott bottles. Scott bottles are the oxygen bottles firefighters carry on their backs. If a firefighter doesn't move for 30 seconds, the sensors on the bottles detect stillness and start to chirp. This helps notify the other men that a man might be down or injured. There had to be *hundreds* of chirps. And then the reality set in. I was witnessing nothing less than a disaster.

Beneath the North Bridge on West Street

I told myself, "This can't be the same place."

I was completely disoriented. On one side of the tunnel it had been 80 degrees and a nice day. On the other side, I was in the middle of 110-degree hell. Smoke was hovering over Manhattan. The hijacked American Airlines Flight 11 had blown out all four walls in the north tower's 94th floor and created an air pocket. The air pocket allowed oxygen to get in and the heat was over 2,000 degrees, enough to melt steel.

I was looking underneath battered vehicles and doorways for someone to rescue. Dozens of hospital workers, paramedics, doctors, and nurses were standing by with empty stretchers. You could see the frustration in their faces, but there was no one to help. I just wanted to find one person to bring to those stretchers, but that wasn't going to happen.

I came across the group of firemen I came in with, and they said, "Mike, what we really need you to do since you're a big guy, is to help us lift some of these girders and beams so that we can get the trapped bodies out."

As the men gathered together I noticed a man in shorts and sneakers. He looked like he was lost. I said to him, "Hey, you okay, buddy?"

He replied, "I'm looking for my company of men. I'm a fireman."

I told him, "I'm a medic, and I'll help you."

That was the beginning of a day that never ended. The man in the shorts and sneakers was firefighter Bob Barrett. He was looking for people to rescue and for his men of Ladder 20.

I said, "Bob, the best way to do this is to start at the beginning and work our way in."

Plane fuselage on West Street before the towers collapsed

Bob Barrett
Retired Firefighter, Ladder Co. 20
Fire Department City of New York

The first plane flew by my firehouse, Ladder 20, in Lower Manhattan. The members were standing out in front. It was during the change of tours. The night tour was getting off and the day tour was coming on. A plane flew right overhead. They immediately realized something was wrong. This was not the normal flight pattern for a jumbo jet flying low and down Lafayette Street.

When they all heard the bang, the fire chief told the men to respond. "Don't wait to be called, go see who you can help."

It was my day off. I was home at the time, and I had just driven my wife Kathy to work. We live in Brooklyn, and on a normal day I'm about 30 minutes from my firehouse in Manhattan.

She called me from work, and asked, "Bob, do you know what's going on?"

I said, "No."

She said, "Turn on the TV."

I put on the TV and saw that the first plane had hit the World Trade Center's north tower. I called my firehouse. Someone picked up the phone. I asked, already knowing in my heart, if my company was at the towers.

Building 5 starting to burn up

The answer was, of course, "Yes."

I felt like a parent might feel when their children aren't home. I worried for my brother firefighters.

I left my house and reported to the nearest firehouse in Marine Park Brooklyn on Flatbush Avenue. Many firefighters reported to that firehouse. We took over a city bus and had the bus driver head for Manhattan. Getting there was not easy. All of the bridges were filled with people evacuating the city. The tunnels were filled with abandoned cars and people doing their best to get away from the horror.

Corner of Vesey and Church Street

Church Street

Corner of Vesey and Church Street

Washington Street

As I approached the site at 11:00 a.m. that morning, what I saw resembled nothing of what I can remember from my 28 years as a firefighter in Lower Manhattan. This was a new place, almost a new planet, and I had never been there before.

During that first search for survivors I met several firefighters from my battalion who told me who was working in my company that day. My best friend Dave LaForge was one of them. Dave was the chauffeur. He drove the front of the fire truck and I was normally his tiller-man steering the back. Usually during any month period there is only one day when the two of us didn't work together. September 11th was one of them.

That day, my company went into the World Trade Center to attack a fire. When you're a fireman, you have to be aggressive. You have to attack the fire in order to put it out. You can't lie back in the fire being meek, that's the worst thing you can do. You have to show the fire who's the boss, and the fire has to be put out and put out fast.

Once you lose the room, you lose the apartment. Once you lose the apartment, you lose the hall. Once you lose the hall, you lose the entire floor. Once you lose the floor, you're in risk of losing the entire building. That's why you can't back out and give up anything to the fire. You attack it and keep it from going anywhere. My company ran up the stairs of the north tower. They were seen on the 42nd floor.

I lost my best friend Dave LaForge on September 11th, and I met Mike Bellone that morning. We were both searching for someone to rescue. Mike and I started searching the rubble together. We kept searching for any sign of injured people and found none.

Cortland Street and Church Street

CHAPTER 3
WTC NORTH TOWER

Kenny Escoffery
Firefighter, Ladder Co. 20
Fire Department City of New York

I was scheduled to work on my wedding anniversary, September 10th. I didn't want to ask my mutual partner to switch days, meaning I'd work the 11th instead. So, I told my wife, "I'll work on our anniversary, and we'll celebrate the next day."

The morning of September 11th, George and I had just come off the night tour and were getting ready to leave. Some of the guys were standing out in front of Ladder 20 during the change of tours. In front of the firehouse, the plane came in so low that the guys watched the plane's belly lights as it flew by. The next thing, we heard an explosion. The company was turned out. It didn't wait for the call. They got on the rig and went in the direction of the World Trade Center.

George Kozlowski
Firefighter, Ladder Co. 20
Fire Department City of New York

It was a typical morning at the firehouse. I was in the kitchen b.s.'ing with the guys over coffee and cereal. It was 8:25, 8:30 in the morning. I had just said to John, John Burnside, "Want to take the back?"

He said, "Yeah, yeah, I got you," which means he's now covering the tiller for the day. The rig in our firehouse is called a tiller-rig. It has a driver in the front and a driver in the back.

I slowly walked up the stairs of the firehouse. All of a sudden bells started ringing, going crazy. I have never heard so many bells going off. There must have been twelve bells.

I yelled, "John, what the hell is going on?"

He answered, "A jet just hit the World Trade Center."

The rig pulled out, and those were the last words I heard him say. That was the last time I saw him.

Kenny Escoffery

About four of us were still back at 'quarters after the rig left. Timmy Haskell went upstairs and got the keys to the HAZMAT, hazardous material truck. Timmy had a spare radio in the HAZMAT, and he decided to catch up with his company Squad 18. They took the HAZMAT truck and left.

George and I didn't have any equipment, so we went to the command station that had been set up at the WTC north tower and reported in. We reported to Chief Peter Hayden. Basically, George and I are still standing here today because of Chief Hayden. Because we didn't have equipment, Chief Hayden asked us to stay in the north tower lobby and check to see if anyone was in the elevators and to make sure people weren't stuck. We did that, and then reported back to him.

World Trade Center North Tower

At that moment, someone reported a fire on the Mezzanine Level. So once again Chief Hayden asked George and I to check it out. We got to the Mezzanine floor and jet fuel was coming down the side of the building. There was some fire where we were, but it wasn't really spreading. What happened then was one coincidence after the other. As we got up to the third floor, a Port Authority Officer asked us to help him lift an over 300-pound man who was in the stairwell where people were trying to evacuate.

From there, while we were in the north tower staircase, we heard an explosion. We believe that's when the second plane hit the south tower. We felt a strong suction of wind coming up the staircase. It was a strong burst of wind, like a wind tunnel. George and I kept trying to figure out what it could be. We thought the elevators were falling down the shaft. That was our conclusion.

When we got down to the Mezzanine Level, the door was slammed shut. Debris and dust were everywhere. We kept the stairway door closed so that it wouldn't come up the staircase. At that moment, the lights went out in the staircase, even the emergency lights.

People were now coming down the stairs in complete darkness. Finally a gentleman came down the staircase and he said he knew of a way through to the front. He worked in the building and knew of a hallway that led from the back staircase to the front staircase. We were in the rear of the tower by West Side Highway.

World Trade Center North Tower

Kenny Escoffery

As we followed our way out, we felt our way through the darkness and found our way to the front staircase. Behind us, we had a long line of people holding hands. That line kept moving for probably at least 30 minutes as George and I evacuated them. Finally some firemen came with flashlights to shine light inside the staircase for people.

I think the reason that there wasn't a lot of panic in the staircase at that point was because the people were in a closed environment. They couldn't see what was happening outside. If you were on the floor below the floor that got hit, you really didn't know the damage. It wasn't until people got outside and began stepping over bodies that they knew of the devastation.

As soon as George and I got outside, we could see people falling from the towers. It was just like you were in the Valley of Death. I can't explain the feeling. It was a really scary, emotional feeling to know that people were falling, and we couldn't do anything to help them. That was the hardest part. As firemen, we couldn't help them. George and I didn't even have a radio or a mask. Even when we were in the staircase and the dust was coming up the staircase, we had to take a feed off of the masks from firemen going up. George was in the back taking feeds of oxygen from Engine 5 as they came through.

As we evacuated people to the outside, we had to actually look up. We had to look up and check to see if the people we were evacuating were going to be hit from the people falling. Between the two buildings, I think probably 1,000 people fell.

After George and I went outside, the chief pointed and told George and me, "I want you there and you here. Direct people in which direction they should walk."

World Trade Center North Tower

George Kozlowski

Kenny and I set up an area in a courtyard outside. As people kept coming out of the building, one of us looked up into the air to determine when it was safe for them to come out. What was happening was like if you were to hold an egg at your waist and then drop it. So many people were falling that it was like a toy flywheel, a pinwheel. Kenny and I had to yell to each other, "O.K! Go! Run!" and keep pushing the people through.

Kenny Escoffery

What stays with me most is the sound of a body crashing into the cement. In the north tower lobby there were so many body parts, their ears, and on and on. I never saw arms, only torsos. From that height when they hit, the smaller limbs blew off. I never saw a head. As people were evacuated and they came down and went outside, they had to step over bodies. Once they saw this, it took them about two minutes to know it was a body. It looked like a war scene.

Then we heard what sounded like an incoming missile. It was the south tower coming down. When it came crashing down, I think the impact knocked me unconscious. Up to then, I didn't even know the second building had been hit. George and I thought it was the elevators falling. When I came to, I laid there, waiting for the building to fall on me. After a few seconds I realized I was okay.

George Kozlowski

Everything came down in seconds. There wasn't even time for me to pray. I went into a fetal position on the ground. The next thing I knew, things were falling on top of me. And then I felt myself being lifted up. It was like I was on a magic carpet from the wind of the collapse. It threw me about 60 feet.

And then I found myself crawling . . . crawling. I just kept crawling. I crawled toward what turned out to be a flicker of a light coming off a Suburban, a Fire Department car. Through all of this the car lights were still on. The car was empty. I tried to decide if I should get in it. I decided, "No," keep crawling. I had to find Kenny.

Kenny Escoffery

I think at that point you're so scared. I was not even thinking about not being able to breathe. I just knew that I had to try to get away from that area. I got up, and there was a fire hose right beside me. I knew the hose led to a pumper, a fire truck that handles water.

I crawled along the hose, but that was too slow. So I squatted and started running, while still squatting, along the hose. I finally got to the pumper on West Side Highway. I washed my face and washed out my mouth. After the building came down it was like someone poured sand into my mouth.

I didn't see George and started yelling for him. I knew he was behind me. But when the building came down, I couldn't even see my hand. I went back for George. I followed the hose back and kept calling for him.

George Kozlowski

The sweetest moment in my life was when I heard Kenny's voice calling my name. And there he was, lifting me up, and he said, "Let's get the hell out of here, Bro."

Kenny Escoffery

I was so glad to hear George answer. George and I made it to the pumper. The air was so bad that the only thing we could do is wet our hoods and put them over our mouths.

George Kozlowski

The sweetest moment in my life was when I heard Kenny's voice calling my name. And there he was, lifting me up, and he said, "Let's get the hell out of here, Bro."

Kenny Escoffery

I was so glad to hear George answer. George and I made it to the pumper. The air was so bad that the only thing we could do is wet our hoods and put them over our mouths.

World Trade Center North Tower

George Kozlowski

The air was filled with asbestos, newspapers . . . and the dust. I was choking, coughing. Once we began to get away from the site it still lingered on for blocks. As we kept walking, cars parked along the streets started exploding. All of a sudden a car would start on fire. They shattered. They lit up and then exploded. It was like we were in the middle of a movie scene.

53

We kept our wet hoods over our faces. It still came through the hood material. It was like we were in the middle of a bomb attack . . . the desolation. You would never think we were in downtown Manhattan. Millions of people were there at that time. And then it's a ghost town. Kenny and I just stood there in awe of what happened. Then the thoughts hit you. The Ladder 20 members, "Where are they?"

Kenny Escoffery

George and I walked for what seemed like 10 blocks before we could breath something close to resembling air. A doctor came over to us and said we should try to wash our skin off because of the contamination. Even with the cloud of dust, you don't realize the devastation. Firemen were now coming in from all over, even the retired guys. They didn't have any equipment. One fireman kept saying, "I gotta get in there." He tried to take the bunker gear off my back so he could go in. One old battalion chief, he must have been 70 years old, grabbed a pair of boots and said he was going in. Everybody was coming in from all over and trying to help.

George Kozlowski

Kenny and I looked up and saw F-16 jets flying by. We said to each other, "What the hell is going on? Are we under attack?" And that's when we started finding out that the Pentagon had been hit and another plane crashed in Pennsylvania.

Kenny Escoffery

We made our way back to the WTC site. We figured Ladder 20 got out around on the other side. We kept searching. We searched for hours. It didn't dawn on us that we wouldn't find our company.

George and I were lucky. It was by the Grace of God that we got out. From that day forward George and I felt like we were born together. We escaped it together, and we have bonded that much closer.

As a firefighter, no one wants to be the first to break or give up. You don't want to be the weak link. That's what makes firefighters strong. No one wants to be the first to weaken. It's what makes a unit. Firefighters die before they give up that line. Never give up. And we don't.

George Kozlowski

The whole stairwell shook. It moved back and forth, and now people were panicking. You have to understand how small the stairwell was. Two normal sized people, if they were shoulder-to-shoulder, could fit in the stairwell. People were trying to evacuate going down the stairs, and firemen with all their equipment were going up.

A woman handed me her flashlight. Kenny and I made a relay to lead the people out. We told the people, "Put your hand on the person in front of you." Kenny was in the front of the line of people, and I was in the back. We told them, "Keep following the light from the flashlight." Kenny and I communicated to each by yelling.

I yelled, "Kenny, are you still there?"

And he yelled back.

World Trade Center North Tower

CHAPTER 4
WTC SOUTH TOWER

Bob Humphrey
Firefighter, Engine Co. 4
Fire Department City of New York

I was on house watch and Scotty Larsen, Ladder 15, relieved me so that I could get something to eat. Jimmy Riches Jr. then relieved Scotty. That was around 8:30 a.m. when the alarm came in.

I was standing in front of 'quarters. The telephone and the teleprinter weren't working. We get alarm calls through the teleprinter. For some reason we were having problems with the phone line and we were trying to get them fixed.

The only other means of getting an alarm was through a voice alarm. The first time we heard the voice alarm, a gentlemen was running down the street yelling, "The World Trade Center got hit!"

We said, "What are you talking about?"

About 10 seconds later we heard an explosion. The voice alarm said it was the Two World Trade Center, the south tower. We later learned it was the One World Trade Center, north tower. We were to standby for assignments. Everybody ran downstairs and got on the rig and got ready. We knew Engine 4 would also be going because we are a unit. I'm the driver of Engine 4, the chauffer.

When we took off, Ladder 15 took a right out of the firehouse. We took a left out of 'quarters with Engine 4. We only took the left because a gentleman said that traffic was very congested toward the right. I looked and saw that the Brooklyn Battery tunnel was congested. It's not unusual for us to take different routes to get someplace, but what was highly unusual is that Ladder 15 went right and we went left.

As I was coming down the block to WTC, we saw a whole bunch of people running out of the north tower building. I pulled down Vesey Street. I was next to WTC Building 6. I parked next to a hydrant and hooked up. I then hooked up to the Siamese. The Siamese is a "connection" to get water flowing into a building

All the members got out of Engine 4, and we had an extra guy on the rig that had just gotten off tour. Ritchie Allen was actually off duty, and he took my mask and went in with the engine company, Jimmy Riches Jr., Tommy Scholaes, Charlie Annaya, and Capt. Joseph Farrelly.

My job is to keep the water going into the building, so I stayed where I was. They went toward West Street, the street in front of the north tower, and into the command center in the lobby. If it's a high-rise building we usually use the lobby for a command center. If there's danger in the lobby, the command center is located someplace else.

I continued making sure that the right amount of pressure was going in, especially since we were dealing with floors going into 80s. I had to make sure I had enough water going to the rise so that when the guys started fighting the fire they had enough pressure to do it.

All the guys were gone, and I couldn't see them anymore. While I manned the engine I was there alone for while, probably four or five minutes. And that's a lot. I don't think there was another company by me until five minutes later.

Then Engine 28 came and they parked on the other side of West Broadway next to Building 7. Then he hooked up. I helped him bring the hose across the street and we hooked up to that standpipe so now we had completed the Siamese. By doing this, now we had a lot of water going into the building.

Jet fuel flowing from the south tower into building 4, causing extreme heat and flames

When the next plane hit the south tower, I was in the middle of Vesey Street. I saw a flash. I didn't know what it was, but it was something… then, BOOM, glass, and debris flying all over the place.

I jumped inside the truck so that it wouldn't land all over me. After that was over I got out, saw the mess in the street, parts of the plane, and then another engine company came in. I think it was 21, and they parked between West Broadway and Church Street. They were up a little further. Now we had three engine companies on that side, right in that area, with a line into the building.

Time was going by, and I was talking to the Engine 28 chauffer. People were standing around and watching. As we were watching the tower, we saw people jumping or falling. Some were trying to hang onto the building and fell. The temperature was so bad that they really didn't know what to do. As they were coming down, you could tell that some of them wished they hadn't jumped. As they were coming down, it looked like they were trying to climb back up again. Some people went in circles and circles and circles as they were coming down. They didn't know what to do.

At that point I'm running back and forth to the engine truck. I couldn't stand by the truck all the time because pieces of metal were falling. I couldn't see if something was going to land on me until it was right on top of me. I had to step back about 50 feet and keep checking if something was going to hit. I ran back and forth to the truck listening to the radio. I heard nothing on where Engine 4 was.

Capt. John Viola and Ladder 15 truck escaped major damage

Engine 4's job is to put out the fire. At that time I did not know what happened to them. I later learned that Engine 4, Engine 28, and Engine 7 were together. They had made it almost all the way up to where they needed to go. They could hear what was happening, the explosions. They were told to evacuate, to get out.

All three companies went down when told to evacuate. When they hit the lobby, the Engine 28 and Engine 7 guys went in one direction, and the Engine 4 guys went in another direction. 28 and 7 got out. Engine 4 got caved.

During the first collapse, I remember that I was with a bunch of people right by the Post Office delivery tunnel. All of a sudden I heard a vibration, a shaking, a rumble. The south tower was coming down and everybody started taking off in all directions.

What I did, and maybe 5 cops, was we went down into the West Broadway delivery tunnel. Everything went black. People were still trying to get into the tunnel. We were pulling people inside into the tunnel.

For myself, it wasn't a bad situation because there were a lot of people with me. We could figure out what to do and try to figure a way out of the tunnel and into the Post Office. The Post Office security guard kept trying to figure it out. We couldn't see, but we had flashlights, policemen had flashlights with them.

We were able to see enough to get up to the first floor. We got to the lobby, and when I got up there, there was a gentleman who was injured. He had a lot of cuts. I asked if the Post Office had a first-aid kit.

Firefighter Bob Humphrey and Engine 4 along side building 4

They said, "No."(This is one of the biggest Post Offices.)

So I asked, "Where is the bathroom?"

They said, "There's none on this floor."

Someone had some water in a bottle, and I sprayed it on a cloth and tried to clean his eyes up. I took him out of the Post Office and found an aid station across from Church Street. I got him washed up, and then took him to Barclay Street. From there I took him to an ambulance. I told him, "You'll be all right now. I have to go back to my truck."

I got back to my truck and there were bodies all over the place. I was trying to help people, put them in ambulances. Other companies had arrived and were resuscitating. I saw someone just lying there on the ground. I went over to try to help him. Half of his head was off.

I went over to my truck and water was shooting across the street to the Post Office. The water was really coming out. I went down the block, shut it off, and made sure the pressure was back to normal.

As I was walking, I came to Engine 21 truck. The truck was coughing. Its engine was running, but ready to stall. I couldn't get it to do anything. I walked across the street to Engine 28, and theirs had completely stopped. It couldn't get started. I said, "It's completely dead. It's probably from the dust in the air."

I asked the 28 chauffer how he got out of the south tower collapse. He had jumped in the truck and closed the windows.

I told him, "It's good that you did that, but if the north tower goes, it's right over our heads."

A minute later, One World Trade Center came down.

There weren't many people on the street where I was. It was him and me, and that's really all who were there. People were gone.

I yelled to him, "Come this way!"

He went the other way.

I went into the same Post Office delivery tunnel I had gone into for the first collapse. I was running down into the tunnel as the north tower collapsed. I was looking behind me. Someone was running, trying to get in, and then I heard the boom… boom. The blast hit me from behind. I got up to where the loading dock was inside the tunnel, and I threw my body over the rail. I hit the cement as the blast came through.

The blast actually moved cars to the side it was so strong. I lay there with my arms over my head and waited. And then I got up. I kind of stood there and said, "Now what do I do?"

It was completely dark. I had no flashlight. No mask. I had given my mask to Ritchie Allen when he went up. I was alone, and it was completely black. I knew I had jumped over the railing. I remembered the railing, that I had seen the railing as we made our way out of the tunnel during the first collapse.

Step by step I moved forward. And then I felt a wall. And then I felt nothing. I realized it was probably an elevator shaft. I almost stepped into it. And then I stopped.

I didn't know which way to go. There was so much smoke coming in. If I faced one way, it was so hot. I said to myself, "I can't go this way because I could be walking into a giant wall of flame."

So I kind of backtracked to get to the railing again. The delivery entrance was half closed. When the tower came down, some of it hit into Building 7, and that went on fire. A lot of debris from that was pushed over to where I was, and that's why I couldn't get out.

I found the wall again, and went straight, all the way to the end. And then I went slowly in the opposite direction of the entrance. I kept following that wall, scaling it, all the way around the building.

Finally, I started to feel some air, like a little wind blowing, I thought, "Maybe this is a way out."

As I kept moving more and more in that direction, the wind increased. All of a sudden I stepped on a little debris. It was maybe a foot high. All of a sudden I saw the opening. It was the opening of another Post Office delivery tunnel on Barclay Street. I had scaled the wall all the way around the entire building.

When I got out, and looked up, I couldn't see very well from the dust and smoke and being in complete darkness for so long. It was tough to breath. I squinted. I couldn't believe, "I'm out of here."

10:03 a.m. collapsing of the South Tower

I walked north for a couple of blocks and the air was clearing. I was the only one on the street except for some filmmakers who saw me coming down the street. I had just made it out, and I was thinking, "Who is this guy taking pictures of me… just filming, and he doesn't ask if I'm all right?"

61

As I kept walking, I saw a friend of mine.

He said, "Hey Bob, is that you?"

I said, "Yeah."

He said, "Let me get you to the new command center. They have a bunch of busses. They'll get you cleaned up."

They gave me oxygen and cleaned my eyes and my face. When I was done, I went back to the site. I was trying to find people, anyone I knew. I was hoping the other guys weren't dead.

I ran into Frank Vasis, the chauffer from Ladder 15. I asked what happened to him when they went to the right and we went to the left out of the firehouse. He did run into traffic. They went around the traffic, but had to drive over a median. One of the brake lines got cut. He didn't have any breaks.

That happened about two blocks away from the World Trade Center, the rest of the unit walked in. The officer told Frank to stay with the rig, try to get it fixed, and then come to the WTC.

He did the best he could. The rig could run, but that was about it. He took his tools, left the rig, and went on his own to try to find his company. By the time he got there, his unit was already up in the south tower.

Ladder Co. 15
Fire Department City of New York

Radio Communications
9:25 a.m.

Ladder 15: "Go ahead, Irons."

Ladder 15 Irons: "Just got a report from the director of Morgan Stanley. Seventy-eight seems to have taken the brunt of this stuff, there's a lot of bodies, they say the stairway is clear all the way up, though."

Ladder 15: "Alright, ten-four, ***. What, what floor are you on?"

Ladder 15 Irons: "Forty-eight right now."

Ladder 15: "Alright, we're coming up behind you."

9:31 a.m.

Battalion Seven Aide: "Battalion Seven, you want me to relay?"

Ladder 15: "Yeah, *** tell Chief *** they got reports that there's more planes in the area, we may have to go back down here."

Battalion Seven Aide: "Ten-four. Seven Alpha to Seven."

Battalion Seven: "***, Seven to Seven Alpha."

Ladder 15: "Fifteen to 15 Roof. Fifteen Roof."

Ladder 15: "We got reports of another incoming plane. We may have to take cover. Stay in the stairwell."

Ladder 15 Roof: "Ten-four."

Ladder 15: "Fifteen to 15 Roof. That plane's ours. I repeat. It's ours. What floor are you on, ***?"

10:03 a.m. collapsing of the South Tower

Ladder 15 Roof: "Fifty-four."

Ladder 15: "Alright. Keep making your way up. We're behind you."

Ladder 15 Roof: "Ten-four."

9:37 a.m.

Ladder 15 Lieutenant: "***, listen carefully. I'm sending all the injured down to you on 40. You're going to have to get 'em down to the elevator. There's about 10 to 15 people coming down to you."

Ladder 15 Firefighter: "Okay."

Ladder 15 Lieutenant: "Ten civilians coming down. Fifteen to OV."

Ladder 15 Firefighter: "Got that, I'm on 40 right now, Lieu."

9:39 a.m.

Ladder 15 Lieutenant: "Alright, ***, when you take people down to the lobby, try to get an EMS crew back."

Ladder 15 Firefighter: "Definitely."

9:43 a.m.

Battalion Seven Chief: "Battalion Seven to Ladder 15 Roof, what's your progress?"

Ladder 15 Roof: "Sixty-three, Battalion."

Battalion Seven Chief: "Ten-four."

Battalion Nine Chief: ""Battalion Nine to Battalion Seven."

Battalion Seven Chief: "Go ahead Battalion Nine."

Battalion Nine Chief: "*** I couldn't find a bank (elevator shaft) to bring you up any higher. I'm on the 40th floor, what can I do for you?"

Battalion Seven Chief: "We're going to have to hoof it. I'm on 69 now, but we need a higher bank, ***."

Battalion Nine Chief: "What stairway you in ***?"

Battalion Seven Chief: "The center of the building, Boy, Boy."

"Tac One to Tac One Alpha."

Battalion Seven Chief: "Battalion Seven to Ladder 15 Roof, what floor?"

Battalion Nine Chief: "Battalion Nine to Battalion Seven."

Battalion Seven Chief: "… Battalion Nine."

Battalion Nine Chief: "***, I'm going to try and get a couple of CFRD engines on the 40th floor so send any victims down here, I'll start up a staging area."

Battalion Seven Chief: "…find a fireman service elevator close to 40, if we get some more cars in that bank, we'll be alright."

9:48 a.m.

Ladder 15: "Battalion Fifteen to Battalion Seven."

Battalion Seven: "Go Ladder 15."

Ladder 15: "What do you got up there, Chief?"

Battalion Seven Chief: "I'm still in Boy stair 74th floor. No smoke or fire problems, walls are breached, so be careful."

Ladder 15: "Yeah, ten-four, I saw that on 68. Alright, we're on 71 we're coming up behind you."

Battalion Seven Chief: "Ten-four. Six more to go."

Ladder 15: "Let me know when you see more fire."

Battalion Seven Chief: "I found a marshal on 75."

9:49 a.m.

Ladder 15: "Fifteen to 15 OV. Fifteen to 15 OV."

"Fifteen OV."

Ladder 15: "***, have you made it back down to the lobby yet?"

Ladder 15 OV: "The elevator's screwed up."

Ladder 15: "You can't move it?"

Ladder 15 OV: "I don't want to get stuck in the shaft."

9:50 a.m.

Ladder 15: "Alright ***. It's imperative that you go down to the lobby command post and get some people up to 40. We got injured people up here on 70. If you make it to the lobby command post see if they can somehow get elevators past the 40th floor. We got people injured all the way up here."

Battalion Seven Aide: "Battalion Seven Alpha to Seven."

Battalion Seven Chief: "Go ***."

Battalion Seven Aide: "Yeah Chief, I'm on 55, I got to rest. I'll try to get up there as soon as possible."

Battalion Seven Chief: "Ten-four."

9:50 a.m.

"Anybody see the highway one car? Highway one car we need it for an escort to the hospital for a fireman."

Battalion Seven Chief: "Battalion Seven to Ladder 15."

"15 Irons."

Ladder 15: "Fifteen to 15 Roof and Irons."

Battalion Six Chief: "Battalion Six to command post."

9:52 a.m.

Battalion Seven Chief: "Battalion Seven to Battalion Seven Alpha."

"***, come on over. ****, come on over by us."

Battalion Seven Chief: "Battalion Seven… Ladder 15, we've got two isolated pockets of fire. We should be able to knock it down with two lines. Radio that, 78th floor numerous 10-45 Code Ones."

Ladder 15: "What stair are you in, ***?"

Battalion Seven Aide: "Seven Alpha to lobby command post."

Ladder Fifteen: "Fifteen to Battalion Seven."

Battalion Seven Chief: "… Ladder 15."

Ladder 15: "Chief, what stair you in?"

Battalion Seven Chief: "South stairway Adam, South Tower."

Ladder 15: "Floor 78?"

Battalion Seven Chief: "Ten-four, numerous civilians, we gonna need two engines up here."

Ladder 15: "Alright ten-four, we're on our way."

9:52 a.m.

Battalion Seven Aide: "Seven Alpha for Battalion Seven."

Battalion Seven Chief: "South tower, ***, south tower, tell them… Tower one. Battalion Seven to Ladder 15."

Ladder 15: "Fifteen."

Battalion Seven Chief: "I'm going to need two of your firefighters Adam stairway to knock down two fires. We have a house line stretched we could use some water on it, knock it down, ***."

Ladder 15: "Alright, ten-four, we're coming up the stairs. We're on 77 now in the B stair, I'll be right to you."

Ladder 15 Roof: "Fifteen Roof to 15. We're on 71. We're coming right up."

9:57 a.m.

"Division 3 … lobby command, to the Fieldcom command post."

Battalion Seven Chief: "Operations Tower One to floor above Battalion Nine."

Battalion Nine Chief: "Battalion Nine to command post."

Battalion Seven Operations Tower One: "Battalion Seven Operations Tower One to Battalion Nine, need you on floor above 79. We have access stairs going up to 79, ***."

Battalion Nine: "Alright, I'm on my way up, ***."

Ladder 15 OV: "Fifteen OV to Fifteen."

Ladder 15: "Go ahead Fifteen OV, Battalion Seven Operations Tower One."

Ladder 15 OV: "Stuck in the elevator, in the elevator shaft, you're going to have to get a different elevator. We're chopping through the wall to get out."

Battalion Seven Chief: "Radio lobby command with that Tower One."

9:58 a.m.

Battalion Seven Chief: "Battalion Seven to Ladder 15."

(END OF TAPE)

John S. Viola
Captain Ladder 15, Engine 4
Fire Department, City of New York

Tuesday morning, September 11 -- I had just returned home from a 24-hour tour at Ladder 15. As I walked in the door, my phone was ringing. It was a friend, informing me of what was happening at the World Trade Center. As I turned on my television and saw the first pictures, I knew this was more than a stray airplane hitting a building. I knew right there that this was a terrorist attack.

I had to get back to the firehouse. I had to make sure that the fourteen brave men I had just said good-bye to a few hours earlier were okay. After the experience of leaving my car and hitching rides from a police car, ambulance and finally a city tow truck, I was back at the quarters of the L-14, E-4 on South Street in lower Manhattan.

11:00 a.m. -- I first checked the dispatch computer to confirm that both companies responded. I then grabbed what little gear was left and reported over to the scene. By this time, both towers had fallen. As I approached the remains of the South Tower, I had, for the first time in my career, a complete feeling of helplessness. There were buildings burning with no signs of hose lines anywhere. There were bodies everywhere I looked. As I continued to walk, I almost tripped over a piece of an airplane landing gear. Next to this piece was a body part of an infant. It was then and there that I truly understood the magnitude of what had happened and what I needed to do.

12:00 noon -- I started to locate the members of my company that had also responded from their homes. We needed to organize a search and rescue party with what little resources we had. We stayed together, searching for survivors and marking the areas we had searched. As the day progressed it became painfully obvious that finding victims alive would diminish as the hours ticked on.

10:03 a.m. collapsing of the South Tower

2:00 p.m. -- I located the chauffeur from Ladder 15. He confirmed my fears; both Companies were inside the towers at the time of collapse. Ladder 15, under the command of Lt. Joseph Leavey, was responding to the initial alarm when their rig lost air pressure and the brakes locked up. The members repaired an air line and continued on. Just before reaching the South Tower, the brakes locked up again. It was at this point that the South Tower was hit by the second plane. Lt. Leavey ordered all of his members to take all of their equipment and respond to the South Tower on foot. He left orders for his chauffer to stay with the rig and try to repair it. Once accomplished, he would catch up with the Company. That never happened. At 10:05 a.m. with the heroes of Ladder 15 working on the floor of impact, the South Tower collapsed.

4:00 p.m. — I located the chauffer from Engine 4. He informed me that the members of Engine 4 had been walking in the North Tower at the time of collapse.

9:00 p.m. — After searching all day, it became obvious that we needed to contact the families of our missing members. This was one of the hardest things I have ever done.

September 12, 1:00 a.m. — We located Ladder 15's rig (see photo). It was surrounded by collapsed buildings, yet it seemed to be a miracle that it stood, untouched. We needed water on the fire and somehow FDNY members were able to stretch a hose line from a fireboat on the Hudson River to Ladder 15's location. That seemed to be one of the first master streams placed into operation.

As the hours and days went on, every hour seemed to bring a new challenge. One day while we were searching, one of my members seriously injured his left arm in one of the tunnels that we dug by hand. He didn't want to leave, however, the search dogs that were working with us kept losing their scents due to his severe bleeding. I had to have him leave the tunnel for medical attention. He was stitched up on a street corner by a woman who claimed to be a nurse—24 stitches. He returned within the hour and continued searching. What could I say? These were his brothers that were missing.

The surviving members of Ladder 15 and Engine 4 worked tirelessly over the next several months, with the help of so many volunteers from the FDNY as well as many outside volunteers. Our motto was that we would not stop searching until we brought all our brothers home. I was honored to see how they supported and cared for the families of our missing. They showed care and professionalism at both the memorials and the funerals. I was most pleased of how they escorted their fallen brothers from the remains of the once proud Twin Towers.

10:03 a.m. collapsing of the South Tower

CHAPTER 5
THREE SECONDS TO LIVE

Tom Fenech
Firefighter, Engine Co. 7 Ladder Co. 1
Fire Department City of New York

I could see the ball of flame above the tower. I didn't see the plane go into the building. All I could see was fire and black smoke above the north end of the north tower. I thought a transformer had blown.

I was a fireman in the Air Force for four years before I joined the New York Fire Department. All of my life it's been like a calling. I was on my way to work that day, and I was supposed to be working on Spring Street. As I was getting onto the Brooklyn Bridge, the first plane had already hit. Everything came to a halt on the bridge, and my first instinct was to get a news station on the radio. Reports were coming in that a plane had hit the World Trade Center. I'm thinking to myself, "Okay, it's a small Cessna or a news helicopter." I didn't think it was a major incident.

As I came into Manhattan from the bridge ramp I could see that it wasn't a small aircraft. In knowing about airplanes and crashes, how much fire comes from a small plane versus a large aircraft, I concluded it was a 747, something that held a lot of gas.

I pulled up by St. Peter's Church because it was the only place I could park. People were running through the streets and being trampled. I started picking people up off the ground. I couldn't go any further because the police, FBI, ambulances, ESU, and emergency service vehicles were all crowded around Church and Vesey. I continued to help pedestrians, and I used St. Pete's as a triage area. It looked like it was safe because it is made out of stone. I figured St. Pete's had been standing there for 100 years and would probably be there for another 100.

I stayed for about 30 minutes helping people, and then, before you knew it, the second plane hit. The second tower was a little behind the first tower so I didn't see the hit. I was standing at the next intersection. I was thinking maybe it was a secondary explosion from the first aircraft, but then people started running again.

People were running and screaming, "The second plane hit! The second plane hit!"

When the second plane came in, its aircraft motor went through the building and came out all the way across to Barclay Street and landed 60 feet away from me.

I said to myself, "Well, the starboard engine just went through the building. Centrifugal force kept it going, and that probably means that it never left the floor. When it fell, it broke the wing, but the engine itself went through the floor of the World Trade Center and actually landed on Barclay Street."

I stood there looking at the engine.

I said to myself, "That was the second aircraft. Something is definitely wrong."

When the first plane hit, people ran into the stores and bought disposable cameras. They were outside gawking like, "Take a photograph of this. This doesn't happen all the time. It's one of those freak things."

There weren't as many people when the second plane hit. The streets were packed with people when the first plane hit because it was nine o'clock in the morning in Manhattan.

When the second plane hit, those were the people who lost it. This is the worst that can happen and now you see the worst happen again right in front of you. They started running like animals.

Everyone pitching in to recover the victims

The medical teams arrived at St. Peter's and began staging it. I walked over by the towers. The towers were still standing at that time. Fire was roaring out of both of them. I walked over to the north tower and came around by Vesey Street.

A lot of people were dropping out of the building. People below were screaming and crying. They didn't know what to do when the debris kept falling. I tried to get into the north tower lobby and they wouldn't let me in. I didn't have my gear with me. I was wearing a regular light blue shirt with the Fire Department emblem.

I saw an orange construction helmet and I picked it up because I figured it might save me. It was better than nothing. I went over to the command center on West Street. They were using a garage entrance ramp for a staging area. All of the companies were coming in, and there was a lot of traffic from emergency vehicles.

The radios? They weren't working that well. If the guys on the outside wanted to get through they could talk to each other, but the guys on the inside of the buildings, no. They couldn't get through, because there was so much steel and metal around them. It just didn't work. Even what we call the "Repeater System" didn't work. I think that was down when the first plane hit.

I was told to go to the Engine 10 and Ladder 10 Firehouse on Liberty Street right across from the World Trade Center. I came around from the back and walked past the second building, the south tower. I stepped over body parts lying on the ground. It looked like people had been sliced through a shredder. The body parts fell outward because the plane pierced into the building. The entire street was covered with bodies, parts of the plane, and broken glass.

Eventually, I made it to the 10 and 10. The door was open in the back of the firehouse. Everything was gone including all the gear. Everyone who was off duty had picked through it so they could go in. I exited the firehouse and walked toward Church Street.

Church St. looking South of the Devastation

A rig was parked about 50 feet away on the corner of Greenwich. The fire truck was running and it was empty. The men were already inside the tower.

I thought maybe I'd find some extra gear on the rig, because chauffeurs usually leave some gear. As I was walking toward the rig, a cop in uniform flew by me and yelled, "It's coming down!"

He dove underneath the rig.

I looked up, and I could see the top 12 floors coming down at me in slow motion. The floors were breaking away from the top of the building. I had a falling building coming at me, and I had maybe three seconds, not even. There wasn't enough time to run and duck for cover.

I jumped up onto the back step of the fire truck, below the hoses, and I pulled as much hose over me as I could. I blanketed myself with hose and it worked. Otherwise I wouldn't be here.

Then came a horrific sound. I could hear the bang, bang, bang. It was the "pan caking" of the floors coming down. A 10-story section of building was coming at me and it angled itself as it came down. Eventually it came straight down. When it did, it took the 100 floors underneath it.

I listened in horror to the, "Chi chi chi chi chi chi." It was like a large coughing noise as each floor compressed into the next one at a very rapid pace.

Greenwich St. looking south

Then all of a sudden came the steel. The ripping of steel from a floor, and then the steel hitting the ground, and the ground shaking, and everything moving, and people screaming… human voices screaming in terror.

I thought about the "old timers", the guys in World War II. They'll tell you. When they got torpedoed, the ship's sailors knew the sound of a buckling ship when the water comes in. They know the sound of metal twisting and turning and people screaming. Those who survived still have horrors about it.

I said to myself, "This is one of those stories that I'm going to have to live with for the rest of my life. I'm going to have to say to myself, 'I can't believe I lived through it.'"

When the building was down, the screaming subsided. I thought it was time to leave the area, but I had forgotten about the cop underneath the truck. The rig was still running. From underneath the truck, the cop reached for my ankles.

He said, "Get me out of here. Get me out of here."

I didn't think he was still alive. I really didn't. I removed the debris and pulled him out. Once he got out, he asked, "How do I get out of here?"

I said, "Put one foot on the curb and one foot on the street." I gave him a push and said, "Go this way." I figured the rear of the truck was facing away from the buildings.

I began checking the truck's compartments to see if there was some type of breathing apparatus I could use, but the compartments were empty. All I could do was use my shirt. I covered my mouth and used that as a mask.

I walked down by Beekman Street and found a restaurant that was open. It wasn't open for business, but it was open. I went into the bathroom, washed my face, and cleaned out my mouth as best I could.

I went back outside and began walking over to the north tower. I must have been a block and a half away from it. Just before I could get to it, the north tower was coming down.

I could see the arch of the top of the building falling, but I couldn't see anything else. Then all of a sudden, from both sides of the building, a major dust cloud comes at me. I got caught again.

I said to myself, "I'm not having a great day. I'm not having a great day. This is the last call, gentlemen. This is it."

There was no way to go back, and I was pretty much out of it. I had so much debris in my eyes from the particles of the building that I couldn't even see in front of me.

But then I was by a cab. The cab driver was taking people to the hospital. I told him, "I have to get to the hospital."

He said, "Jump in. I'll take you."

When I got into the hospital they said that all of their mobile equipment was out of service. They were highly staffed that day because a lot of people had come in, but they couldn't mobilize the team. They had no equipment to take them there. They gave me some antibiotics.

I can't remember if I went back to Ground Zero or to the firehouse. It was still early in the day. It was only 10 a.m., now it was 12:30, lunchtime. I did end up back at the firehouse that day. I must have gone back to Division Street. That's what I did. No, I can't remember what I did that day. I can't remember.

Rubble in the streets

CHAPTER 6
EVACUATION LOWER MANHATTAN

Lt. Claudio Fernandez
New York City Highway Patrol

I worked the midnight shift, and I got off at 6:35 in the morning. I left and went home. At approximately 7:30 a.m. I arrived at my house. At about 8:00 a.m. I decided to go to bed, and I slid into bed with my wife Pamela and our precious 11-month old daughter Ashley Nicole. At approximately 8:55 I got a call from Highway 3 where I work, telling me that there had been a plane crash at the WTC in Manhattan. I was to report back to work immediately.

As I was rather startled from that information, the phone rang again, and it was my mother. She was crying. She was in downtown Manhattan and saw the commotion and smoke. She informed me that my younger brother was in that same neighborhood, at college on Chamber Street. She was very worried about him. I told her not to worry, and that I'm on my way back to work. I'd go down to look for him if necessary.

Within minutes I was dressed, and I kissed my wife and daughter goodbye. I ran to my truck and made it to work in 20 minutes by running a few red lights. By 9:30-9:35 I was at work again.

When I got to work there was chaos. I had heard on the news there were other attacks. The second tower was hit as I was changing into my uniform. At Highway 3 we didn't even have to listen to the radio or TV because cops were calling in for help over our police radios.

My own personal thought at the moment was that we were definitely under attack, like war. I imagined chaos at the scene. The cops in the Highway 3 station house looked like they were in shock. I would have expected more chaos, but we rise to the occasion when called upon.

They understood the orders that I was barking at them, and they performed their tasks with efficiency under the circumstances. What we ended up doing was lining up a motorcade that consisted of a dozen vehicles and upwards to 30 motorcycles. We then proceeded to leave the station house all together, and went down to the highway toward Manhattan. At which time, when we were crossing over the Long Island Expressway, we were able to see the two buildings on fire. They looked like cigarettes on fire. At approximately 10:00 a.m. we were on the road moving toward Manhattan.

At about 10:20 a.m. we were by the West Side Highway. I believe a building had already collapsed or was collapsing. Some of us were running for cover.

Our basic mission was to evacuate everybody from the location. We were able to commandeer over 50 public and private busses to assist us with the evacuation. I continued supervising the operation of evacuation.

I had to literally go into the Ground Zero area to identify the best locations as to where the busses could get down as far as possible, and where they'd be able to turn around. My own personal thoughts were, "This is hell. This is chaos. This is surreal."

I felt like it was a volcano erupting. It didn't even look like a building had collapsed. Ashes came down on me, but it felt like it was snowing. I was wearing black leather boots and dark blue pants. They turned completely gray.

Civilians running up Vesey St. past Broadway

I was able to assign a motorcycle to each bus, and I was yelling to all the civilians to get on the busses. When more information came over the radio and told us there may be more collapses, we pulled back to the location of Canal and Broadway Street. We ran the Operation from that location.

I estimated that we removed approximately 20,000 people from the area and relocated them as far as 59th Street and Columbus circle. Again, my own personal thoughts were that I was dealing with people walking up to us with a lot of blood on their heads and arms. Older women sat down on the concrete because they didn't know what was going on.

I was getting a lot of questions from the public. Some of the questions were as simple as, "Is Brooklyn still there?"

"If I get on this bus, will it take me home?"

Civilians running onto the Brooklyn Bridge

They were very confused questions from people in shock.

On some occasions I had to literally order people or yell at them to get on the busses. They didn't understand that they needed to get on the bus to get away from the area. They wanted to go to Brooklyn or New Jersey.

They had questions like, "Do we have to pay to get on the bus?"

"Do we use our metro card?"

I told them, "Just get on the bus and don't worry about it."

During the initial 48 hours, the mission was to evacuate all persons and potential victims from the area, render aide and rescue personnel. Our mission then turned to one of recovery. Our Base of Operations coordinated the various types of equipment and machines needing to be transported to Ground Zero for the recovery efforts.

Civilians coming off Brooklyn Bridge into Brooklyn

I estimate that by three in the afternoon we were able to evacuate all of the civilian population in Lower Manhattan. I estimate that I personally evacuated 20,000 people.

That day a particular event made an impact on me. A cloud of dust was coming north of Broadway. I recognized Sean Veeraten, an officer I had worked with. He was injured because he was dragging his leg. His hair and uniform were covered in gray and white. I went to assist him. He seemed to be in some type of shock. I placed him in back of my police car and told him to rest. I needed to find him something to drink and eat. Across the street, a pizza shop was still open.

I brought water and a pizza slice to the officer, left my car, and continued to evacuate people. I later learned that the officer had torn ligaments and other tendons in his legs. Eventually I got him to the hospital, but not before we evacuated everyone.

His injuries were internal, but the most interesting thing about this officer occurred down at the World Trade Center. When the first plane hit at approximately 8:53 a.m., this officer was in his car that was parked a block away from WTC. Apparently some of the jet fuel came down on his car and burnt it to a crisp. He was able to dive away from the vehicle as parts were falling from the building. That is how he sustained his injuries.

Lt. Claudio Fernandez's NYPD Highway Patrol car

As he was trying to escape his car, and was running away from the collapse of the tower, he ran into another police officer running in the opposite direction. After colliding into each other, they continued running in their same directions.

Glenn Pettit, a Member of the Police Academy Video Unit, mistakenly ran toward the World Trade Center. Glenn Pettit perished in the worst terrorist attack on American soil since Pearl Harbor.

Later that day we reunited all the officers a little further away from the Ground Zero scene so that we could gain a better perspective about what was going on. We rendezvoused on the West Highway at a place called Pier 40. We commandeered Pier 40 for our operations.

All that time, I was thinking about my mother and my family. I was able to reach my mother and she told me that my brother was all right.

My concerns then turned to my best friend, a firefighter with Engine 24 Ladder 5. His firehouse is very close to the World Trade Center, and reports had come back that a lot of firemen and police officers had lost their lives during the attack. I was unable to reach him for approximately three days. I later learned that he did survive the impacts, but eight of his fellow firefighters were killed in the line of duty that day.

Corner of Vesey and West Street

Vincent LeVien
Director of New York State
Senator Martin Connor's,
Emergency Task Force,
Ground Zero

I was running a campaign in Brooklyn for Brooklyn District Attorney Charles J. Hynes. I was at the campaign headquarters when somebody ran in and said, "Turn on the radio."

When I first turned on the radio they said that a plane hit the World Trade Center. At that moment, my father, Doug LeVien, who has a view of the towers from his Brooklyn office, called me. He said we were under attack and to stay where I am. They were evacuating all buildings at that moment, and F-16's were patrolling the air space. All bridges and tunnels had been closed.

I put four senate employees in my campaign van and proceeded to try to get into Manhattan. When I reached the U.S. Federal Court House at Tilary Street and Adam Street where the Brooklyn Bridge starts, two U.S. marshals told me that the only way into Manhattan was to walk or to get into an emergency vehicle. At that point I was trying to reach my boss Senator Connor, because he was dropping off his son at Stiverson High School that morning. It's five blocks north of the World Trade Center.

Senator Connor has a retired NYPD police officer for security. I was notified that Senator Connor's his driver raced him to the Manhattan Bridge, walked Senator Connor and his son over the bridge, with his gun in his hand not knowing if they would take out the bridges.

Later that night about midnight I was able to meet up with Senator Connor, and he told me that when the first building came down, his security personnel threw him underneath a stairwell to save his life.

The next morning, September 12, I grabbed my New York Senate ID and shield and drove to the Brooklyn District Attorney's office. I had the Brooklyn Attorney's detectives drive me into Manhattan to pick up Senator Connor's car, which was still at the base of the Manhattan Bridge. After I escorted all of the senator's senior staff out of New York City I drove back into Manhattan. That evening I met up with Tobias Russo at my senate office two blocks away from the World Trade Center. Toby and I walked down to St. Peter's Church, and I said a prayer.

I met Capt. Campbell from the Salvation Army, which had a cantina outside of St. Peter's church. I proceeded to work through the night with Toby, handling logistics for the Salvation Army and rescue workers. The next morning I brought in five senate employees to volunteer down at Ground Zero. On September 13, Senator Connor formed an emergency task force, of which I became director.

L to R: Vincent Le Vien and Phil De Vane

CHAPTER 7
ALL CHILDREN
ACCOUNTED FOR

Chief Robert Crawford
Department of Transportation
Student Passenger Transport
City of New York

Tuesday September 11, 2001 started as a clear September morning, following a late summer heat wave that had just grasped the City of New York. On 1010 WINS AM radio the main topics of the day were the projected voter turn-out for the Primary Election and the New York Giants football team loss of their season opener the night before to the Denver Broncos.

As I did every day, I passed the WTC on the West Side Highway at about 6:45AM on my way to work with the New York City Department of Transportation (NYCDOT) located at the Battery Maritime Building (BMB), shared with the Governor's Island Ferry Terminal and adjacent to the Staten Island Ferry Terminal and US Coast Guard Terminal at the very tip of lower Manhattan - within blocks of the WTC. As I drove passed under the walkway that attached the WTC with the World Financial Center I looked up marveling at the sight of the "Twin Towers" against the morning sun, not knowing this would be the last time in my life that I would be able to gaze upon them untouched in all their infinite glory.

At that time, I was Chief of Oversight and Enforcement of the Passenger Transport Division, Pre-K Student Transportation Program. The NYCDOT administered the Pre-K Student Transportation Program in coordination with the New York City Department of Education (NYCDOE) and the New York City Department of Health (NYCDOH); overseeing 240 contracts with more than 40 private transportation vendors with an excess of 1,500 school buses to provide transportation services for one of the most fragile population within the City; 18,000 disabled children from birth to five years of age receiving Special Education Services. The Pre-K Program was coupled into the NYCDOE Office of Pupil Transportation system which provided transportation of approximately 170,000 young students and students with special needs aged out of the Pre-K Transportation Program. The NYC Department of Education operates the largest public school system in the United States, serving 1.1 million students in five boroughs of the City of New York: Manhattan, Brooklyn, Queens, Staten Island and the Bronx.

I was also charged with assisting in the inspection operation of the Surface Transit Subsidized Franchise Bus System, which at that time was the fourth largest commuter bus system in the nation, and I was one of the emergency management coordinators for the Passenger Transport Division which included the Private Ferry and Staten Island Ferry operations.

That morning I conducted roll call and dispatched the unit's transportation inspectors to the "field" at various educational sites throughout the City to perform road side inspections of the school buses performing on Pre-K contracts. Some staff from other units was in early too including people from Pre-K Customer Service, Pre-K Contract Management, Surface Transit, Private Ferry, Alternate Fuels Program and the Executive Director of Pre-K Student Transportation Program.

As I was getting my breakfast at a nearby deli on Water Street sometime after 8:50 a.m., the NYCDOT Traffic Management Center (TMC) transmitted an advisory from the NYC Office of Emergency Management, that a twin-engine Cessna plane accidentally hit the North Tower of the WTC, there was debris falling from the building; and to use caution within the vicinity. I responded to Church Street and Vesey Street to view the incident. People everywhere were looking upward, shards of glass and concrete were strewed all over the area. Port Authority Police, NYPD and FDNY vehicles were responding, initiating a shutdown of traffic flow on Church Street, so I immediately reported back to the BMB. Monitoring the event via two-way radio, it began to take shape that this was a very bad accident; and a request for more citywide response apparatus to report to the WTC was made. It wasn't until the second plane hit the South Tower at approximately 9:03AM that it became apparent this was no accident; that in some way the City of New York was "under attack".

Directing his team from the department of transportation

The two-radio became "alive" with multiple transmissions requesting more information on the event, asking if any staff from DOT were on-scene with live updates. The first 30 minutes were very confusing to everyone; no one really knew what was going on. All highways, tunnels and bridges leading to lower Manhattan were shut-down except for emergency vehicles; all Interstates leading in and out of New York City were closed. Outside our windows and on the veranda of the BMB you can see smoke coming from both towers, as sirens echoed through the corridors of lower Manhattan, it was surreal. The DOT Inspectors who were in the field called in confused based on upon hearing multiple different stories. They contacted me for verification as well as guidance on what to do. I ordered all Inspectors to stay away from lower Manhattan and to stand by at their assigned location until otherwise instructed.

At this point I grabbed my gear and communication equipment and proceeded to respond back to the WTC but as I was leaving I was confronted by my Executive Director. She asked me what I was doing and I replied I was going out to help with the emergency. She told me that my services would be better served assisting in coordinating a "joint effort" between DOT and Pre-K units than in the field. I passionately and strongly responded back to her that I felt I needed to go assist in any rescue needed and that I was leaving. She became upset and fiercely ordered me not to leave, saying that if I left I would be violating a direct order. Filled with mixed emotions, I dropped my gear and proceeded to the conference room to plan our strategy; not knowing until later, that this encounter probably saved my life.

Boats used in transporting civilians

The Passenger Transport Division initiated emergency operations, from alerting all Surface Transit bus operators to detour from lower Manhattan, implementing operations between DOT and other agencies to coordinate a mass evacuation from lower Manhattan and to determine the attendance of Pre-K pupil ridership that morning. During these operations at 9:59AM, a terrible thunderous noise was heard shaking the office; it was assumed one of the tops of the towers had fallen off "sideways". Some staff went to the veranda while I went downstairs to the street level to try to understand what had occurred, it was then I observed people running from all directions from the West Side of Lower Manhattan where the towers stood, and behind them what appeared to be a "massive wave" of ashy, grey cloudy smoke pouring through the corridors of lower Manhattan. I began to bring people into the building that were standing on the Governor's Island Ferry slips, attempting to shield them from the ashy dark cloud, but this smoky, ashy dark cloud penetrated the BMB through doors and windows smelling like burnt material burning my eyes. It was difficult to see, the natural light of the sun was blocked. There was zero visibility for a couple of moments.

By the time the smoke cleared everything in the office was covered in this "chalky ash debris", the smell was horrible. The 2-way radio was silent and everyone in the office was in fear. The Pre-K Customer Service Director was also a pastor of his church, asked everyone to gather around, fifteen people held hands in a circle as he began a prayer; trying to build our confidence and reassuring that though this was a dark hour, we were all going to be ok. I believe this moment will be treasured by all present and believe we all found, for a split second, peace. As soon as the moment was over, the executive decision was made to get all children transported back home. It was apparent there was a lot of work to be done.

Boats used in transporting civilians

Shortly thereafter, the unit was advised an evacuation of Lower Manhattan was ordered; and that various MTA and Port Authority PATH train tunnels were possibly destroyed by the collapse. The official stance was that everyone should evacuate; and of the twenty people in the office, fifteen stayed and began coordinating a massive operation. Even after the NYPD arrived at the BMB to declare the building be evacuated immediately; the fifteen of us ignored that order and pressed on, being that the BMB was one of the few buildings at that moment in Lower Manhattan to still have both electrical power and phone service.

Our unit was able to contact its counterparts at the NYC Department of Education Office of Pupil Transportation, identifying the educational sites south of Canal Street assisting in the coordination of the evacuation of the Pre-K sites along with 7 other public school sites and nearly 9,000 other DOE pupils closest to ground zero. Staff from Surface Transit and Pre-K then performed the tedious job of contacting over 250 other Pre-K school sites, and urging that all children remain at the school sites until it could be verified that there was a parent or guardian present to receive each child in light of the fact parents or guardians may have just perished.

Most schools wanted to close so their teachers could get home but we reminded the school administrators that we didn't know if someone was home to receive the children, and that the schools had food, water, medicines and trained personnel for the children which would not be available on a bus ride that could take hours. Over 50 school bus vendors were also contacted and ordered to return to all school facilities and stand by at the sites and wait for children who have been cleared to go home. Field Inspectors coordinated between sites and buses to construct new routes and maximize vehicle usage.

Buses used in transporting the children

The Surface Transit and Alternative Fuels staff developed a system of franchise expresses buses to transport people out of lower Manhattan and carry in emergency responders; along with Private Ferry operators working side by side with the Staten Island Ferry and various tour boat companies assisting in evacuating all citizens from Pier 11 and other lower Manhattan piers. The Staten Island Ferry Terminal was turned into a triage center for victims.

As these operations were going on the North tower collapsed at 10:28 am, again a wave of ash and debris swept over lower Manhattan, this time the electricity flickered as the building shook. The windows turned dark as the dark grey-brown ash took over the sky. As we were being advised of the lower Manhattan electrical grid being down, the BMB and the Staten Island Ferry Terminal still had electrical power generated from the US Coast Guard terminal allowing us to continue performing our duties. This was very fortunate for our unit, because the filters on the air conditioners allowed us to continue working – although we kept masks on whenever possible.

For hours thousands of citizens both on buses and walking proceeded pass the BMB onto the FDR Drive Northbound to cross the Brooklyn Bridge into Brooklyn; we continued to work in smoke and debris covered offices until after 5:00 pm when all Pre-K Special Education children were accounted for and received by a family member and emergency bus routes were functioning accordingly. Due to the closings of all bridges and tunnels to non-emergency vehicles, some children in schools in Manhattan but living in outer boroughs were taken home by ambulance.

Abandoned bicycle

The NYC DOT Commissioner was escorted to an undisclosed location in Washington Heights in upper Manhattan; and agency operations were conducted from the DOT Mobile Command Center where all emergency response personnel assembled.

The next operation I was involved in was the transportation of essential NYCDOT TMC staff from the outer-boroughs to the Control Center located at 28-11 Queens Plaza North. Since all highways and transportation systems were shut down, essential staff was trapped in the outside boroughs with no way of getting to the Control Center. I quickly utilized my response vehicle, traveled to various locations between the ends of upper Manhattan and the Bronx collecting these individuals and transported them to the Control Center. While conducting this movement at 5:21PM, we had learned the New York City also lost 7 World Trade along with the City's Office of Emergency Management Main Operations Center.

By evening's time the NYCDOT TMC was fully staffed, all children had been transported home and were accounted for, and a hundreds of Police, Fire and EMS personnel were systematically being shuttled into ground zero. Private Ferries became the mode of transportation between lower Manhattan and the surrounding boroughs and the BMB, still having electrical power was transformed into the temporary DOT Field Headquarters.

At 9:57 p.m., Mayor Giuliani announced the Chancellor's decision to close New York City public schools and Pre-K educational sites on Wednesday September 12, 2001.

Five vehicles, one from each borough, motor-pooling Pre-K staff returned to the BMB on Thursday September 13, 2001 to a different world. Smoke still filled the air, jet fighters were flying over head, Battery Park was a military encampment with tents everywhere; and other than emergency response personnel we were the only office open for business. All of lower Manhattan was engulfed in the "chalky ash debris", and on the horizon was a huge black cloud of fiery smoke emanating from hundreds of feet of smashed and twisted iron and metal on the footprints of where the twin towers once stood

They say the sense of smell is one of the strongest senses to ignite memory. I will never forget the smell of that smoke nor the ankle high ash debris that contain hundreds of different types of materials and chemicals along with the remains of thousands of innocent civilians and fallen heroes.

Robert Crawford at a ceremony

CHAPTER 8
AIR

Mike Bellone
Honorary Firefighter, Ladder Co. 20
Fire Department City of New York

During all the chaos, sometimes Bob and I would lose each other. Sometimes we would reunite. During that first time we were apart, I found my first body. It was the body of a man underneath a beam. Six of us tried to lift the beam so that we could pull the man out. I realized there weren't going to be any rescues made, only recoveries.

Someone handed me a paper painter's mask to put on. I later realized when I took the mask off that my nose was bleeding. I took some cotton painter's masks, ripped them up, and stuck them in my nose to stop the bleeding. Now I could only breathe through my mouth. I later realized my nose was bleeding because of all the toxins and glass in the air. I couldn't single out one contamination from the other.

The plume of toxins settle as the smoked rises

When you stepped up to the plate, there was no turning back. I wanted to be angry, but I couldn't. I had to stay focused and keep my eye on the ball and not let my emotions run away from me. There was no time to cry. No time to be upset. There wasn't even any time to think. There was only just enough time to react to the next call, whether it be an empty bucket, lift up this piece of concrete, pull out this beam, or "spot me" if I'm going down into a void.

Collapse of the north tower. covering a wide area in lower Manhattan

Bob Barrett
Retired Firefighter, Ladder Co. 20
Fire Department City of New York

The air was so thick you could chew it. I was coughing, but I believe everybody down at the site had a respiratory problem. People were getting nosebleeds, and just about everyone I spoke to was coughing.

As a firefighter I have tasted all varieties of smoke. I've learned to distinguish one from the other. For instance, smoke from an oil burner has its own particular flavor. The same is true of wood or electrical or rubbish fires. This was a new one for me. I did not recognize this odor to be any I had experienced before, and I hope I will never again experience it in my lifetime.

Some firefighters were dressed in full equipment, others had partial protection, and some of us were void of any equipment. At that point, the only protection being handed out was paper painter's masks, which are inadequate for this type of contamination. This was also about the only protection that civilians were wearing.

The plume starts to roll down lower Manhattan, to the north

It struck me that this could turn out to be a serious health disaster in the making. I am not a doctor, but I suspect that somewhere down the line, serious health consequences will stem from this horrible concoction of hazardous materials.

In the back of my mind I wondered, "Will I bring any of this contamination home with me?" I knew I would have to isolate myself from my family for days until I was sure it was safe

94

to go home. This was one of the reasons I didn't go home for approximately five days, and then only for a hug and a kiss from my wife and my three children. And to remind myself there was a life outside of this tragedy still going on. It was a life I would have to rejoin sometime in the future. Right now life was on hold. I knew it would be strictly recovery from then on and there weren't going to be any miracle rescues.

The plume heads out towards the water, contaminating the Hudson River and surrounding waters

Solange "Hollywood" Schwalbe
Office of Strategic Services
Award-Winning Sound Editor

Since 1981, I have been a Motion Picture Sound Editor in Feature Films in Los Angeles. I have over 150 Feature Credits to my name. All of them theatrical releases.

In 1980 I moved to New York City. My dream. In 1981, I got my first feature in Hollywood. What, I have to move back to LA?

From then on, New York City became my Christmas present every year. I would hook up with my best friend, and his best friend, and we would pal around Manhattan like three kids. We would do all of the Christmas Traditions in Midtown, including the Rock, the Tree, and Santaland at Macy's. I would then INSIST on going to the top of the World Trade Center. They pointed out that the Empire State Building was right across the street. I didn't care because the Empire State Building was TOO SHORT... Off we went to Lower Manhattan to experience the most incredible view on the planet! Every Christmas!

The plume picks up speed with force, like a sandstorm

In 2001, I was working at Disney on "Snow Dogs." I was awakened by my radio alarm set to the news that announced, "The Towers have been hit!" I do not remember getting up to turn on my TV. Suddenly, the tears started flowing. It was like my best friend had been shot. Little did I know that I was about to witness its death. Needless to say, I got a call 2 hours later saying that the Disney lot was closed, just like every other studio in Hollywood. I sat in front of the TV, alone, for 7 hours before I could get up.

That Christmas, I went on my annual trip to New York City, without the Towers. The first place we went to was the top of the Empire State Building. It was awful. Lower Manhattan looked like a huge football stadium. The next day we went down to the WTC Site where thousands of people were wandering around trying to figure out what had happened. On Broadway, I found myself taking photos of what use to be there. Nothing. I was taking photos of nothing! That's when I realized I wanted to help. I took the subway to Brooklyn to the Red Cross Headquarters to inquire about volunteering. They said the Salvation Army was in charge of the Respite Center where they feed the rescue workers 24-hours a day. Back to Manhattan, I found the Salvation Army Headquarters on 14th St and walked in. "We don't take volunteers off the streets. You have to be a part of the Salvation Army around the country." Well, as it turns out, it's the week of the New Year. The Volunteer List was empty starting January 2nd, 2002. So I signed up!

I was on the breakfast shift 7am-3pm. I have never FELT so much in my life. Everything was magnified. Bigger than life. The rescue workers became my best friends. Bussing tables never meant so much to me. I would seek out those who were willing to put up with me to hear about their day (or in this case, night). I became friends with the same crowd that were there during my shift. In fact, I had become friends with so many people that it made my supervisor very angry. She didn't think I was doing a good job. She put me behind the food line where I couldn't socialize. I thought that was part of our job! Oh well. Just before my two weeks were up, an older gentleman came up to me and said, "I've been watching you for the last week and I really like the way you interact with the rescue workers. You want a job?" Shocked, I said, "Excuse me, I'm a Motion Picture Sound Editor in Feature Films. I don't belong here. I've never worn a hard hat in my entire life." He said, "Don't worry, I'll get you trained and certified. It's that MOUTH of yours..." OMG.

January 14th was my first day to enter the pit. My boss wrapped around a ladder that went down the west slurry wall. I can't even tell you the last time I was on any kind of a ladder. I wrapped myself around the ladder and slowly started down. Looking straight into the slurry wall, I started crying out of fear. "What the hell am I doing?" From that moment forward, Ground Zero became my life. The life I previously had was put into a box, shoved in a closet and the door slammed closed. Ground Zero is now my life.

For the next four months, I was a safety Monitor in WTC6. Tower 1 collapsed on WTC6. The debris pile was so huge that they could not get access to the North Slurry Wall to drill tie-backs to stabilize the wall so it would not collapse. The Contractor that I worked for had two contracts. Confined Space and Freon Monitoring. What? The drillers doing the tie-backs were working UNDERNEATH the debris pile. My job? To monitor their safety 24-hours a day. We split the shifts to days or nights, 7-7. I worked days. We had to inspect each worker for correct gear, inspect the environment and the air. We had meters reading air, carbon monoxide, poisonous gas and explosives, 24-hours a day. I was the only one on the Freon Contract. I would read Freon in the NW corner of the "Bathtub". That's where the Chiller Tanks were located, on the bottom floor. There was no way to know their conditions until we could reach them, 6 floors down beneath; over 30 floors worth of debris.

The people I worked with are now family for life. We call, we write, and we see each other every 9/11 Anniversary and Christmas. I was really lucky. I don't seem to have any adverse effects from my time there. Not physically anyway. Unlike my dearest friend, Mike Bellone, who unconditionally worked at the site for no pay, ate and slept at St. Paul's, and made himself available to the Fire Department with his ATV 24-hours a day, for the entire clean-up efforts. He hitched a ride from Brooklyn to the site on 9/11 and never left.

The engulfing plume of toxins roll north, like a tsunami

One very windy, freezing cold morning, I was limping to the Respite Center to warm up. I had shin splints from the huge amount of walking I was doing every day. No one was around. It was gloomy, overcast skies. Suddenly, an ATV roared up from behind and asked me if I wanted a ride. Little did I know this was the beginning of a very incredible friendship that would last a lifetime. Mike and I are now family. I have worked with his wife Julie, I have spent so much incredible time with his daughter Meaghan, and share everything we went through during our time at Ground Zero. He has been my shoulder to cry on, my inspiration to learn from, and my way in to many elements of the Pit I would never have seen without him. He has introduced me to some of the most incredible people from Ground Zero that I am still friends with today.

He is now in a wheelchair and suffers from no oxygen in his system and blood poisoning. Yet, he spent years after Ground Zero traveling the country teaching children about 9/11. He is so amazing. Ask him, if he knew then what he knows now, would he do it again? Ask any firefighter, any rescue worker, anyone who was there. I would do it again. In a heartbeat.

Immediately following the collapse. the trail leaves remnants of destruction

On the other hand, none of the "non-uniformed" workers had the opportunity to get re-acclimated to our normal lives. It just ended. Done. That's it. "See you at the First Anniversary." I went back to LA and buried myself in all things Ground Zero. I had an electric current running through my veins that would not let me sleep or think without Ground Zero. My career in the film industry was gone. I had nowhere to live because I couldn't get a job. I moved home with my Dad with the hopes of getting my career back. Nothing. In 2002, I returned to New York City seven times. In 2003, it was worse. After the Second Anniversary, my Dad's wife physically threw me out of the house. She was sick of me. I ended up in a hotel room in Glendale not knowing what to do. I had just finished the LARGEST thing I will ever do. My career was gone. My friends can't understand me, and I really had no reason to be around. I didn't want to "kill" myself, I just didn't want to be around any more. For what? What's the point? I'm done.

Solange "Hollywood" preparing to take air quality measurements at Ground Zero

CHAPTER 9
MILITARY RESPONSE

Michael Bellone
Honorary Firefighter, Ladder Co. 20
Fire Department City of New York

While sifting through the rubble after the collapse, I started to notice an army of men, camouflaged suits, M16 rifles, half tracks, tanks, Humvees; it felt like we were at war. But the focus was still on finding anyone alive. I remember walking towards the Hudson River marina to the only public restroom and I was watching the servicemen guarding the perimeter of Ground Zero. I did kind of make me feel safe.

I spoke to some of them who came from Fort Drum and asked, "How long are you here for?"

His answer, "As long as you are here."

They explained how the area was on lockdown and only those with specific credentials could gain access. I was already approved to be on site.

The F-16s were flying overhead. We weren't nervous to hear this air traffic because we knew they were protecting us and not attacking us.

Military personnel posted around City Hall

Top & Bottom: Military personnel covering the perimeter of Ground Zero

Military covering the perimeter of Ground Zero

Military urn perimeter of Ground Zero checking access tags

Top & Bottom: Military posted around City Hall

CHAPTER 10
WHAT'S THE PLAN?

Lou Chinal
Firefighter, Engine Co. 152
Fire Department City of New York

I was home lying in bed, and oddly enough, I had just been at the World Trade Center at about 2:00 a.m. that morning. I had a part time job, went home, and went to bed at about 9:00 a.m.

My wife woke me up and said, "A plane hit the World Trade Center."

I watched it on TV for a while. Everything happened in slow motion. The atmosphere was so strange. There was no rush. I live two blocks from my firehouse, and I walked up. At this time the second plane hadn't hit. Everyone thought it was a freak accident. Our fire company covers the north shore of Staten Island so we weren't initially called until the Total Recall went into effect.

Vesey & Church St.

We watched it on television at the firehouse. Then the second plane hit. Then the panic started to set in, the urgency of it all. The dispatcher and the radio were going like crazy. There were calls coming in from all over the city.

I went and got my uniform on. Other guys were driving by our firehouse from other boroughs to borrow gear. And then the dispatcher came over the TV and said there was a Recall, a Total Recall. I don't think they've ever done that before.

Because of the physical location of my firehouse at the north end of Staten Island, we could look right across the harbor. We could see the smoke. It was so strange to be watching it on TV, then duck your head out the front door and see it, and then watch it on television in real time. Then all the bridges and the tunnels were shut down. No one could get there and move in. But the one thing that was still running was the Staten Island Ferry.

A regular city bus pulled up in front of our firehouse. We all piled on, and said, "Let's go." We went down to the Staten Island Ferry, and it was pretty much, "What's the PLAN?"

I heard one fire chief say, "I'm LISTENING."

Everybody was open to suggestions. We had no tools. We only had our turnout gear, which are the heavy coats, boots, and helmets. We went down into the ferry's engine room and stole a couple of axes that were on the boat. It was bizarre.

Unexpected water main break

We were told that a fireboat was tied up to the bottom of Liberty Street and ran across from where the south tower was from the river, up to the Federal Reserve Bank. We had a fireboat at Liberty Street, an unlimited source of water, guys coming in from all over the city, and I foolishly thought, "We're going to be here all day, but eventually we're going to make some sort of progress with this."

Lou Chinal at 10 & 1o firehouse

When we were pulling into the slip there was a lot of smoke, and to tell you the truth, I'm not sure if the towers had fallen down. It's like sensory overload. The towers were there when we got on the boat. We were watching. We could see the towers clearly, and then it was like they disappeared. It was surreal. It was like if I had spent two years preparing to go to the moon, and then you drop me off on the moon, I could have told you what was on the moon. But I couldn't tell you exactly when the WTC towers fell.

Washing off toxins before lunch

I believe what saved me that day was when we started directing some people into a parking garage across from West Street, Battery Park. I vividly remember being in there. I recall walking down a street and seeing the landing gear from a plane and stepping over it. It was definitely gear from a plane. I also vividly recall stepping on bodies, dozens of them, to the point where it was like trying to do a Mexican hat dance. People were everywhere, whether they had jumped from the building or were blown out by the plane, I didn't know. There were just pieces everywhere. I had seen bodies before, but this number was beyond imagination.

Trying to maneuver the rubble

A lonely stretcher never utilized during the rescue

Murray St.

Vesey and Washington Street

There was another building on West Street that was a roaring inferno, and we somehow got involved with trying to extinguish that fire. All the fire apparatus was basically unusable because of all the dust. The carburetors couldn't get restarted. The dust was everywhere and it was in everything. I guess that's when the onlookers started coming out, the photographers, people with sandwiches and bottles of sodas in their hands.

As far as my part that day, I contributed nothing, absolutely nothing. I just stood there and asked, "What do we do now?" At 2 a.m. that morning I saw a fire chief I knew. I almost jokingly asked him, "Hey Chief, I thought you retired, what are you doing here?"

He said, "I'm looking for my son. He was in the towers."

It was then that it hit me. I knew guys got killed, but I knew it on an intellectual level. I hadn't accepted it on an emotional level. My mind thought, "The kid got out. Of course he got out. He's in a hotel, or in Brooklyn, or somewhere." There are so many who are now dust. We never found any parts from a lot of the people.

I don't think I was doing very well. At about 3 a.m. a cop came up to me and asked me, "Where are you staying?"

I replied, "Staten Island."

South Bridge to the World Financial Center

He says, "Listen, I have to take this car back to a precinct in Staten Island."

I knew it was just an excuse to get me off the Pile and get me home. I just can't say enough good about what that cop did for me, and for what all the cops did down there.

When they later put out a call for volunteers to go back, I said, "I know the area. I used to work in downtown Manhattan." I went up to headquarters and saw an old chief I knew. He thought about it for about 10 seconds. A piece of paper came out of the computer, and he said, "Sign now, and here's where you go."

I was detailed to Ladder Company 10, which oddly enough did not have a fire truck. I don't think anybody knew what the plan was. They lost five people in that firehouse. When I got there we had a job called the GPS Unit, Global Positioning System. We had little hand-held computers and every time a body part was found, we stood over it and scanned a tab. The tag went into the bag with the body part.

That's what I did at Ground Zero. We found body parts all over the place. A flight attendant's pair of hands that were tied together was found on the roof of the firehouse. We tried to make it as dignified as possible. Whenever we found bodies or parts of bodies, we covered them with an American Flag. We all saluted as the body was brought out.

Checking the voids for victims

113

Lou Chinal on West St. after the collapse

Searching, searching and searching

A particular event stands out in my mind. There was an Episcopalian Bishop named Gerry Wolf. We found bones and a pair of pants. A wallet was in the pants along with an ID. Bishop Wolf said kind words over what was left of this poor kid. The body parts and bones went into one bag. The contaminated pants went into another, and the wallet into another bag. It took fourteen months to reunite all those parts.

The kid's brother called me on the phone. I don't even know how he found me. He wanted to know what happened to his brother, and "What did I see?" I told him that on October 10, 2001, I found his brother. It seemed very important for him to talk to someone who was really there.

A perimeter was set up in the first couple of days. Before you came to the perimeter, people's relatives put pictures in your hands. They asked us to look for this person, for that person. They had no idea that what we were finding were fingers, toes, and eyes. Walking past the perimeter we got a salute from five Marines. It was a strange dichotomy of emotions. People were grasping at straws, and the military was trying to make some sense of it all.

As people stood there, it felt like you were in a dream, more like a nightmare

CHAPTER 11
MAYBE IT WAS A DREAM

Ralph Shakarian
Laborer

At 8:45 a.m. I was changing cables on the mid-span on top of the George Washington Bridge. The guys with the walkie-talkies yelled, "They hit the tower! They hit the tower!"

We didn't know what was happening. All of a sudden the crane went down and they closed the bridge. Police were all over the place, and I looked south. I saw big smoke, black smoke, and I thought it was a fire.

We strapped ourselves to the wire, scaled the GWB with our cables, slid down, and got to the bottom of the bridge. We stood there and talked to each other and couldn't believe what was happening.

Photo By
Det. Greg Semendinger
NYC Police Aviation Unit

The first iron workers arrived by boat from the George Washington Bridge

Iron workers cutting up steel so rescue workers can get in

There was a big commotion, noise, police, and ambulances. Everybody was going toward the World Trade Center. We wanted to go help. A police boat took us over to the shore. We arrived by boat at approximately 12:30 p.m.

There was a heavy dark midst, and I couldn't see. We had such poor visibility. It had been a sunny day with not even a patch of a cloud. I couldn't make out what was going on. I couldn't comprehend it. We came off the boat and there was no sign of the towers. We looked at each other with our mouths open. I don't know how to put it into words. Maybe I was in shock.

We made our way down to the site and found an opening to it on the north side by the Verizon building. We saw beams sticking out of the pile of steel. And then we saw the bodies. Beams had skewered the people when they fell.

We climbed up to the beams. There was an old man with a torch in his hand, but he was too shaken to cut the beam. I asked him for the torch. I climbed the beam. We cut the beam and the bodies slid down off the beam. That is how we helped recover the first two bodies.

I just didn't know what to make out of it. Right next to it, there was another beam with four bodies on it. We cut that beam and came down.

There were lots of police and firefighters. I believe they were all like me, confused, because I know I was. I still couldn't comprehend or make myself believe what happened.

Top & Bottom: Without the iron workers the task of recovery was impossible

Without the iron workers the task of recovery was impossible

This guy and me started to help out by picking up body parts. I didn't know where to start or where to end. I saw a lot of firemen trying to pick up bodies and there'd be only half a body. Body bags were everywhere.

What actually got to me the most was a boy. He must have been not more than 12-years-old. A quarter of his body was missing. He was stuck underneath a beam with chairs, desks, and rubble on top of him. As we cleared the debris off him... when I saw him... I just broke down.

Maybe I was too tired. Maybe I was not ready... until this day. Maybe it was a dream. But I tell you this. It's a horrible dream to have.

I told my partner, who picked up the boy out of my hands, and kneeled at the edge of the beam, and screamed, "OH, JESUS!" Tears were pouring down his face. I was sobbing.

I had to leave. I went home and took a shower. It was a cold one. I stayed under the shower for about half an hour.

I later went back to work at Ground Zero. I told a friend that if I go back, I'm going back to prove that we are better than they are... whoever they are.

Now I have said it. I said it because I had to say it.

Maybe the nightmares will go away.

Maybe now it can be over.

CHAPTER 12
WHY ARE WE STILL HERE?

Mike Bellone
Honorary Firefighter, Ladder Co. 20
Fire Department City of New York

I came across a friend of mine, Derrick Greenberg, who was an ironworker. He had just brought in one of his cranes. We decided that we, and the group of firemen and Bob, would form a team and try to find as many people as possible.

Derrick hooked up a beam to remove it, and as he pulled the beam up, we found two people underneath. The firemen handed me the person's ID to hold while they picked up the body and put it into a black bag. I put the ID in the bag with the man.

Everyone was still holding onto the hope we would find survivors to rescue. As a firefighter Bob had spent 28 years running into burning buildings looking for people to rescue. I knew Bob was still holding onto hope that some of his men were still alive.

We kept searching. Maybe during the collapse, citizens, police, rescue workers, and firefighters sought protection inside the trucks. Maybe they were still trapped inside. Maybe someone was still alive. Maybe. As I searched through debris, I hoped I would stumble upon one of Bob's men. But that would not happen today. I thought of my kids and my family and hoped they were safe. I realized what I was missing, and that was my family.

The crane needed to be relocated, so Bob and I walked over to see if we could help by Vesey and Church Street. Bob and I made our way around the corner of Church Street and took a left onto Vesey. Bob, myself, and five firefighters walked towards what was about to happen.

We were about halfway past the Federal Building and approaching Building 7. I remember hearing a screeching, churning sound of steel rubbing against each other like a train pulling into a train station. The ground started to shake.

That afternoon Building 7 came crashing down around us.

We all stood still. Nobody talked. Nobody moved.

When the dust and smoke cleared, I looked up. The same men I was standing with, were still standing. We all looked at each other frozen in time. We could read each other's minds.

"Why are we still here?"

I later realized I was still here so that I could talk about it. A certain bond was formed that day between Bob and me. It is something different than a friendship or a family. It is something far more than that. I knew right then and there that this was the place I had to be all the time. It was the start of a day that lasted 257 days.

Firefighter Bob Barrett and Honorary Firefighter Mike Bellone

Firefighter Bob Barrett and Honorary Firefighter Mike Bellone searching for victims

Greenwich Street, looking south at building 7

Bob Barrett
Retired Firefighter, Ladder Co. 20
Fire Department City of New York

I think I was in a state of shock trying to grasp the situation and to understand the gravity of what just happened. This would take some time. It all had to sink in. I don't know to this day if I have fathomed the entirety of this tragedy.

I spent that day lost in a cocktail of emotions. I was afraid, anxious, sad, solemn, and confused. Time was unconnected. I felt like there was nobody real there except me. I was the world, and others were part of the landscape, drifting in and out of my consciousness. I was there, people were with me, but yet they weren't. My mind was in another place, on another plane, and I refused to accept the fact that the towers had come down.

I looked for the towers through the smoke, through the debris, trying to wish them back out of the dust. My mind was filled with computer-like messages and images that were too numerous for me to make sense of. I stumbled along trying to grab hold of whatever strength I could muster.

Building 7

It was left to me to be bigger than myself. At one point I thought of something my son said to me when he was young. We were talking about superheroes and my son said to me, "Dad, let's use our powers for good not evil." At that moment in time I wanted to be a good guy, and it was to be my driving credo.

That day, 343 firefighters died responding to the "five-alarmer" at WTC. We lost 15 members in all from our firehouse, seven in the truck Ladder 20, seven in Squad 18, and one Fire Marshal. We lost all of our rigs including the Deputy Chief's sedan. That day the Fire Department lost 126 fire trucks and all the equipment that was on them.

We didn't have any fire trucks or equipment, but still we were on an around-the-clock shift working 24 hours a day. About a week later we received a spare truck and went on a 24-on, 24-off shift, which meant I worked 24 hours in the firehouse covering our district and also did search and recovery. On my 24 hours off I went down to the site to work.

For the first four or five days I stayed at the site only leaving to walk over to our firehouse to see the surviving members of my company and to check with our officers as to how we were to proceed.

I didn't know when the day started or when it would end. It became one continuous and unending day that lasted 257 days.

On the left, Saint John's Dormitory

CHAPTER 13
NDMS

Jay Schnitzer, M.D., PhD
Massachusetts General Hospital
Department of Pediatric Surgery
NDMS, IMSuRT
Boston, Massachusetts

When the planes hit the towers, I was in my office in Boston getting ready to go to a conference in Italy. One of our secretaries came in and asked, "Did you hear the news that an airplane crashed in New York?"

At first I thought she might be joking. Then I saw the expression on her face. I turned on the television and saw the reports. That was Tuesday morning just after the first plane hit, but before the second hit. Then as we were watching the television, the second plane hit. Soon after that there was something going on at the Pentagon. The news was very sketchy at that time, but I knew it was obviously a disaster. It was likely that the disaster teams would be called up shortly.

Searching the pile with the rescue dogs

I belong to NDMS, the National Disaster Medical System. We are a Boston-based team that also belongs to the IMSuRT, National Medical Surgical Response Team. I called the head of our team Dr. Susan Briggs, and she already knew something was going on. Soon thereafter she got a call from Washington and she was to get her team ready and mobilized.

Behind the scenes, on the ground, the President authorized activation of the Stafford Act. The sequence of a disaster response is 1) Initial response is local FDNY NYPD and 2) If overwhelmed, the Stafford Act is empowered.

This authorizes the President to offer Federal assistance to state and local governments. FEMA, Federal Emergency Management Agency, is the lead agency. The government's response is then organized under the Federal Response Plan. The Federal Response Plan establishes a process and structure for the systematic, coordinated, and effective delivery of Federal assistance to address the consequences of any major disaster or emergency declared under the Robert T. Stafford Disaster Relief and Emergency Assistance Act. This is put into operation when there is a major disaster, manmade or natural that exceeds the capability of local assets to respond effectively. The order of command at that time was:

U.S. Department of Health and Human Services (HHS)

Office of Emergency Preparedness (OEP)

National Disaster Medical System (NDMS)

Disaster Medical Assistance Team Metro-Boston (our team)

Disaster Medical Assistance Team standing by on ready-alert to respond for assistance on the pile

When the Stafford Act was activated, they wanted the closest available teams. On September 11th, we readied ourselves to head out later that day. In Boston we have a regular DMAT, Disaster Medical Assistance Team, but we also have three specialty teams. Boston is rather unique, and Dr. Briggs heads all. We have a Pediatric Team, a Burn Team, and an IMSuRT. This was the first international team of the NDMS system. Some of us are members of all four teams.

Our team was deployed between 12 Noon and 1 p.m. on September 11. We gathered the whole group together by 5 p.m. We formed a convoy of vehicles and headed up to Stewart Air Force Base in New York. We spent the night at Stewart in a large hanger with lots of cots, and by the following morning there were several thousand people there ready to help.

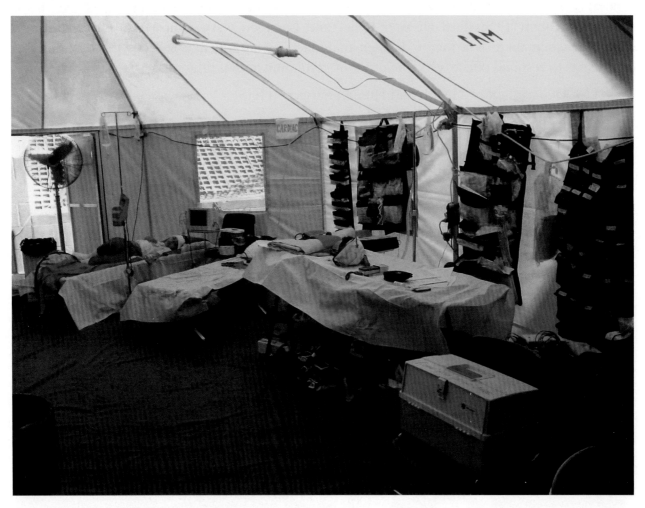

Disaster Medical Assistance Team tents specifically for workers, so doctors and nurses could tend to the victims

The original plan had been to set up a large triage hospital at Stewart with the assumption we were dealing a mass casualty event of injured people. As the situation rapidly progressed, it became apparent that it was, in fact, a mass fatality event and not a mass casualty event. As a result, there was no need for a large triage hospital or a need for intensive care beds or regional or national hospitals. All of which were being set up at the same time with the expectation there would be mass casualties.

Since we were now dealing with a mass fatality event, the people in charge tried to determine what the needs were at the site in terms of medical assistance. It was decided that there was a need for medical care at the site for the rescue workers. The NDMS teams were deployed to New York City. On Thursday morning we arrived first at Chelsea Pier where a medical station had already been set up. This location was too far, too remote, from Ground Zero to be of any use at that point. We had expected mass casualties, which is why the Chelsea medical area was set up. It was obvious this was no longer needed.

We moved at about midnight to what was known as Medical Station Number One, which was set up in the courtyard of the community college about one block from Ground Zero, across the street from the Stiverson High School. We set up that station in the courtyard between midnight and 7 a.m., and it was operational and ready to receive patients by 7 a.m. on Friday.

Disaster Medical Assistance Team tents specifically for workers, so doctors and nurses could tend to the victims

This was still a little too far away, so over the next three days we set up a series of four medical stations in a ring around Ground Zero. These were then staffed in eight-hour shifts by the NDMS DMATS that had by then been deployed to New York to join us.

One of our medical stations was located in a delicatessen on the south edge of the site. We used their refrigerated section, which had previously been used for salads, desserts, sodas, and water. We dispensed over-the-counter medications and other supplies that people needed, like Tylenol, Advil, and bandages. The back part of the deli was converted to a real medical station

129

triage area complete with stretchers. We also had Advanced Life Support systems if they were needed.

The reason why we set up the medical stations so close to the "pile," was so that the rescue workers would have easy access to care. This way they wouldn't have to interrupt their work any longer than absolutely necessary. We knew that the only thing they wanted to do was to keep working.

The U.S. Naval Medical Hospital Ship, "Comfort", docks at Pier 19 for stress management

My job was to patch them up and get them back to work. The most common types of injuries we saw were what we called "the walking wounded." This included eye irritation and foreign bodies in the eye, foot problems (especially blisters), some cases of dehydration because of the intense heat, and upper respiratory tract problems brought on by all the smoke and other articulates in the air and occasional minor wounds.

We also saw a small number of serious medical trauma related problems. Most of those cases were chest pain or worsening underlying respiratory problems, people with chronic pulmonary disease. We saw a handful of more serious trauma from either falls or explosions or burns. Everybody had psychology responses to the stress and fatigue.

The NDMS also includes a Veterinary Medical Assistance Team (VMAT), which helped take care of the search and rescue dogs. The Canine Unit was amazing. The dogs were part of the search and rescue and also the search and recovery teams. They became incredibly frustrated because they couldn't find any survivors. The dogs literally worked until they dropped and then had to be taken care of. We saw a large number of exhausted and dehydrated dogs. You couldn't stop the dogs, they could sense something terrible had happened and just kept going.

My team was there for two weeks. We left to go back to Boston on September 28 when our teams were relieved from DMATS from other locations in the country. During that first couple of weeks, we saw over 4,000 patients.

The U.S. Naval Medical Hospital Ship, "Comfort", docks at Pier 19 for stress management

CHAPTER 14
CONSOLING EACH OTHER

Debbie Meshejian
Mental Health Counselor

On September 13, I started volunteering for the Red Cross as a mental health counselor for Family Assistance at the Armory. The Red Cross had 20 counselors for every 50 family members. Once the families filed a death certificate for their loved ones, the families had an option to go see the site. From Pier 94 they were brought to the site by ferryboat. Each counselor pretty much stayed with one family and there were usually three to four people in a family.

From the Armory I then volunteered at the Red Cross Respite Center located at St. John's church. This center was for the workers. It was a place where they could go to relax and get something to eat.

I struck up conversations with the workers, and the goal was to try to get their head out of the Pile. Ground Zero was first referred to as "the Pile." Then it was "the Pit," and then "the Hole."

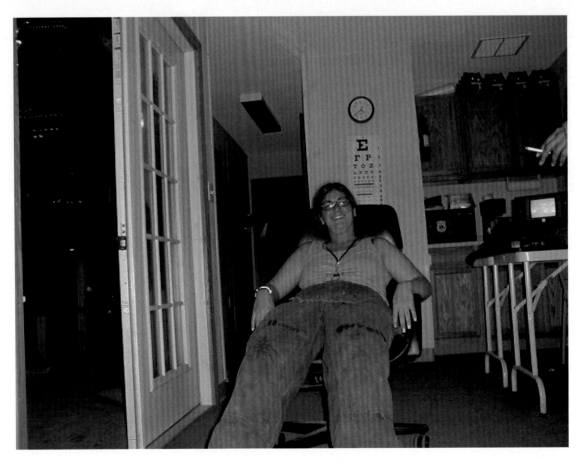

Grief counselor, Debbie Zimm

A company that provided medical services out of the site later hired me as their mental health counselor for the workers. They tested people for respirators and saw people for physical accidents, or anything medical. If workers needed stitches, they stitched them there, and for anything serious they were sent to the hospital.

I was working six or seven days a week, 12 hour shifts, and went out and around the workers. It took a couple of months for me to get to know them. Counseling is all about forming relationships and building trust. I let them know that I was there everyday, and eventually they saw me as one of them. I saw what they saw. I felt what they felt.

Generally it was a matter of listening to them and being there. Regular conversation took its own course. One man told me that he was having trouble sleeping. He was having dreams that he didn't want to have. He didn't want to go to sleep because of the dreams.

Debbie Zimm on site

One of the biggest things I advised the workers, was to "not keep it inside." Many of them had built a big fence in not wanting to tell their families and friends what they were seeing or experiencing. They didn't want to add to their family's fears. When you carry it around, it's like a weight and can keep you down. You have to get it out, tell someone, or write it. Tell your pet, because your pet isn't going to get hurt by what you say. If you write it down, burn it afterwards, burn it out of your life. Take it off your shoulders and put it on the shelf of experience. Tell yourself you're going to learn from it and that you'll be better for it.

We were all working so hard, 7 days a week, 12 hours. The joke at Ground Zero was someone saying, "I got five hours sleep," and the other person would say, "I'm so jealous." Everyone was emotionally and physically exhausted.

As a counselor, I knew that it wasn't going to really sink in until we were all done doing recoveries. I told them, "After it's done, start writing and put it on a shelf of experience."

I met Mike Bellone when one of our mutual friends asked me to meet him. Mike and I hit it off. Mike brought people to me. He was like my liaison to the men. He and I built a nice friendship.

As a counselor, it was nice to have someone to talk to. We relied on each other while we were there. Mike was definitely there for me as much as I was there for him.

While I was at Ground Zero I met the families and the workers, and they were the most incredible people. I learned the most valuable lesson in my life, and it has changed me. To see the good in human nature, the collective spirit, and how everyone can come together and be there for each other.

Debbie with co-worker

Bob Barrett
Retired Firefighter, Ladder Co. 20
Fire Department City of New York

While we were working at the firehouse and also doing recoveries, we had mandatory counseling. I didn't think it was the time, nor did I have time to dedicate to a counselor. I was busy making recoveries. So, I did not wish to speak to a counselor. I had Mike and the other members of my company to talk to and tell them what I was feeling. What we were all feeling.

We vented our emotions to each other, especially with Mike. Mike and I shared our feelings with each other. We had been and were going through it together. We supported one another and could continue to work at the same time. We weren't ready for formal counseling. It was just too early. We actually found great solace with one another. We counseled one another.

Several counselors came to the firehouse and spoke to us individually and as a group. But again, it didn't feel like the time was right for it. We were still wrapped up in our emotions.

We couldn't step "back" from it because it was still happening. We were in the midst of it all. It was impossible for someone who wasn't there to pluck our emotions from us. Our emotions were still raw and the wounds fresh. The time for healing had not come.

Mike and I still do not go to professional counseling. We keep in close contact with each other and the other rescue workers. That's who we talk to.

Debbie with her colleagues

Mike Bellone
Honorary Firefighter, Ladder Co. 20
Fire Department City of New York

I think counseling is a great thing. The first time I was asked to go see a counselor I was sent to St. John's College on West Street right near the site. It was a respite center. I never talked to Debbie as a counselor.

At the request of some of the chiefs, they wanted me to see a counselor because of all I had seen and done. They thought it appropriate that I see someone.

I sat in a room. They sent in a Red Cross counselor. After speaking to her for 10 minutes, I saw tears running down her face.

She was very upset. I started to help her. After I left my counseling session, I felt like I had just spoken to someone I would normally speak to on the site, and help. This didn't do anything for me other than the fact I was able to help someone.

When asked how the counseling went, I just said, "It was great. If there's anyone else you want me to help, let me know."

Three months later, after some difficult times I was going through by losing both my parents, and the fact I was working even harder, they thought it was time for me to get some more counseling.

This time I saw a counselor from another organization. And again, this person became hysterical. I hugged this person, and told them, "Everything will be all right."

The third time I saw a counselor I had spoken to over at St. Paul's. She was new and eager to help. I gave her a few names of people that I would send to her. But she insisted on talking to me.

After ten minutes I knew where our conversation was headed.

I said, "Before this gets any further, let me get someone in here for you."

While I was getting someone for the counselor, a guy started ribbing me and said, "Hey Mike, you gotta stop destroying all the counselors before we run out of counselors."

And I simply said, "These counselors are great. They just can't do anything for me. They don't understand where I am or where I'm going."

I found it a lot easier to talk to the men I worked with down in the Pit. They understood where I was going and where I was coming from.

Anyone who says men can't be emotional, are so wrong. There were nothing but emotions down there.

Debbie Zimm working in the west hut

CHAPTER 15
PIER 94

Mike Bellone
Honorary Firefighter, Ladder Co. 20
Fire Department City of New York

For a temporary command center, this area, Pier 94, looked like it had been in operation for years and years. This huge area was divided into sections. There was the FDNY, NYPD, PAPD, OSS (Office of Strategic Services), OEM (Office of Emergency Management), FEMA, US Armed Forces (all branches), FBI and many other civil and federal branches of service. There was also a section for grief counseling, for the victims' families and any others who were in need. There was funding for families and housing for those who had to be removed from the Ground Zero area and perimeter.

Pier 94 personnel assisting in child service, monetary compensations,
counseling, strategic services and operation headquarters

Everyone who worked there was polite, respectful, informative, and made things happen quickly. Amidst all the chaos, grief and confusion, Pier 94 worked like a perfect engine. All information given by the workers there was swift and accurate. Pier 94 was heaven's annex and all the workers were hand-picked angels.

Top & Bottom: Pier 94 personnel assisting in child services, monetary
compensations, counseling, strategic services and operation headquarters

CHAPTER 16
COLLATERAL DAMAGE

Mike Bellone
Honorary Firefighter, Ladder Co. 20
Fire Department City of New York

Working on the pile, one thing that I had noticed was all the perimeter of the buildings being damaged. One building had two pins to help it from toppling over. The pins were placed near the perimeter buildings a few days after the initial collapse. A laser beam was shot between the pins and any break in the beam would sound an alarm that the building had moved or shifted. This would help identify any other unstable buildings and prevent further loss. Buildings that suffered significant damage included the American Express building, The Atrium, Verizon, St. John's University dormitory, 90 West Street, Deutsch Bank, Century 21 Department Store, Millennium Hotel and Zuccoti Park. These buildings were considered highly toxic and unstable, though we still searched them for victims and evidence.

Brooks Brothers Department store

Building on Liberty Street

World Market Tower

World Financial Center Atrium

Fire Truck split in half

Engine 76

Deutch Bank building

Top: Building #5 Bottom: Parts of aircraft engine

145

CHAPTER 17
DOCUMENTING DEVASTATION

Rob Miller
Photojournalist
New York Post

I remember exactly everything I did before it happened, but once it happened, it's a blur. I had an early assignment on September 11, 2001. I was to seek out Lizzie Grubman's apartment and take photos as she left and headed to court. It was one of our big stories of the day.

I got to her place at seven in the morning. I remember taking a taxi, getting a bagel with butter, walking over by her apartment, planting myself, and waiting. Another photographer was there from another paper. We were both standing outside. At one point he tapped me on the shoulder.

He said, "Hey, Rob, that plane is flying really low."

He looked up. I just shrugged. It was just another day in the city. I didn't think twice about it. About ten minutes later he got a call from his desk. They told him that they thought a plane crashed downtown, near the World Trade Center. He had to go.

I called my desk and spoke to my editor. He said, "I want you to go down and try to get into the Empire State Building. We think a plane crashed into the World Trade Center or Battery Park."

My editor thought it was a little Cessna, so I picked up and left. I remember walking to the subway and hearing all the sirens. I was on Lexington Avenue and it was filled with traffic and sirens. I knew something had happened. I got onto the subway and took it to 34th Street. I got out on Broadway and Herald Square. When I came out, I looked up and saw smoke and thought, "Wow, this is bigger than a Cessna."

I started heading towards the World Trade Center. People were talking on cell phones. Telephone booths were backed up with people waiting for a phone.

I tried to get into the Empire State Building. The security guard told me it was closed. I told him, "I'm with the press. There's a plane crash, and I need to get up to the top." He told me I had to leave.

It was now very crowded on the streets. I realized that I really did have to leave. Arguing about it would be pointless. I half understood why everyone was leaving, but at the same time I thought they would let people back in.

I tried to get a taxi, but I couldn't get one by myself. I asked someone if I could jump in with him and we'd share the fare. We headed downtown to 5th Avenue. I remember seeing a tour bus filled with people looking up at the Empire State Building while all this was happening.

I thought, "This is not going to be good, this is going to be bad."

The devastation

The devastation

When we got below 14th Street, the traffic was moving so slow that I jumped out and started walking. I tried to get into a nearby building so I could get up to the roof and shoot from there. I knew I had to get high as fast as I could for a better vantage point. I talked to the doorman, but he said the building was closed and only open to residents. I left that building and tried another one. I talked with the maintenance man, told him I was with the press, and he said he'd escort me up to the rooftop.

We took the elevator and walked up another few flights to the elevator room. We opened the window and climbed out onto the water tower on top of the roof. We made it that far, only to find out that a wall blocked the view. So I had to leave that building and find another one.

The devastation

I walked down toward Washington Square about a half a mile away from the towers. I got part way when I found a building with an unobstructed view. People were standing out in front. A man told me that he lived there, and he would allow me into the building but that his view was obstructed. I took him up on the offer, and once in, I thought I'd be able to find someone else who had a better view.

He took me up to about the 16th floor, and I started knocking on doors. I found an apartment with somebody home, and when the man answered I told him why I wanted to come in and I was with the press. The first thing he said to me was, "A second plane just hit."

I thought, "Shit, we're under attack."

I ran over to the window, and I was just looking. I wasn't taking pictures for what seemed like a few minutes. More smoke was coming out, a thick black smoke. I thought of those poor people in the towers.

A number of people were in the apartment, and I was told I could take pictures from the terrace facing the towers. I walked out onto the terrace, and I could clearly see, while I was looking for this view, that a second plane had hit.

And then for some reason I went downstairs. I don't know why I was on the streets. Then the first building collapsed. I heard a rumble, but I had no idea what it was. I looked at the people and saw the look on their faces. I just knew something terrible had happened. People were putting their hands on their mouths in shock by what they saw.

Ground floor perspective

I remember lifting my camera and taking pictures of a guy with his hand over his mouth. After I took those pictures, I learned that the south tower was coming down. I spent some time taking pictures of people's reactions. All of a sudden I was hearing news blaring out of car radios.

In shock, I went back up into the building. When I reached the apartment, people were in tears. A girl sat on the couch crying. An older man who seemed pretty composed was talking on the phone. From the television in the background we heard that a plane crashed in Pennsylvania.

Huge amounts of smoke were coming from the second tower. I could see pieces of it falling off. The tower was going to fall. It seemed like the south tower snapped from the middle. As I was looking through the camera and thinking of those poor people, I wept as I took pictures of the building coming down.

But I knew I had to do it. I had to take those pictures. I also knew there was nothing more I could do to help them. I felt helpless taking pictures at a moment like that. I know it sounds cliché, but I knew I was a "reporter." I had to document the history. As a reporter it was my job, despite the terrible circumstances. Taking photographs while this was happening was not automatic for me. I had to force myself to keep the camera straight and keep shooting. I had to keep looking at the building as it collapsed.

After taking the photos I then had to do "the routine". I called my editor and reported to him. I had to report what I saw. The first thing my editor asked was, "Are you all right?"

I said, "I'm safe."

After both towers collapsed I didn't put my cameras down right away. I took pictures of the whole horizon, panoramic views with the wide lens. I remember seeing all the smoke, and then my cell phone didn't work. When that didn't work, I used the landline in the apartment. I went back and forth on the phone with my editor. He wanted me to come in with what I had.

Part of me wanted to stay and go down to the site, but another part of me after seeing what just happened… it just seemed unbearable to go near it. I didn't know the building went straight down. I thought it went all over the place and everything was destroyed. I was told to go back to the paper, and I did. Strangers took me back up town.

I was numb, in shock. As if I never, ever thought those buildings would collapse. Total shock. I thought anything could happen now, but for some reason I felt safe. I felt guilty about feeling safe.

When I walked into the New York Post I saw another photographer. He was covered in dust. It looked like he should have been dead.

When I got inside there was chaos and noise. Everyone was rushing into the back room with their film and talking about what they had just seen. My editor told me that my mother called and she was very concerned. He wanted me to call her right away. She was so glad to hear I was fine.

Ground floor perspective

CHAPTER 18
BUCKET BRIGADE

Mike Bellone
Honorary Firefighter, Ladder Co. 20
Fire Department City of New York

I was passing buckets. We started to get buckets and made lines of people with maybe 50 or more in a line. We sent an empty bucket in, and a bucket of debris came back. All of the contents in the buckets were searched. I remember when someone accidentally spilled a bucket. What fell out of it was a hand, an ID, a shoe with a foot in it, a bracelet, and a once again reminder that this was a recovery operation. I couldn't see anyone walking away from what happened.

As the buckets were passed, I was on the side where the buckets were full. Different odors were coming out of the buckets as they passed by. I smelled toxins. I then realized that besides all of the other things I had noticed in the dust, what about all the freon, the mercury, the lead? All of the different types of chemicals used to keep a building of that size cool in the summer and hot in the winter. The toxic odor was as though someone had taken all of those ingredients, put them in a plastic bag, and shaken them up.

After hours on the bucket brigade, a few of us broke into groups of six and jumped into voids that were once windows in the World Trade Center. We call them voids because they led down into an area that you did not know and couldn't see. We tried to listen for noises, but heard nothing.

We tried to pull out what were any signs of property or identification to see if anyone was down there. We were finding make-up kits, handbags, shoes, and sneakers. Some shoes and sneakers had legs and feet inside of them.

Bob Barrett
Retired Firefighter, Ladder Co. 20
Fire Department City of New York

Although any reasonable person would have assumed there would be no survivors, my mind would not let me be reasonable. I still hoped that civilians, all the emergency services, and my men would be found. It was probably not until the next day that I surrendered to the fact, to the reality, that my company was gone under that twisted 110 floors of steel and concrete.

As I stood there surveying the landscape, I couldn't help but visualize the people I had worked with for so many years. Firefighters I knew not only from my company, but also from a number of companies throughout the city. I had thoughts running through my head. "Who was working? Who had the day off? How many of us responded?"

We didn't know who among us was still alive.

The site was excavated the first two weeks, mainly by buckets

Thousands of buckets

153

I wanted to rescue at least one person that day, but it never happened. We found no one alive. I quickly realized that recoveries were important. Recoveries are critically important for families because it allows them to grieve their loved ones with something tangible. Anyone's remains that could be identified were later turned over to the families.

Initially we acted as individuals more or less, but as firefighters our natural instinct is to form units and help one another. Therefore, our prior experiences helped us to band together in searches and work as units even though we were without leadership.

In the initial phases, we picked up the pieces that were strewn across the landscape. There were units checking any void where they thought someone might still be alive. This was still a precarious situation because fires were still burning. Beams were hot, and there was always a possibility of further collapse. One had to be particularly cautious not to also become a victim.

We were finding and picking up anything at all and putting it into buckets. The buckets were sent up where they were emptied and then inspected for anything and everything. Pieces, fragments of human remains, were transported by hundreds of rescue workers to a place where the victims could be sorted through and identified.

Mike and I used our bare hands and basically worked without any tools. I was dressed in shorts and sneakers and looked like I was headed for the beach on a sunny day. It wasn't until that night that I returned to the firehouse to pick up some of my protective clothing.

Buckets everywhere

Passing the bucket

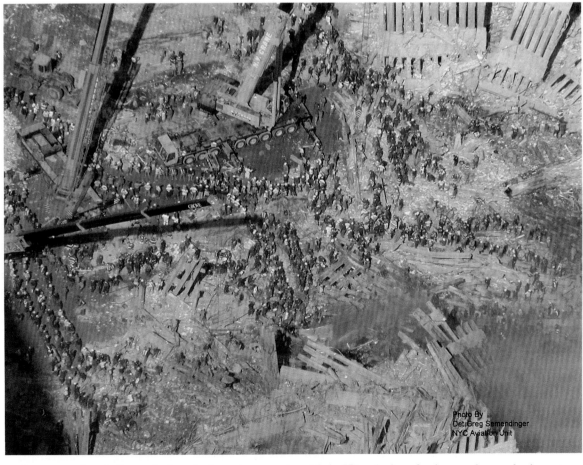

Rescue workers in lines of a hundred or more, passing debris, ID's, airplane fuselage and many body parts

CHAPTER 19
ORDINARY HEROES

Mike Bellone
Honorary Firefighter, Ladder Co. 20
Fire Department City of New York

As I passed buckets to the next person in line, the firemen I came in with on the first day came by and asked me how I was doing.

I said, "I'm fine."

They looked at me, and one of them told me, "We're all going to grab a sandwich. They're making sandwiches for us. You eat with us."

Civilians handing out food and water to the workers

I felt accepted. It made me feel like a part and made me want to do more. That is one reason I couldn't leave. It is what helped motivate me to do more.

As it got closer to the morning, after hours of digging and finding more bodies, Bob and I decided to take a rest. We slept on a curb near the AMEX, the American Express building by the marina. When I awoke the sun was out, but the smoke still smoldered. I got up and continued where I left off a couple of hours before. I ran into Derrick and we decided to communicate back and forth on walkie-talkies and use his crane for recoveries. Derrick was more than obliging, and we had a very good team of players with all the same intent: to recover everybody.

Tony Award Winner Bernadette Peters handing out sandwiches and water bottles to the rescue workers

There was no way anyone was going to survive in those towers after what just happened. There were only a handful of people who survived after both towers came down, including men from Ladder 6. They survived because they were in the third floor south tower stairwell with Captain Jonas.

I thought about my kids, my wife, my family, and realized how lucky I was that they didn't have to go through the horrible grief I was witnessing. I began to really miss them. I was a medic and Bob was a fireman. Between the two of us, one would think that with all those years of experience we would be able to help many people. But we couldn't find any. There weren't any people to help.

I was in the lobby of the south tower when I discovered the girl. I found the body of a young girl who had been skewered by a rebar pole of solid steel. When I saw her, I thought of my daughter and how lucky I was. It was then I realized we're only here a short time and have to make the most of the time we have. I wasn't doing that with my kids. I swore that after this recovery was over, I was going to make sure I never wasted a minute with my children or my family.

As an emergency worker you never know what to expect when you arrive on any scene, but you're somewhat prepared. This was not a scene you could prepare for. There were no bosses. There were no chiefs. They were all gone. There was no plan. We took everything upon ourselves to do the best we could with what we had, which was nothing except our hearts.

There was no hesitation as to who was going in. No hesitation as to who was jumping into a void. This was the sight of ordinary people whether they were firemen, policemen, ironworkers, construction workers, medics, or civilians who were doing extraordinary things under extraordinary circumstances.

At one point, Bob called me over and said, "Mike, you need some water."

I said, "Sure."

Bob said, "Can you believe this? This guy has to be about 50 years old and he walked all the way to Chambers Street to get a bucket of ice and cold water."

In our eyes, this man is our hero. Without that water to drink, to rinse our eyes out, to pour down our backs, to cool off our bodies, we couldn't get our job done. We seemed to work like a perfect engine. No matter how little the task, if you missed that task, it threw the whole engine off like it was missing a spark plug.

I wish I could find that man to thank him for the incredible job he did by bringing us water. No matter how little you may think that job is, it was a giant, heroic feat to us.

Academy Award Nominee actor Harrison Ford gave up his afternoon to help feed the rescue workers

Civilians bravely attempt to put the fire out of the burning ambulance

Civilians handing out food and water to rescue workers

CHAPTER 20
ON THE THIRD DAY

Frank Silecchia
Concrete/Excavation Specialist

I had watched the towers fall from the Jersey shore, but the first day I couldn't get down there. That night I went to sleep with the news of the World Trade Center. The next morning a phone call woke me up. They were still taking volunteers. I ate, got dressed, and made my way into the City. I do excavation, pick-and-shovel and heavy machinery. I handle anything to do with utilities, concrete, foundations, bridges, storm sewers, and tunnels.

The second day, I pursued my pilgrimage to get down to the World Trade Center. I waited all day. At the end of the day I finally managed to get down to the site by traveling along with provisions that were being brought through. Once I finally got there I was hoping to find survivors. Unfortunately, I didn't find one.

On that second day, I went into Building 6 with firefighters as a rescue operation. The fire chief allowed me to follow along with them. He broke us into divisions of three with about 12 guys to a division. I suggested that we turn on car headlights to illuminate the area. This helped us find our way while we searched. We found no survivors but discovered two deceased. We bagged them and brought them up.

We were in Building 6 on the floor above the garage level. It was a high-level security area along with high-level surveillance equipment used by Custom Agents. For personnel such as myself, the chief's orders were to remove the bodies through on stokes, and then haul them up. A stoke litter is a fiberglass or aluminum basket used by firefighters and rescue workers that holds an injured or deceased person.

It was now pre-dawn on the third day of devastation. I was on the top of the stoke line, two and a half stories up at the edge of the loading dock area. Below me, pieces of the north tower had created a large open area in Building 6 from its beams plunging through it. Below me, firefighters loaded body bags into stokes.

As daylight began to illuminate the open-air crevassed area, to what looked like a newly created atrium, I began to make out images below me. What I was looking at was the interior of Building 6 totally crushed from the north tower's debris. As it grew lighter, I saw what was below me.

I became overwhelmed.

When the north tower fell into Building 6, as Building 6 collapsed, some of its iron beams were severed.

Below me, I saw not one, but three crosses.

The first iron cross was standing upright in the middle of a large debris pile inside the "atrium". On the horizontal part of the cross, it looked like a "shroud" had been draped over it.

The Cross was found standing in Building #4

The two other crosses were in the background of the first cross, which to me gave it the affect of "Calvary."

It brought me to my knees. I wept for 20 minutes.

In being a Born-Again Christian, I understood the significance of the setting and what I was looking at. Death and destruction were all around me, and in front of me stood the meaning of my faith.

I have a Christian faith and I understand the meaning of God and the purpose of his Son. I understand that God's Son should suffer for man's sins. As I looked upon the three crosses, I knew I was to understand that what I found would not only bring comfort to me, but would bring comfort to many.

To be able to see the images of the three crosses through the early morning light on the beginning of the third day of devastation was such a privilege for me. It was and is an honor for me to be given this opportunity to spread the word of my faith to a grieving country.

I saw the firefighters looking upon the scene in tears. We all cried and wept in anguish because of the dead bodies, but in being able to see the crosses lifted our sprits. It allowed me to realize that if it did this to me, there is a nation that needs the same medicine. I then proclaimed from that moment forward I would to try to preserve this cross so that it can bring comfort to others.

Left to Right -- Frank Silecchia, Andrew Macchio and Father Jordan

The cross was erected on top of the north walkway cement slab as a sign of hope

CHAPTER 21
MOUNTAINS OF DEBRIS

Mike Bellone
Honorary Firefighter, Ladder 20
Fire Department City of New York

I had to ask myself, "How are we going to find a way to safely travel underneath all the debris in order to find these people?"

Bob Barrett
Retired Firefighter, Ladder 20
Fire Department city of New York

In trying to explain it, it might be similar to the way one would clean a room. You start out with the little pieces, picking up whatever is around, until you get to the part when you move the furniture. Our furniture was steel, concrete, and debris.

Building #7 reduced to a pile

Jiri Boudnik
Architect, ERMACS (Emergency Response Multi-Agency Communications Systems)
Written by Jiri Boudnik, edited by Gail Swanson

I had been in a weekly Tuesday morning meeting when I got a call that a plane, presumably a small Cessna had hit the World Trade Center's north tower. At the time I was working as a project manager with J.A. Jones Construction at the entrance to the Brooklyn Bridge on a Federal Courthouse and Post Office construction site. I said, "I'm in a meeting, I'll call you back," when only a few minutes later the door flew open.

The construction superintendent shouted, "Everybody out, another plane flew into the second tower. This is some kind of an attack on the United States and this is Federal property, so everybody out!"

When I got out of the building I had a clear view of the towers burning. As an architect I realized that the tremendous heat being generated by those fires would buckle the steel. Since our site was being evacuated, I grabbed my hardhat, a portable radio, and headed over the Brooklyn Bridge into Manhattan. When I was in the middle of the bridge the south tower started collapsing.

Light travels faster than sound, and it took a few seconds for the thunderous noise to reach the bridge. There were thousands of people walking against me with their backs to the towers. When the sound finally reached them, the south tower was already down.

This pile of debris was 70 feet high

165

A few minutes later I heard on my portable radio that the next potential targets would be bridges and tunnels. There were military planes in the air, and I prayed they were ours. I returned to the Brooklyn side of the bridge for fear of being blown up in the middle of the bridge. When I realized the planes were American, I started crossing the bridge for the second time.

The north tower collapsed when I reached Manhattan. This time the cloud of dust reached all the way to City Hall. Everyone was covered in white powder with dark spots around their eyes and nostrils. That day the closest I could get to the World Trade Center site was Chambers and West Street.

The next morning I went to work in Brooklyn where a group of construction workers were assembling, determined to go help with the rescue operations and debris removal. We convinced police officers that were guarding the entrance to the bridge to provide us with a police van, which then escorted us over the deserted bridge and through the empty streets of Lower Manhattan. We were dropped off at the corner of Albany Street and Gateway Plaza.

The city looked like a museum. All of the buildings looked like giant objects on display in a beautiful morning light. Everything seemed frozen by this golden glow but without any sound. When we stepped out of the van, we stepped into the reality of devastation and an irrepressible odor filling the air. Like some moonscape, a white dust covered everything, and we discerned twisted carcasses of fire engines, police vans, and countless cars. Fire hoses twisted under our feet like giant water snakes and the water in the streets sometimes reached up to our knees.

The pile of steel exceeded 200 feet

166

Assessing Building #6

As we were passing pieces of debris I was trying to make sense of the site. I remembered many visits to the World Trade Center, but now I could not see any signs of the towers in the dusty air. Only when I got closer could I recognize the arched columns of the outer skin of the towers.

Firemen were crawling in and out of holes trying to find people to rescue. It was hard to tell whether vertical openings were stairwells, elevator shafts, or just random spaces created by the debris piled on top of it. We knew that if there were any survivors they would be in these vertical pockets of space. I started to search along with the firemen because as an architect I would have a good idea on which spaces were safer to access.

I asked if anyone had plans of the World Trade Center and was told that any plans that existed before were now destroyed in the collapse. Even the Office of Emergency Management, which was located on the 25th floor of WTC 7, was gone.

Building #5

I decided to find a set of plans to allow for a more coordinated search for survivors. I was finally able to get one set of plans for the Plaza Level all the way to the B 6 Level, the PATH Station on the lowest level, 70 feet below street level. I made seven copies of the set, and I distributed them to FDNY (Fire Department City of New York), DDC, (Department of Design and Construction), OEM (Office of Emergency Management), PAPD (Port Authority Police Department), and FEMA (Federal Emergency Management Agency). With a set of drawings now in hand, it was easier to locate subterranean stairs and passageways.

We all hoped there would be many survivors. It seemed every 30 minutes someone yelled, "Quiet! Quiet!" All work stopped. We stood still straining our ears listening for any sound or cry for help.

Many body parts were trapped between the steel. I found a complete body of a woman lying on her stomach. She seemed physically intact except for a reinforcing bar piercing her chest. We saw-cut the steel so that we could lift her up. When we turned her around, her face was missing. She broke in half when we tried to put her into the body bag. To this day when I see a woman with blond hair in a ponytail I have a flashback to that moment.

Building #5

Over the next few days I worked with the Department of Buildings, which along with some engineering firms, were responsible for the inspection of the surrounding buildings to determine the level of collateral damage. One of the tasks I was given was to inspect the southeast corner of the American Express Building. Pieces of the north tower's exterior columns had pierced the 17th and 21st floors. AMEC Construction, which was responsible for the Northwest Quadrant of the site, was in charge of removing the North pedestrian bridge, spanning between the U.S. Customhouse and the Winter Garden to allow for access of cranes from West Street. There were dozens of construction vehicles lined up along West Street, and the destroyed bridge blocked their access to the site.

The concern was that steel was wedged into the building's façade and it might get loose and fall onto the construction workers working below on the removal of the bridge. A fireman escorted me to the floors that were occupied by the offices of Lehman Brothers. I opened their corner office door and half of the office was missing. In its place was a steel column apparently from the north tower. It was an eerie sight to see papers neatly piled up on a clean desk with framed family pictures, and only inches away lay a pile of twisted steel like some vicious dragon frozen in mid-attack. I realized that the Lehman Brothers employees, like Lawrence Marsh, would never be able to return and retrieve their personal belongings. I took their family pictures and nameplates from the offices, and through Lou Young, a CBS reporter, I found the owners of the items.

I took some photographs of Ground Zero through the missing walls. I didn't know it at the time, but these photos would serve me well when I later constructed the first recovery model of the WTC. One of the buildings I was inspecting was Building 5, the home of Citibank and a day care center. The day care center was in the northwest corner of the building. It was covered in two inches of white powder. Cribs were filled with twisted steel and broken glass and high chairs turned over. It was the first time I broke down and started sobbing uncontrollably.

Piles of steel

At the time I had no idea that all the children got out safely. I later heard there were about 20 children and four caretakers. Since they could not evacuate all the babies at once, the caretakers handed the children over to complete strangers passing by on their way out of the

170

towers. They said, "Take the baby and go to Canal Street. We'll find you there." And they did.

On Thursday evening, September 13, it rained heavily. A lot of the white dust had washed off, and with it also many hopes of finding any survivors. But we still held onto the hope of people making cell phone calls from under the rubble. As irrational as it seems now, we still hoped for some miracle.

On September 15, I attended one of the meetings at the command post at Elementary School I.S. 89. All of the operations were coordinated from there. It was funny in a way to see these big guys, construction managers, engineers, and firemen, sitting on these little baby chairs. Aerial photographs of the disaster covered the walls and right next to them were children's drawings of Winnie the Pooh.

The meetings often turned into heated debates about what to do next. Where to place a crane? Will the existing columns, which are supporting the Plaza, hold a 100-ton crane? Will this type of crane reach into the center of the pit? How big of a piece of debris will it pick up? Which debris should be removed first? Will it cause shifting of another debris? Will it endanger the precarious stability of the slurry wall? Will it put the search and rescue groups in danger?

Mountains of debris

Firemen wanted to continue unobstructed search for the dead. The Mayor's Office wanted some good news. The FBI wanted to keep an eye on every piece of debris leaving the site, and along with that, the Secret Service was concerned about the documents buried under the ruins of Building 6, the U.S. Customhouse, since there were rooms full of firearms, cocaine, and top-secret information.

During the meeting some engineers were confused by the addresses One Liberty Street, One Liberty Plaza, and One World Plaza, etc. They looked at plans of the street level, concourse, and other subterranean floors, and compared information gathered from the site regarding damage to the slabs and location of debris. It was hard to determine which columns were structurally sound, which floors were missing, and which held debris.

Piles of steel

I realized that a model, a three dimensional model of the site, would help orient everyone. That afternoon I took more pictures from the 26th setback floor of the AMEX Building. I called my friend and fellow Cooper Union classmate Kenneth Francis and his wife, architect Sandra Donner, to recruit their help. They immediately volunteered with the building of a cardboard model of the site.

But before that, I had to get the Sanborn map which would serve as a matrix, a base on which we could reconstruct the disaster site. All of the schools and libraries that had copies of this map were closed. I went to Cooper Union, my Alma Mater, in hopes of gaining access to the school's library. The guard told me it would reopen on Monday. I said, "I cannot wait until Monday."

I remembered that the school recently renovated the Stuyvesant-Fish House that serves as the residence for Cooper Union's President, Dr. George Campbell. Dr. Campbell was home, we went to the library, and I made copies of the Sanborn map.

Over the weekend, day and night, we built a precise replica of the World Trade Center on my friend Ann Clements' dining room table reflecting the extent of the damage. It was a model of everything above ground. We delivered the model to the Command Post at I.S. 89 on September 17.

Piles of debris

In the meantime, I knew that a 3D computer model with all the data on the debris and status of slabs and columns would be critically helpful. Ann and I put together a creative team of architects, engineers, and computer experts. We set out to create a digital 3D record of the site as it slowly evolved during the debris removal. While continuously developing the computer model there was a need for a 3D model of the subterranean levels within the "bathtub" showing the condition of the structure and location of debris. I approached Cooper Union archive's Steve Hillier, and he put me in touch with Elizabeth O'Donnell, a professor who then organized a group of students. The students worked on the model between classes and during their midterm exams.

I was getting updated information and drawings from DDC and Port Authority that served as the basis for the three-dimensional interpretation in the Plexiglas model. It took the students only three weeks to finish the model. It was made out of Plexiglas so that one could see through the perimeter slurry walls into each of the six levels of subterranean floors. Through these walls, one could see the extent of the damage to the slabs and columns, and the location of debris, etc. For easy access to the central areas, the model consisted of four quadrants where each floor was removable so that the workers using this model for a visual reference could easily understand the context and extent of their tasks.

Piles of debris

On November 8, 2001 we officially handed over the three-dimensional model to the City of New York. At one time there was a real concern for the safety of the firemen searching in the areas under Building 6. The plan was to take down the building and allow part of the north exterior wall of the north tower, which was leaning against the building, to fall down naturally. The wall was sheared off at the B3 level, and the fall of the wall could have crushed some of the intact slabs directly to the north of it. The engineers worried that some firemen may not heed the call to stay away from those areas.

Because of this, we created a computer-animated version of what may happen when this wall fell. We ran a simplified simulation and applied some of the physical attributes of the slabs and columns. It was then decided that rather than to let the wall fall naturally, the wall would be taken down piece by piece.

One thousand people worked each shift at Ground Zero and there were three shifts a day. But out of all those people at the site, Mike Bellone's a guy who's hard to miss. I met Mike Bellone and Bob Barrett while we were working at the site. Mike was working with the firemen, removing debris by hand and searching for human remains. He seemed tireless, as if every pound on his body represented thousands of workers.

Pile of debris

CHAPTER 22
SHOULDER-TO-SHOULDER

Mike Bellone
Honorary Firefighter, Ladder Co. 20
Fire Department City of New York

We had no water, no water pressure, and debris in our eyes, noses, and throats. Someone came with a bucket of water and a ladle. Homeless people kept begging to help the firefighters who had lost 126 trucks and all the tools. We never found one entire fire truck. They melted. One truck was severed by an eye-beam. There were no phone lines, no computers. We were communication deaf.

Building 4 was a charcoal briquette in seven days. All of the office equipment had melted on the floors and fused together in the middle. Five and Six Block burned for days and days. Cars at the bottom were melted like plastic. The frames were charred metal.

The Hudson River was our only source of water. We lost all of our fire chiefs and all of our hoses. At that point, there was no more paperwork, and the job worked better without paperwork. We had to rescue and recover whatever we could. The beams remained hot until January.

Lt. Claudio Fernandez
New York City Highway Patrol

The fire was still simmering as hot as ever the third day. I received an emergency call from a Con Edison worker who told me that he needed a vacuum truck to be brought to Ground Zero because there was some type of petroleum leak. The vacuum truck had the ability to suck up all the petroleum at a high rate of speed to avoid further explosion and catastrophe.

No one was allowed to go into Ground Zero without our approval and a police escort. How we accomplished this, was that every motor vehicle was given a ground escort down to Ground Zero.

An escort is when a vehicle is designated as the lead vehicle and brings any type of vehicle or equipment into a certain location. I had no more motorcycles left when they needed the vacuum truck. I personally went over to Walker and West Broadway to escort the vacuum truck to Vesey Street and West Street.

Vincent LaTerra
Labor Foreman
Bovis Lend Lease

That morning on September 11, I was on the Ritz Carlton job on 6th Avenue. It must have been coffee time, because I overheard the guys talking. A plane hit a building, and I didn't think much about it. Then another plane hit. We were on a construction floor with no radios or televisions. I ran down to an engineer's shanty. He had a little TV on, and all of a sudden we heard the news that it was more like an attack than an accident. A slight panic started happening with everybody.

Each foreman is responsible for his men, and we quickly tried to account for the men within each trade. We have an evacuation plan and accounting for men and where to meet is part of that procedure. I remember going up to the roof, and I gathered some of the men to take them down to the shanty.

From that vantage point I was able to look down 6th Avenue, and I saw one of the towers fall. I had a clear shot of it down 6th Avenue. It was chilling. I watched as a mass exodus of people fled the city. The avenues and streets were filled with corridors of people.

Searching for victims

I told the men, "If you want to go home, go home. But if you want to come with me, I'm going down there."

The atmosphere of slight panic intensified.

I was able to get a hold of our boss Jim Abadie at Bovis Lend Lease. Jim and I best friends. He already knew without my telling him, that I was going down there. I knew without Jim telling me, he was going down there.

We said, "Let's get some of the boys together and try to help."

We all met at a central location by Columbus Circle. We had about 50 guys coming with us. We put together baskets of tools, masks, shovels, chopping guns, and more. We recruited a city bus to take us, and none of us knew what the hell we were walking into.

The bus went downtown and we got as far as 14th Street. The police stopped the bus.

They said, "We can't let you go any further."

We climbed into the back of a pick up truck, and the driver took us in little further. We came up to Building 7, which at that point was burning. We couldn't get too close to it, so we skirted around to West Street.

Searching through Building 5

Then the reality hit. After all that walking, I had thoughts going through my mind, "I want to go down, but what the hell am I doing here?"

I kept trying to think logically. I thought of my mother. In the middle of this disastrous chaos, I thought to myself, "I don't think my mother would want me to go down there. But I'm going down there."

I saw a hoard of firefighters. Something kept drawing me down closer. Supplies were going through on West Street; bottles of water, oxygen tanks. Nobody knew what was coming next.

I left the guys. I walked away. The moment was too much for me. I needed to be by myself. Everything was empty. The people were gone. I started getting the feeling of being in unreality.

I was on West Street looking up at Building 7. All of a sudden Building 7's windows popped. Pop, pop, pop. I watched as the whole top of Building 7 became crippled, and then it just collapsed.

And that freakin' toxic cloud. That circle. It rolled like a ball. It was like a whirlwind. I ran from it but it kept catching up with me. I kept running and I passed the north bridge that had already collapsed. I somehow made my way around to the other end of the site on Albany Street.

Strategizing

My cell phone worked sporadically. I'd hear from Jim, and he told me things like, "The firemen just lost 300 men." Or, "We're trying to clear streets."

I met up with Jim at the south end. Jim tried to start organizing things. He met with firefighters and the DDC, Department of Design and Construction. We asked each other, "What is our next move? How are we going to handle this whole thing?"

It must have been noon by then. Then it was night. Then it was another day. We just didn't know what was coming next, and we didn't know how to handle it.

We tried to figure out what we needed. We were in a position to help. We called in all our subcontractors. We had the equipment and the labor. We said, "What we have here is a demolition job on our hands. Everything is already down."

It began to get a little clearer on what we should do. We knew it needed to be organized so that nobody else got hurt. Steel needed to be cut. Cranes needed to be brought in so that the rescue workers could try to find people.

Soon thereafter, the access to the site was limited. Everybody's heart was in the right place, they wanted to help, but it looked like we were in the middle of a Schwarzenegger movie happening all around us.

Bringing in the heavy equipment

It was like everybody wanted to fight on the "front lines" of Ground Zero. We just couldn't let everybody be on the pile. It was far too dangerous. There were other ways that people could help, and they pitched in. When we were cold, wet, and shivering, they brought us dry clothes. When we were thirsty, they gave us something to drink. We just couldn't stop. We had to keep going.Until you started noticing, really noticing, what it really looked like, you couldn't even find a pen in that rubble. It looked like no human being had ever inhabited the area. Everything was pulverized. No desks, no pieces of glass, no pieces of sheetrock. It was powder and steel. All of the electrical work looked like steel spaghetti.

What people probably don't realize is that one full story of building got compressed into 12 inches. When we really understood what we were looking at, we realized how hard it was going to be.

I went over to the north side of the site and set up a trailer. We had our two-way radios so that we could communicate. At that point we had already been down there three nights in a row without any sleep. Jimmy Lomma brought down his R.V. so that the guys could took turns sleeping in the R.V. for a couple of hours.

Bringing in the heavy equipment

Around the fourth night, I set up a trailer on Pier 40 to handle things from there. I'd get a call for 20 ironworkers for the shift. If I needed 20 ironworkers, 40 were waiting to go in. Ironworkers were instrumental in cutting steel and torching out areas. We needed excavators. We needed pick-and-ax. Laborers. Cranes. Operating Engineers. I had about 100 men waiting outside my door wanting to go in and help. We bused them into the site.

We all started working together, the contractors, the subcontractors. Without everybody doing his job, we wouldn't have gotten anywhere. It wasn't a NYPD site, and it wasn't a FDNY site. From the beginning, contractors joined together. Everyone went shoulder-to-shoulder, and said, "Let's do this together."

The City divided the site into quadrants. The City's Department of Development Design and Construction (DDC) oversaw all four main contractors. Bovis was in charge of the southwest corner. We had Grace Excavators and all of their equipment. Tully had a lot of his own equipment. D.H. Griffin was a really good demolition contractor from the south who acted as our demolition consultant.

We said, "Let's divide up this side, and we'll start cleaning out this area."

I was personally responsible for 80 guys on a shift, two shifts a day, 7 days a week, 12 hour shifts. Everyone was so dedicated that it became kind of a job to get people to go home. I didn't want to leave the site. We couldn't get Jim to go home.

My friends Mark and Bob finally convinced me to leave the site for a few hours. We stopped at a bar for a beer. It was my first beer in three weeks. I remember getting all teary-eyed because I felt like I was around family. I felt like I could cry on their shoulders. They were like my brothers.

In a way, I think all the men had a strong sense of personal responsibility as to what was happening down there. It wasn't like a job where one might not finish the day's work, put papers in a "to do basket", and do it the next day. If someone didn't get his job done at Ground Zero, it made it harder for the next guy.

This wasn't going away. There was no time to stop for you. No matter what was happening outside of that site, it was all chicken-shit compared to what these men had to deal with.

Working there heightened every one of our senses. The site became "everything" to us. It encompassed our whole being. We couldn't escape it. Not down there. We knew what each of us was going through.

I used to walk into the "Green Tarp Restaurant." It was a blown-out deli with a green tarp thrown over it. I'd be sitting there eating by myself, and I'd ask the person next to me, "Are you all right?"

They'd answer, "I'm all right. Are YOU all right?" We really weren't all right, but we felt better when someone asked us.

One night I walked into the Green Tarp and asked someone for mashed potatoes. It was Candice Bergen. She gave me a kiss, and I felt better.

There was another time when late at night I was helping to direct one of the crane operators. I remember running up to the top of the crane, that huge one, the one right in the middle of the site, and I sort of had to push a guy aside in order to talk to the crane operator. I had just pushed Alan Alda.

He said, "Hey, do you know who you just pushed away?"

As quick as those types of things happened, at the same time, you'd turn around and spot a pocketbook in the rubble or someone's Driver's License. Ten minutes after finding the pocketbook, we discovered the woman's body that it belonged to. That was the only time I knew who the victim was.

Another time at Ground Zero, Jim came to me and said, "We have to get some 55 gallon drums together. You have to dig some dirt from the site and put it into the drums."

I think we put together about 8 or 10 drums.

I asked, "What do you want me to do with them?"

Nobody knew.

A couple of days later, I said, "Look, we have to get a hold of someone and get these drums where they need to go."

My friend Vinnie had an old pick up truck. He said, "Hey, I'll help you."

I said, "I'll get the list to see where they go."

As it turned out, we delivered the drums to chapels all over New York City, a drum to each chapel. What I think they were doing with the Ground Zero soil, was putting it into little urns to give to people. This way people could have some type of closure. It was like giving them a lost loved one, something to hold onto.

Bringing in the heavy equipment

It's the "not knowing" part that is so hard. If this helped soothe some of the sorrow, we were very glad to do so.

It was all just so horrifying. Do you know how many body parts were strewn on rooftops? We found plane seats. We found a jet engine by Building 2, on the north side of the Vista hotel.

I met Mike Bellone down on the site. Mike was the liaison between the firefighters and the contractors. One day Mike came to me and asked if there was a way we could make a "sifter". He drew an idea on a piece of cardboard.

I told him, "I can make a box with a handle on each end with a very fine screen on the bottom."

Mike said, "That would be fine, I need 20 of them."

In one hour I called Mike, and he came to pick up 20 sifters. We must have made hundreds of sifters. Using the sifters was like panning for gold. Instead of finding gold, we were finding people.

I think that one of the reasons I, and so many others, had trouble leaving the site was because finally, for once in your life, you have real purpose in your work and what you were doing for other people, and yourself. That sense of responsibility is what kept you coming back until every stone was unturned.

I finally understood why my uncle's best friend, who was a Green Beret in Vietnam, made it out of there alive, got out, Purple Heart, decorated with Honors, and then he re-enlisted. He went back into Viet Nam and was killed.

For years I wondered why. I thought, "You fool!"

Now I know why he did it. We were in the middle of a war in downtown Manhattan. It was a short war, but it was a war. I understood what his purpose was in going back to Viet Nam and what he had to do. Like a soldier who goes in for the sake of freedom, we were going BACK for the sake of finding a missing loved one.

Honorary Firefighter Michael Bellone, Church Street & Liberty on September 11, 2001

CHAPTER 23
A.T.V. UNIT

September 11, 2001 – June 12, 2002

Nicholas DeMasi
Firefighter, Engine Co. 261
Fire Department City of New York

I got a call from a friend, and he told me, "Turn on the TV, a plane just hit the World Trade Center."

I responded to my firehouse. I then went to the Fire Department area at Shea Stadium and got on the first bus going down. On the way there, the second building was coming down. When we arrived, a staging area had been set up and there was supposed to be a team of four to five firemen and an officer. We were to stay in that area until they told us to go in. Another firefighter and myself didn't wait. We went in.

We started rescue efforts and searched for people. We moved some of the apparatus that was damaged. We needed tools to work with and we didn't have any. In order to get a tool, we had to walk back to the staging area where all the rigs were parked. It was a long walk and would have taken close to an hour to get a tool. So I figured if I had my personal A.T.V. (All Terrain Vehicle) with me, I could go get the tool and bring it back right away.

So many tools were needed, ones we didn't even have. There were so many people supplying things like ropes, masks, and torches, etc. People were bringing in tool supplies, but the supplies were so far away from the site that it would have taken us forever to get them.

The next day I came back with my A.T.V.'s. I had four of them because that's what I do on my time off. I go to A.T.V. rodeos, and I use them for hunting and for pleasure. Two guys from the firehouse, and my nephew and I put the A.T.V.'s on a trailer and brought them down to the site. We immediately started running tools and men to where they needed to go.

Ground Zero was so spread out, but by driving around the site we learned where everything was. We knew where to get supplies, how to get back to the site, and how to get into the site. It started catching on with all the firefighters, officers, and the chiefs. "If you needed anything, go ask the 'A.T.V. Guys,' they're the gopher guys." After a week everybody was saying, "Call A.T.V. Nick," and we brought what was needed.

The Fire Department issued us radios so that any of the officers or chiefs could call us and tell us what they needed. Within minutes we delivered, whether it was a paper clip or 200 bottles of gas for the torches.

There were several command posts around the site, and we went around and checked on every one of them to see what they needed. On our downtime, when we weren't getting supplies for men or officers, we dug for survivors. We also transported families of the missing firefighters to the command posts, and tried to make them feel comfortable when they wanted to see the site.

Firefighter Mike Basil picking up tools

We did this for several weeks until I remembered I had a friend who had a Honda dealership. Lt. McBrian and Lt. Beoncovela from Engine 261 and Ladder 116 helped get me through the channels to set up a Firefighter A.T.V. Unit. Jay Johanas and Harry Vass of New York Honda, Long Island City, donated five A.T.V.'s to Ground Zero.

Lt. McBrian and I were assigned to this new unit. Chief Hayden asked me to head the unit and recruit five firefighters. I made sure that an A.T.V. guy covered each shift. We had four shifts, and we used three A.T.V.'s each shift. One A.T.V. was reserved for the Department Chief to get around the site.

Jim Cody was the first guy I hired for the unit. I thought I was doing a tremendous job until Jim came on. He was really good. He broke his ass down there. That was the attitude of everybody down there, but he really stood out. He was such a hard worker as was everybody. Jim Cody was above and beyond anybody I've ever worked with.

What really stands out in my mind are the faces of the people who lost somebody. We took the families down to where their loved ones were lost. They returned at different times, for different reasons, such as birthdays. They brought flowers or balloons, and we took them to get something to eat. For me, that really stands out in my mind the most.

Firefighter Nick DeMasi picking up a load of batteries

I felt like the A.T.V. Unit was very resourceful. Whatever you needed, we could get it for you. Everybody pulled together and helped each other out. You could feel it in the air. You could feel it around you. I think everyone wished the world could be like that all the time. It was just the greatest atmosphere of people helping people. I've never seen guys so dedicated and who worked so hard, the firefighters, ironworkers, chiefs, etc. I never saw a group of people work so efficiently. Everyone was polite, and they'd do anything for each other. People couldn't give enough, and they couldn't do enough.

I miss it. I miss the camaraderie of all the guys and working together. I miss helping out where I know I can be the most useful. Not that I would ever want to see anything like that happen again, but I felt like I was at my best. Everyone was at his and her best.

Many times movie stars came down to give us a moral boost. I took them around on my A.T.V., and wherever we found a group of men or women working, we stopped to chat. Christie Brinkley was there, John Travolta, Tom Cruise, and others.

At one point I was assigned to take Federal Agents around the site to search for the black boxes from the planes. We were getting ready to go out. My A.T.V. was parked at the top of the stairs at the Brooks Brothers entrance area. We loaded up about a million dollars worth of equipment and strapped it into the A.T.V. When we got into the A.T.V. to take off, the agent accidentally pushed me forward. The A.T.V. was already in reverse, and my foot went down on the gas pedal. We went down the stairs in reverse. Fortunately, everything was okay. There were a total of four black boxes. We found three.

Firefighter Nick DeMasi riding through the toxic pool

Mike Bellone was always helping out. He started filling in on the A.T.V. Unit. We always had one firefighter assigned to each tour, and Mike was with whoever was on that tour of duty. Not too long after that, Mike became known as "A.T.V. Mike." Eventually he was assigned specific duties with the unit.

One day we found 23 bodies in 24 hours. Everybody felt so good about that. That was the best day down there. Another time, a recovery was made and they tried to notify the family their loved one was found. The family was on their way to Atlantic City, New Jersey. The New Jersey State Police located the family on 95-South, intercepted them, and then escorted them to the site.

189

L to R: Honorary Firefighter Mike Bellone, Deputy Chief Jim Riches, Firefighter Bob Barrett

Volunteer firefighters came in from all over the country. They all wanted to help out. Many times I brought them to the ramp after someone was found. They were very proud to stand at attention in the Honor Guard. It was a big help to us.

During the time spent at Ground Zero, it became a challenge to me when someone asked me for something that we didn't have. They would ask for something crazy like, "Get me a jackhammer."

I said, "Come on, give me a challenge. I can get a jackhammer in a minute."

I don't think there was one thing we couldn't get. And if we had to find something, we didn't just stay at the site. We went as far as Midtown Manhattan to get what we needed.

It felt really good when the A.T.V. Unit started to get known. Everybody knew that when you went down to Ground Zero, to just get in touch with the A.T.V. Unit. "They'll show you where everything is or get you what you need."

It made me feel good, because I had the opportunity to start the unit. I felt like I started my own unit in the Fire Department. If another disaster happens, God forbid if it did, I hope they'll activate an A.T.V. Unit.

What is the most important tool of all? A bucket. Ground Zero was excavated bucket-by-bucket.

Firefighter John Masera

Mike Bellone
Honorary Firefighter, Ladder Co. 20
Fire Department City of New York

When the towers came down, the Fire Department lost 126 trucks. For the first 48 hours, we all called it the "CFD: the Cody Fire Department." This was because Jimmy Cody kept using his van to go back and forth all over the place to pick up the tools and equipment we needed for the recoveries.

Jimmy Cody
Firefighter, Ladder Co. 24
Fire Department City of New York

Whenever we saw Nick DeMasi, he was covered from head to toe. He looked like one of those guys on TV who does mud racing. He didn't care. The only time you'd see him stop is when he had to get gas in the A.T.V. The word got around, "This guy Nick on the A.T.V. can get us stuff so we don't have to walk a half a mile."

Nick never said no to anybody. He did what he had to do to get what they needed. I never saw him in the hut eating. I never saw him putting his head down to rest. The guy just never stopped. When time went on, I saw what Nicky was trying to do.

I said, "This is the only way to do it. To walk a half a mile to get a hose is ridiculous; it would stop the men from digging."

When Nick started the A.T.V. Unit, he asked me, "Do you want to do this?"

I wanted to stay at Ground Zero. They were rotating everybody out after thirty days. I didn't want to leave until the job was done.

I said, "I'll do whatever it takes to get this done."

I had a lot of friends that I lost. We owed this to them and their families. All of the guys who perished would have done it for us.

For so long, it just didn't seem real. Your heart doesn't want to accept it. I wasn't letting it register in my brain. It really did happen. We really did lose all those people.

I was close to Father Mychal Judge from St. Francis of Assisi. He had married my wife and me. When Father Mychal Judge died in the north tower, they brought him uptown, and put his body in my firehouse. Once the reality of that set in, I thought, "How are we going to get through this without him?" Father Mychal had gotten us through so much before.

St. Francis was right across the street from our firehouse. The window in Father Mychal's room looked right at the firehouse. The phone would ring, and he'd say, "What do you have the "Probies" doing today?" I'd look up and Father Mychal Judge would be looking at me from his window. He was the greatest guy.

We would take turns driving Father Mychal around to the funerals he needed to get to. It was our way of trying to take some of the pressure off of him. One of the first times I drove him, I said, "I have to tell you that I'm not a really religious person."

He said, "Too much religion is no good."

I said, "We'll get along just fine."

L to R -- Firefighter Mike Basil, Hon. Firefighter Mike Bellone, Firefighter Nick DeMasi on the way to a recovery

Firefighter John Masera, HAZMAT Specialist Eric Joyner and Honorary Firefighter Mike Bellone

Whatever kind of problem you had, the man was always willing to listen for as long as it took. That was one of the tough parts, losing him. Father Mychal was one of a kind. He was always there. He was the guy who got us through the hardest time. No matter what it was, he got us through.

Ladder 24... yeah, deep down, those guys had to know it wasn't good. They had to know there was a good chance they'd never see their families again. I lost my good friend Stephen Belson, firefighter, Ladder 24. We lost our Capt. Daniel Brethel. He had just gotten off that morning before they got the call. He jumped in the car and drove Father Mychal Judge down there. We lost Lt. Andy Desperito, Engine 1. Firefighter Michael Weinberg, Engine 1. Danny, Andy, and Father Mychal Judge were found within the first 48 hours.

Steve and I had worked together for 18 years. Steve was a Chiefs Aide because he had a back injury. He was driving Chief Orio Palmer, the 7th Battalion Chief over to the World Trade Center. We had gotten reports that the guys had seen him here or there. It was a really big thing for me to try to find Steve. I know Stevie would have never given up. He was never found. They never found Chief Orio Palmer either.

In the A.T.V. Unit, we did the things that "they" couldn't do. We did what we had to do to get the job done. Nothing mattered but getting the job done and getting the brothers and the civilians out. Then we could go home.

Honorary Firefighter Mike Bellone and Firefighter Jimmy Cody

Honorary Firefighter Mike Bellone down below the street level

There are people who are followers, and there are people who get things done. We tried to be the guys who got things done. Whatever anybody needed in order to do the recoveries, we tried to get for them, or we did it ourselves.

Whatever it took to get to the victims, there were no rules. There were rules after awhile, but we didn't play by them. It all goes back to, whatever it took to get the bodies out, when the last body got out, that's when we go home.

That part of it never ended. There were so many bodies. Unless you stayed there for the nine months we were there, if you didn't live it, if you didn't see it, you don't know. You just don't know. For the first six months, if you saw some article written about Ground Zero, you'd think, "Who wrote this? Where did you get your information? And why didn't anybody decide to correct it? Why did they let them print that?" It's a shame, it really is.

Firefighter Nick DeMasi and Honorary Firefighter Mike Bellone delivering tools to a recovery

I used to be in construction, so I could get a little creative when we needed something done. My conscious knew the importance of finding everybody.

In the beginning, nobody knew Mike Bellone's name. He was known as the "Mystery Man with the Green Gator" who was always willing to give the teams a ride to the hut or to get water. All of a sudden, you'd turn about, and he was there. As time went on, Mike and I became like brothers. If I thought we needed something, I'd turn around and Mike would already have it. We knew what each other were thinking.

I never heard the man say no. If called Mike on the radio and said, "I need you to yank the sun down here because I need more light," I figured he could do it.

Top & Bottom: Honorary Firefighter Mike Bellone

Like if you needed a torch to cut metal. The chiefs would say, "We need a torch. How are we going to find one? There's no torch around." Before the chief could count to 10, a hose came sliding down with a torch attached to the end of it.

I'd say, "Relax Chief. The A.T.V. Unit's got it." They'd say, "But where did it come from?" I'd say, "It's from A.T.V. Mike."

Then you'd hear Mike's voice from up above, "What else do you need?"

One time, the site's stadium lights needed to be moved over to the northwest corner of the pit because there wasn't enough light for the guys to do recoveries. The bodies were there, but they couldn't see. It was an immediate situation. We couldn't wait.

The lights were in the southeast corner next to the Salvation Army hut. The lights needed to be brought all the way over to the other side. You have to understand, the lights are on a big huge truck that has to be driven. And, it has to be hooked up to a huge generator that supplies the electric generator for the lights, which is a separate truck. The tower went up 7-8 stories. When it was boomed up, it looked like something you'd see at a football or baseball stadium. It was massive. It was the biggest set of lights on the site.

Mike and I knew it needed to be moved... like now, and we always did our best work "under the cover of darkness." Our plan was to wait until dark.

The guys who actually manned the truck were not from New York. We needed them to disconnect the power from the generator, bring the lights, bed them in the truck, and then drive it. Mike and I "sweet-talked" them into it.

After moving some parts of the Salvation Army's hut, a little bit, which is as much as I'll admit to, we got the guys, the guys not from New York, to drive it out. Basically, if anybody asked any questions, we said, "Chief (mumble, mumble) said to move it, now."

It wasn't a fast operation. We were walking faster than the truck was moving. We stopped traffic with the A.T.V.'s to let the truck through. This is a very, very expensive piece of equipment. You couldn't make a sharp turn.

We got it moved. We got that massive thing over to the northwest corner. We had the light truck, but then we needed the generator. Next, we had to come up with a truck to tow-the huge generator. Along the way, we almost slipped next to the scaffolding. Nothing major happened. Nobody else would have done it. We barely got the guys not from New York to do it.

It was rough on all of us family-wise. We did get what they call "tunnel-vision. I felt bad about Mike not being able to see his family, but he didn't stop.

I used to say, "If I had to walk through hell, I know Mike would be right behind me the whole way." And once we got there, Mike and I would find some way to make a deal with the devil to get anything we needed while we were there.

I'm just hoping Father Mychal still has his foot in heaven's door for us. Father Mychal Judge would say, "Wait. Wait! I've just got one more!"

With Mike right behind me, then I'd put my foot in the door for him. Mike should be very proud of what he did. I know I'm very proud of him. I'm proud of everybody. Ground Zero was hard for everybody.

Dave McCalaster and Rory from Angel Aerial were the guys with the water trucks. They also brought in the light towers. For their "normal" work, Dave and Rory work on movie and TV set locations. For instance, when the TV show The Sopranos needs a rain scene, Dave and Rory hose down the streets. To us, Dave and Rory were the stars.

Honorary Firefighter Mike Bellone

None of the water hydrants worked, so Dave and Rory brought in big water tankers with spare cannons to remotely shoot. The EPA wanted them there, because if the dust got too bad, the area needed to be sprayed down.

Dave, Rory, Mike and I made up hose fittings to fit to their trucks. That way we could use our hoses to put out small pocket fires so that we could keep digging.
Dave was great. He was a magician with a torch. Dave was another one who never said,"No."

Whatever it was, he'd say, "We're on our way."

They were a tremendous help from day one right to the end.

Vinnie LaTerra never said, "No" either. Whatever we needed, he said, "Take it."

These guys could never do enough. All the trades worked together. The grapplers drove the big heavy machinery that looks like a tank. The machine has an arm with a claw on the end of it. They'd put the claw into rubble and then pulled up layers for us one at a time. Then they'd pick up the debris and move it to an area so that we could go through it. Then they put the debris into a truck when we were done going through it. I

With the way the floors were pan caked, there was no way we could have done it all. The Ironworkers were right there with us. The Laborers. The truck drivers who put up with us walking aimlessly about the place, watching out for us so that we wouldn't get run over. That had to be mentally exhausting just looking out for us. Without the Trades, we couldn't have found as many as we did. The guys would have dug with their hands until they dropped dead, but without those machines . . .

L to R: Firefighter Jimmy Cody, Firefighter Sal Scarentino, Ladder 24

Mike Bellone
Honorary Firefighter, Ladder Co. 20
Fire Department City of New York

Being down at Ground Zero required you to wear many hats. While working on the A.T.V. Unit, you never knew which hat you were going to wear. I met Jim Cody early on in the recovery effort. He's the guy, that when you're a little kid and you want to be somebody, like the president or astronaut, I would have wanted to be Jim Cody.

Jim Cody taught me everything I needed to know, from changing a flat tire to putting a fire truck together.

I remember one day he told me, "We have to put a fire truck together today."

When he said that, I didn't realize that we were actually going to physically put a fire truck together. Not the body or chassis, but equip the whole thing tool-by-tool, from each compartment door to the hose bed. He taught me every nozzle, fitting, and tool.

After we put the truck together, he said, "Now we can bring this over to the West Side Highway and use it in case of a small fire."

Jimmy Cody taught me other invaluable lessons. Not just technical, but emotional. I learned to suffer his pain and loss because of all the time we spent together every day. We gave each other updates and kept a list of who we found and when and where we found them. When people asked us to perform certain tasks, they knew we would accomplish them, because between the two of us there was always a way. Jimmy and I usually ate together at four in the morning, somewhere, and we talked about tackling the next task.

Hon. Firefighter Mike Bellone and Firefighter Nick DeMasi

We also had, what we called, "the best hidden secret on the site," which was Angel Aerial water. Dave McCalaster and Rory were always there to back us up no matter what we were up to and at a moment's notice.

I remember when Jimmy and I were in the north tower and we found Father Mychal Judge's bunker jacket. Jimmy put it in a bag and said to me, "Go and hide this. This has to go to the proper place."

I felt honored just to hold it in my hands. We didn't want it to get lost within the thousands upon thousands of recovered items. I tucked the jacket away until the proper time when I was called on returning it. It was never the physical work, but the emotional work that often laid a heavy burden on us.

We did crazy things like calling Bovis in the middle of the night with an idea to make the west hut warmer in the middle of winter. Bovis had many, many cases of canvas tarps. Jimmy and I climbed up on the roof of the hut. Like a cartoon, the two of us hammered the tarps onto the hut like a big blanket to try and keep the heat in. When the chief came out sweating, he said, "Where did all the heat come from?"

He looked at me and Jimmy, shook his head, and said, "I don't want to know."

When we had to move the stadium lights from the southeast corner to the northwest corner, the chief said, "Where did all the light come from?"

He looked at me and Jimmy, shook his head, and said, "I don't want to know."

If Jimmy and I had a dime for every time a chief shook his head at us and said, "I don't want to know," we could retire.

Jimmy's family came down to the site, and I met his wife Bernadette. I could just see the support she gave to Jimmy. Behind every great man, there's a woman, and in this case

Bernadette certainly fit the bill.

I love and respect Jimmy Cody. He taught me everything I know, and everything I didn't

know. And for that, I am forever grateful.

Bob Barrett
Retired Firefighter, Ladder Co. 20
Fire Department City of New York

Much of my time down in the pit was spent with Mike on an A.T.V. It seemed to me as though it was always raining when I was on the A.T.V. We were forever running through puddles, and I was always getting splashed with muddy water. I used to curse at Mike and tell him, "You never miss a puddle!"

I often waved my arms from side-to-side imitating a windshield wiper since there was no cover or windshield on the A.T.V. I always found myself drenched and in cold, wet clothes. It was a pleasure the few times we had good weather.

We drove the A.T.V. all over the site checking to see if anyone needed any tools, water, etc. It was important for them to have contact with us, and just to see how everyone was doing during their shift. If they needed a tool we drove up to the 10 and 10 firehouse and picked up whatever they needed. If the tools were not available, Mike made arrangements with the construction companies to get the supplies. Usually the tools were readily available somewhere around the site. Considering the fact that there were many different entities involved in trying to acquire necessary tools and supplies, it all ran amazingly well.

Honorary Firefighter Mike Bellone

Jim Riches
Battalion Chief
Fire Department City of New York

Mike Bellone lived at Ground Zero. He was always smiling and asked, "What do you need? Can I help you?"

Mike is like family to me. Over the months he became one of the boys and we accepted him into our fold. He was there as a volunteer and gave up everything during that time in order to help us. He was there for me when I needed him. Mike's a brother and a true friend. I'll never forget him.

Brainstorming the next plan in the West Hut

John Masera
Firefighter, Engine Co. 331
Fire Department City of New York

I was at Ground Zero from September 11, 2001 to October working as a firefighter with the FDNY. I went down on a 30-day detail, and after the detail was up, I volunteered to reassign and stay. When I reassigned, I was asked if I wanted to join the A.T.V. Unit.

Mike Bellone was the liaison between the construction companies and firefighters. We got around on Honda A.T.V. four-wheel quads. They had four-wheel drive capability and were good for getting around the site and down into the hole. We also used Gators to transport tools. Gators are all-terrain-vehicles with a box in the back.

Basically, we had to make sure that the chiefs, firefighters, and everyone working down

there with the Fire Department, had everything they needed. This meant providing dry gloves, bottles of water, or any type of tool they needed in a recovery. If we didn't have something, we would always find it or get it from somewhere.

Everyone always called Mike "A.T.V. Mike." Mike had a radio, and if they needed anything they called whoever was on duty. He was always on duty. He never took a day off. I was there every other day, more or less.

HAZMAT Specialist Eric Joyner

Mike had a thing about him where he would just fall asleep. He would be going all day, and the first second he sat down he fell asleep. You couldn't wake him up. The only way he would wake up is if the radio around his neck went off calling him to do something. He always heard

that radio out of a deep sleep. Even if I was standing next to him, I had to call him on the radio. That's the only way he'd wake up. Another one of Mike's nicknames was "Mud Ball." He didn't mind getting dirty. He was always filthy. His eyeballs were the only things that were clean. At six-feet tall, 300 pounds plus, you can imagine.

OSHA was always yelling at him. He was supposed to wear a respirator, and they wanted to get him thrown off the site because he wouldn't wear the mask. Mike didn't wear one because he wanted to smell for remains. He couldn't do that with a respirator over his face. Mike was like a bloodhound, and they knew they needed him. It was a distinct smell that you will never forget. When you smelled it, you knew you were in the general area of a recovery. Most of the time you found remains.

There was one truck, Ladder 4, where we spent thirty hours digging out the truck to see if anyone was in it. I knew one of the guys who was in Ladder 4. I went to high school with him.

John Tipping. They did find him, and there was a memorial service. That was really nice. We couldn't find everybody who was missing, but the firefighters couldn't have done a better job in trying to find everyone.

In regard to the mental stress of the job, some people who worked down there asked me, "Are you going for help?" I felt strange about that. I was so close to Mike and Bobby. I talked to them if I had something upsetting me. I didn't feel comfortable talking about it with people who weren't there and who didn't experience what I did. How could they possibly understand?

Mike and Bob knew exactly what I was talking about and what was going on in my head. It wasn't easy, but it definitely helped to be able to talk to people you knew and trusted. These were the people who stood right next to me in the Honor Guard. A lot of people didn't stay at

Ground Zero. Most of the personnel left after thirty days, and then a whole new group came in. We stayed the whole time.

Tool Nazi Firefighter Tom Fenech

Eric Joyner
Hazardous Material Specialist

Like any city, fire rescue, ambulance or emergency response company, hazardous materials is also in the private sector. I have been a HAZMAT specialist for twelve years and thought I had experienced everything, until we went to Ground Zero. We didn't know what to expect but it was a shock to see the devastation there. My responsibility there was to see that the rescue workers were completely de-contaminated and clean of hazardous materials.

Having a change of clothes on hand was vital because of the extreme toxins the workers were exposed to. I met Mike Bellone, Jim Cody, Bob Barrett and John Masera at 10&10 where the ATV unit was stationed. These guys lived in the pit. When they came out they were a mess. Like NASCAR, we were a pit stop to de-con the workers as quickly and efficiently as possible. I remember one day it was very dreary. You could feel the tension in the air. Mike Bellone and John Masera came up from the pit after digging for hours and Mike needed a change of clothes. He was very hard to dress because he was so big; it made us have to improvise. After he was undressed and he washed down we left him his clothes to change into. Needless to say all the clothes were size medium and he was a 3X. Watching him try to put on those tiny underwear had everyone hysterically laughing. John and I cut two shirts and duct taped them together for him to wear. It was very rarely you saw anyone even smile, so this was good therapy and a great remedy for the tension and emotions they endured daily. I worked down at the 10&10 house almost every day. I never thought it was possible, but I now have a new family and a new outlook on life. Mike, Jimmy, John and Bob have changed my life, my attitude, and my faith. Not only do I feel better, I am better. Mike was right, from every negative comes a positive.

Joseph Adinolfi
Independent Contractor

It was an event with no status. Everybody did whatever had to be done. I was getting ready for work while listening to Imus in the Morning. They mentioned that a plane crashed into WTC. I put on Fox News, and as I was watching it, I thought, "What a shame. A pilot probably had a heart attack." When I saw the plane crash into the second building, I immediately thought of terrorism.

For the next few hours I was riveted to my television. I followed the story, attempted to get in touch with loved ones and friends, but communication was nonexistent. I felt a sense of aloneness and lost confusion. I felt there was something I could do, but I couldn't identity what it was. I attempted to gain access to the site, but I had no credentials that would gain me access. I was unable to contribute that first day.

After a few weeks, when the confusion got into a more organized state, I became an independent contractor through Bovis and helped Mike Bellone. Mike was the liaison between the contractors and the firemen. This way, there would be no red tape, and tools could be distributed immediately. These tools included light towers, generators, fuel, saw-blades, power tools, rebar cutters, SawZalls, partner saws, ladders, sifters, and on and on.

The sifters were something designed by Mike and the contractors to be used on the site to run the debris through. This separated personal property, body parts, or anything that could be used in making identification. The contractors made the sifters into a 2 x 3 foot boot-box with a handle on each side and a very fine mesh in the middle. Whenever they needed sifters, we sent them down.

We also helped in other ways. At the respite centers we talked with the temporary volunteers. Some of the Red Cross people were volunteers from small, rural areas now lost in the big city. We helped to put things into perspective for them. We also tried to get their minds off the catastrophe for small portions of time.

Working at Ground Zero changed my mentality. I refocused on priorities and what is important in life. How as an American, my single, solitary everyday life became so unimportant as to what we were facing as a city and a nation. I saw people come together in a way I never would have imagined possible before. The term "I" was replaced with the term "we." It was a communal feeling that we were all going through the same thing at the same time. I remember being astounded at the general feeling of optimism, that we will survive this, we will get through it, and we will survive it as a nation and a people.

In the days before I came down to the site and worked, I had a longing and a need to be part of something that would help. I needed it for myself as well as for the event. There was a hole in me, an ache that needed to be filled. Working at the site so many nights put me at ease. It alleviated the ache and gave me a sense that I was contributing. I was working toward a greater purpose, other than my own. I'm thankful for this opportunity, because I'm sure many people didn't get the chance to contribute in this regard.

Honorary Firefighter Mike Bellone and Firefighter Michael LaRosa in A.T.V. Unit

John "Chainsaw" Pasqualicchio
Laborer

I volunteered at Ground Zero from September 15th until maybe the 22nd. After the 22nd they didn't need any more volunteers, so I went back to work.

It was in January when I was called and told that I was needed at Ground Zero. My job was to put utilities on the ground as quickly as possible. We worked 24-hour shifts, seven days a week, because the generators on the site were only for the pit and not for the surrounding buildings. Come summer, those generators couldn't handle all the air conditioners in the buildings nearby.

I met Mike Bellone soon after that. I was working on the ground putting in utilities and found a piece of steel sticking out of the ground. We tried to pull the beam out, and when we did, it went through the water main pipe. We stopped the utility work and tried to stop the water. We needed rain gear, boots, rubber gloves, and there was water up the kazoo. Mike said he'd get what we needed. This was very important, because we did not know where the shut off valves were. We couldn't locate them once we pulled the beam because the towers were obviously on top of it. There was water all over the place.

Once we pulled the beam out, we excavated to the top of the water main. We found the problem. The beam had pierced right through it, a 20-inch water main. We had to put the bucket of the machine over it and call the city to see if they had the plans to locate the shut-off valve. They didn't, so we had to go down three blocks and shut off the whole neighborhood.

By then, all the water went into the utility pipe we had just put in. We got the water under control and went back to the utility pipe. We had to take everything out and start all over again. We were drenched—our boots, socks, everything but our underwear was wet. I asked Mike to help us out again, and he took care of us again.

I continued to dig for utilities for two to three weeks, and also went down into the hole to help with recoveries. I needed a rake, a little shovel, eye protector, and kneepads. I went out of my way to find Mike, and he said, "I'll come down with you." That's when we started working together. He knew his way around more than I did. He was in the mix, in deep, and did a lot of recoveries.

I worked on West and Liberty on more utilities, and that's when my accident happened. I was putting utility pipe in the Timmerman. Next to me was someone operating a chainsaw. He hit a knot in the wood, and it kicked back on him.

That's when I got caught. It caught my leg. It cut through the muscle and the nerve and chipped my bone. There were about 40 people around me. As soon as they found out I was hurt, everybody stopped. Everybody. Trucks stopped. Machine operators came out. They did as much as they could for me, and then an ambulance brought me to St. Vincent's Hospital. Mike called and asked if he could come over to see me. I told him, "Stay where you are because I'm all right where I am. You're needed there."

Three weeks later I went back to Ground Zero. One day I happened to have borrowed the Crime Scene Unit's Gator. They had an A.T.V. that was always parked. I didn't think they were using it at the time. In the meantime, the Crime Scene Unit wondered where their Gator went. They put it out over the loudspeaker, "Whoever has the Gator please return it. It belongs to the Crime Scene Unit."

I thought, "Uh, oh. Now I did it." So, I brought it back.

They told me, "This belongs to the Crime Scene Unit, and don't touch it again." I said, "I was just trying to help the guys down in the hole."

When they found out I was helping out the A.T.V. Unit, they told me, "If you're helping those guys out, just let us know when you need it and how long you need it. Make sure you're the only one who uses it."

24
THE TOOL NAZI

Tom Fenech
Ladder Co. 1 Engine Co. 7
Fire Department City of New York

When things were more organized, I started working out of the 10 and 10 firehouse, Liberty Street across the street from Ground Zero, handling the tools the firefighters needed. Large corporations like Stanley or Black and Decker had trailers near by. We needed equipment and transportation to get at the Pile. We needed something local and we needed right away.

Fire Chief Peter Hayden had noticed me at the site. I must have looked like I was homeless because I didn't have a firehouse to work at. He said, "Why don't you run the cache, tool room?"

When they started the A.T.V. Unit, Mike Bellone came down on his A.T.V. and worked the area with it. We used to call Mike the "Marathon Man" because of all the hours he put in. He hung in there tough. He really did.

Mike was the liaison between the contractors and the firefighters. The firemen wanted to look at every speck of dirt for DNA, and the construction companies were worried about getting the debris out.

Many companies and organizations helped with the tools and supplies that were needed. The Spring Street organization, the WTC Ground Zero Relief effort, a not-for-profit project of Art Science Research Laboratory, really worked hard on supplying us what we needed. Like Mike Bellone, there are certain people and organizations that went above and beyond what they had to do. Some of the organizations really stood out. Mike stood out like a sore thumb. He was everywhere and he knew everybody. He was one of the guys who could really get around.

The WTC Ground Zero Relief organization advertised items that were needed on their web site. Their warehouse was only 15 blocks away at 304 Spring Street. I called over there when we needed something and they delivered it. When the weather was cold, we needed thermals. When it was hot, we needed bright orange tee shirts to replace the heavy vests. You name it, they sent it: boots, rain gear, socks, helmets, or gloves. Just from raking and going through the rebar and sharp glass everything got cut to shreds. For instance if you found a body part and started digging around, you then had to position yourself in that spot. The jacket gets caught in the rebar and it rips or punctures a hole. Then it starts to rain or it's muddy. The water soaks up right through the boots.

My job was to assess what was needed and make sure that the firemen had what they needed for the day. If they needed rain gear, they got rain gear. If they needed socks, they got socks. We went through hundreds of pairs of socks in a day. Instead of keeping socks in packages, I had the volunteers roll them into balls. The balls went into boxes and then on a shelf. I had the carpenters build shelves for inside the tool room and the outside. This way, the general supplies like aspirin, eyewash, nasal spray, or batteries could be easily accessed. Whatever they needed quickly, we gave it to them. Mike and I also made deliveries on the A.T.V.'s.

If it was a dry day and the wind was kicking up, gray matter and papers flew everywhere. I knew I'd be going through gallons of eyewash and nasal spray, face pieces, masks, and filters. After a while the filters got like mud. We went through thousands upon thousands of masks. I never gave out one set of filters. I told them, "Keep the other one for the day." This way they could change a filter every four hours, and they didn't have to make the trip all the way back to the tool shed.

In the first couple of days not everybody had a filtered mask. There weren't enough to go around. That's why a lot of the guys have "the cough" even a couple of years later. Dr. Rodney Liebowitz did a good job. He got his hands on quite a few respirators. Rodney did a hell of a job. I think he was in his office when he first learned about it. He was the first one. He saw everybody coughing, and he knew respirators were needed. It took a while for the city to get it together.

I got the name "Tool Nazi" because in the beginning "things walked out of there." Some people were acting like they were at a department store. So I created a system where they had to leave their ID if they took out a piece of equipment. They got their ID back when they returned it.

Firefighter Tom Fenech

Mike Bellone,
Honorary Firefighter, Ladder Co. 20
Fire Department City of New York

I was sitting by the tool cache and a fireman walked up from the pit. He said, "I need a pair of dry socks."

When he took off his shoes to change them, Tommy looked at his socks and said, "One sock is wet and one sock is dry. You only get one sock."

That was what earned Tommy the title of "Sock Nazi."

Then Tommy started doing it with the tools. We needed blades for the SawZall. He gave us used blades. We knew Tommy had new ones in the back. He then went from being "The Sock Nazi" to "Tommy the Tool Nazi."

But Tommy was right. How do you predict how many blades are going to be needed when you only have so many? We had to get as much out of a tool as we possibly could. Tommy controlled that, and he did it the same with gloves, or shirts, rain gear, and batteries. He had a pretty tight lid on it, and if it weren't for Tommy, we would have run out of supplies by November.

Firefighter Tom Fenech and Honorary Firefighter Mike Bellone

CHAPTER 25
RECOVERIES

Rob Miller
Photojournalist
New York Post

Later on I was assigned to do a story on Mike Bellone. My editor came to me and said, "Go to Ground Zero. I have an interesting story for you." That's how I met Mike.

Mike immediately offered to take me to wherever I wanted to take pictures. I asked if we could go into Ground Zero. There had been a lot of other journalists trying to get into the site. I knew it was a burial site, but I also saw it as a Holocaust. It had to be recorded and documented. This could not be forgotten.

Mike understood this, and I think that is why he felt he could reach out to me and offer this opportunity. He understood that, for the sake of history, this needed to be recorded.

I was with Mike at Ground Zero a number of times, but there was one particular Sunday. I telephoned Mike to see if anything was happening. He told me that there might be a recovery of a fire truck. Later that day a piece from a fire truck was identified.

It seemed as though Mike was able to piece together where the fire truck had been lost and knew exactly where it was. He knew it was Engine 55 truck.

He told me, "I'll come up from the hole and pick you up."

I was across the street at the 10 and 10 firehouse. Before Mike and I went out, I had to gear-up. Mike got me a mask and a helmet. The next thing I knew I was on the back of Mike's A.T.V. It was a bright sunny day, and we headed toward this large, what seemed like from above, group of ants all over a pile. What I was looking at were firemen searching.

They were on top of a pile where they thought they would make a recovery. Firemen were all over it digging furiously.

It was well organized. One was digging, one was straining, and it was very quiet. Nobody talked. It seemed like they knew exactly what to do without talking. Buckets were passed. One guy was digging with his hands and putting it into a bucket. Someone else handed him an empty bucket so he could keep going.

Once the victim was placed on the stokes in a black bag, an American flag was draped over the victim.

Mike started to dig with his hands. I looked over and saw Mike with a jacket, a fireman's jacket. The jacket appeared very flat, dirty, brittle, and one-dimensional. I remember watching Mike put his hand inside the jacket.

Mike's reaction always appeared to be internal. There were very few words. Mike was on his knees and he had the jacket in both of his hands. He cradled it like a baby. It seemed like he was examining it. I didn't know it at the time, but he was looking for a name. Mike found a firemen's tag in the jacket, and that's when it was confirmed that it was from Engine 55 Company.

Mike said, "Now we can call his family. Having this will make them feel better. Now they can have a funeral."

I remember seeing a part of something in another area. It was a bone with cloth around it. I could tell by all of the activity around this cloth that they had just found one of the firemen. They put all of the remains on a stretcher and placed an American flag over it. This went into a small truck, and there was a pause. The men stood in silent reverence and then looked out over the site. It was a moment of silence and a moment of peace for them. That is what they had all been working for, to bring each other home.

During recoveries, a stokes (slang for stretcher) was placed near the victim

Mike Bellone
Honorary Firefighter, Ladder Co. 20
Fire Department City of New York

I was standing by with a rebar cutter. We knew by the scent in the air that this was a 100 percent recovery. Captain Jerry Summerville, who ran the GPS Unit that day, was on his knees digging in the hole. I had the rebar cutter and was trying to clear away some of the debris. He had just yelled that he needed a hand, and my first reaction was to respond to that call, but I hesitated. I knew the firemen should be there first.

Capt. Summerville, since I was so close, said, "Mike, come here and help me." We tried to lift some debris off of a bunker jacket. As I lifted the debris, the jacket came clear. Capt. Summerville asked me to help him open the snaps of the jacket.

My emotions were running very, very high. I tried to stay focused, because I knew this was someone's father, someone's son, and someone's husband. As Capt. Summerville held the jacket open, I checked to see if I could find a name. Sometimes we used ammonia to rub on the stitching to enhance the name. I whispered the firefighter's name to Captain Summerville.

I put the shirt down and closed the snaps. I cradled the jacket like a baby. As badly as I wanted to cry, I had to stay focused. Capt. Summerville said, "We're ready."

On "three" we would lift him up and place him into a black bag.

During recoveries, a stokes (or stretcher) was placed near the victim

As we were doing this, Capt. Summerville and I had a conversation with this firefighter and told him that he was going home. We told him what a great job he did. We also told him that we would never forget. We would make sure that everyone would, "Never Forget."

When the bag was lying by itself on the plastic stoke, and we opened up the flag to cover him, I knew this would be his final goodnight as he was tucked away.

I said, "Goodnight Firefighter," and I kissed the flag.

I then stepped back when it was time for him to be picked up and placed for the Honor Guard. I walked to the ramp, stood in the Honor Guard line, and gave my last respects.

Paying my last respects was something I had already done hundreds of times.

The victim was then marched up the ramp in an honor guard by all rescue workers and construction workers

Bob Barrett
Retired Firefighter, Ladder Co. 20
Fire Department City of New York

That first day as I looked out over an inconceivable landscape, I saw an almost blank stare on the faces of the firefighters, asking, "What has happened here? Who did this? Why did this happen? What do we do now?"

I don't think that anyone was able to comprehend the enormous tragedy that occurred before our eyes. For the first time in my life, I actually witnessed dry tears. Men who would not cry were yet balling their eyes out. I saw a woman whose tears could barely wash the dust from her face, and yet I felt like she was crying for me. And I felt better.

All the tears across the nation being shed for this tragedy helped us. We could not cry. The nation cried for us. I wanted to cry. I really wanted to cry, but there wasn't even time to cry. Crying comes later when the work is done.

When the victim reached the top of the ramp, a chaplain said a final prayer and
the deceased was placed in an ambulance and taken to the temporary morgue

Maybe that's what I want to do now by writing this. I want to cry. I need to cry. The firefighters had to hold it inside. We hugged, we embraced, but we watched as the wives and children shed their tears. We shared the grief, but we still had to remain strong. It was our duty. But we are only human. At some point, each in his own time will give in and let the tears flow to wash away our grief.

As we searched for survivors or victims, each one of the victims became a personal friend of mine. Most of the people we recovered were not immediately identifiable. Never in any of the recoveries I made were people immediately identifiable. Therefore, each and every one of them was my "Brother." By that I mean that there were no faces for me to look upon. Only the apparel they were wearing gave them a generic identity.

Many of the firefighters we found had been wearing their bunker gear, which bore fire department patches and IDs. Civilians were usually wearing dresses, slacks, or suits, and some had IDs. I found wallets with pictures of, no doubt, their husbands, wives, and children.

When we carried the bodies out of the site, we actually talked to them. If there were pictures, I showed the pictures to the victim.

I said, "John, come on. We're taking you home now. Look at your lovely wife and kids. We're bringing you home to them."

This was a way to help us always remember that these were human beings who deserved our respect and honor. Everyone was treated the same.

Mike Bellone
Honorary Firefighter, Ladder Co. 20
Fire Department City of New York

When we made a recovery, when we found someone, there was total silence, from day one to the last day. The person was put into a black bag and covered with an American Flag. Right there, at the site, an Honor Guard was formed with all working in the pit and around the perimeter. A Chaplain said a prayer at the foot of the ramp where everyone lined up and stood at attention, saluting the victim. You could hear a pin drop. The victim was carried up the ramp and placed in an ambulance and taken to the morgue.

Lt. Claudio Fernandez
New York City Highway Patrol

In addition to providing escorts to the different agencies that needed to get into Ground Zero, we took on a new mission. A week after 9/11 we decided that our mission was to bring every Member of the Service home in escort mode. Our "home" was to be the New York City Morgue. This was because any body or body parts that were recovered at Ground Zero had to be brought to the morgue for properly identifications and then reunited with the families.

We felt that these heroes gave so much that the least we could do is to give them the respect and honor they deserved. How we accomplished this was by conducting a pseudo-funeral escort. A person's recovered remains were put into an ambulance. In front, six motorcycles escorted the ambulance. The respective agency vehicles followed the ambulance in the rears. If a firefighter had been found, fire trucks were in back of the ambulance. If it was a policeman, police cars were in the back of the ambulance.

One thing that I demanded of all police officers at Ground Zero for security purposes was that they salute the heroes as they were brought from Ground Zero to the morgue.

The Highway Patrol is always thought of as "the devil in the rearview mirror," because they only come around when someone is speeding. But one of our most proud duties is to escort a fallen loved one to their final resting place. We felt we were accomplishing this each and every day working down at Ground Zero.

I often felt compelled to want to give the same respect and honor to all those who were killed on 9/11. For the Highway Patrol it was physically impossible to do every single escort with the resources. We made a pact with the New York State Troopers that they would provide all the civilians with an escort from Ground Zero to the morgue. Everyone deserves their final respects, and that day everyone gave all they had. The least we could do is recognize that, and do the right thing.

Joe Adinolfi
Independent Contractor

The moment of greatest impact I can recall was the first time I was allowed to stand in the Honor Guard for the removal of a recovered body at the site. There was a long wooden ramp that was built to facilitate this. Everybody lined up on both sides of the ramp. The body was carried between us at full salute. At the top of the ramp, the body was placed in an ambulance to be escorted off the site. I can't convey the emotion and the feeling of respect I had for the victims. It is an event I will never forget as long as I live. It helped me to put everything into a context that affords me now to live my daily life.

I carry the memorial card for the one I lost. Jesus N. Cabezas worked for me when I owned a restaurant in Brooklyn in the 1980s. He was among those lost that tragic day. Jesus Cabezas was a hard-working chef who worked in Windows of the World. I owe it to him and all those who lost their lives that day, to never forget.

Bob Barrett
Retired Firefighter, Ladder Co. 20
Fire Department City of New York

I was always in awe of all the firefighter's wives, because they always maintained such pose. They looked regal to me. I spoke very little except to offer my condolences, and to explain to them that they belonged to a large family of firefighters. Their loss was on all our minds and in all our hearts.

I couldn't bring myself to say more than a few words to any of the widows, even though inside I was ready to explode. I felt that my silence and my hugs were speaking for me in a way no words could ever have expressed. All the wives were very special people, and I'm sure they felt the same way about us. It didn't require words from either one of us. Our love was in the air around us. To me, each wife emanated an aura of dignity of which I was proud to be around. The best had married the best.

Lou Chinal
Firefighter, Engine Co. 152
Fire Department City of New York

When we weren't working, we attended funerals. I remember the Gregg Atlas funeral. He was a Lieutenant in Engine Company 10. We all wore our dress uniforms and got on a bus. They brought us up to Middletown, NY, and when we got off the bus, the bagpipes were playing Amazing Grace. I think I had already heard Amazing Grace 1,000 times. I couldn't stand it anymore. We did the hand salute and we all piled into the church.

His wife got up and told everyone what a wonderful husband Gregg Atlas was. His kids got up and said what a wonderful father he was. His brother got up and said what a wonderful brother he was.

And then a woman got up.

She said, "I don't know him. I only talked to him for about a minute or two. wo minutes. But he saved our lives that morning. Part of the ceiling had fallen down and it was blocking the doorway. Gregg Atlas just stood there and held it up."

That woman had walked by him and told him, "I'm glad the Fire Department hired big, strong guys."

He said, "I have to be. My name is Atlas."

Atlas may not have held up the world, but Atlas held up Manhattan for a few minutes.

Once the victims were placed on the stokes in a black bag, an American flag was draped over them

CHAPTER 26
WINGS

This chapter is dedicated to Sara Low and all the Crew Members and their families and all the Passengers and their families of American Airlines Flight 11.

Mike Bellone
Honorary Firefighter, Ladder Co. 20
Fire Department City of New York

Toward the beginning of the recovery effort I was working on e day with Chief Riches. We were digging on the west side of the site. I called over to Chief riches and said "I think I have something here, it looks like a dark blue uniform, possibly a female". We carefully dug around her outline so as not to damage any remains. As we brushed off her clothes we saw something shiny attached to her jacket. We soon realized it was pin shaped like wings with the "AA" insignia. This was the emblem for American Airlines and presumed this was a flight attendant. We said a prayer for her and her family and carefully placed her on the stokes for her honor guard. She was taken to the temporary morgue onsite which was protocol. I drove there on my ATV and asked Reverend Mitties DeChamplain to please take extra care of this special lady.

One time I found a little compact of makeup amongst the ruins. It made me sit and wonder. The compact once belonged to a woman who, for what it meant to me, wanted to make herself look pretty, not for just everyone, but for herself. The thought of what she must have looked like, and now amongst those ruins, brought tears to my eyes.

Sometimes the slightest things I picked up gave me a feeling that this little "thing" would probably mean the whole world to the person connected to that loved one. Maybe her husband or boyfriend would want that compact because it belonged to her. It broke my heart because I didn't know who to give it to. It made me cry.

Another time I was digging in the north tower and out popped this little Irish or English cloth doll. I couldn't believe how beat up it was, but it managed to survive. I thought to myself, "This doll must have come from someone's desk," and I wished I knew the history behind it. Was it a gift? Something they won? Had they liked and purchased it? It was heartbreaking to know I had someone's possession and I couldn't return it.

It was a dark night in Building 6. I was with Chief Manes, and he said, "Mike, I found an odd disk."

Generally, you can get things back to the right owner.

He said, "See what you can do with this."

It was a very large, round, brass plate that was very badly bent, distorted, and fire-scorned.

I called my friend from the Secret Service and met him for a cup of coffee. I asked him if he knew what it was. He looked at it and said that on the 6th floor of Building 6, it was the emblem, the seal that was on the main door of the A.T.F., Alcohol, Tobacco and Fire Arms agency.

Presenting Edward Domeneche with the seal of the ATF Agency where they were located in Building 6

I asked him, "How can I get this back to its rightful owner?"

He made a few phone calls, came back to me, and said, "You have to go down to where they relocated in Brooklyn and speak to Edward Domeneche. He is the Special Agent in charge and he's expecting you. I did not tell him why you're coming, but that you have something for him."

When I got there, I introduced myself and met Mr. Domeneche. I said, "I found something

in Building 6 about 40 feet below street level with Chief Manes. We felt it was only right to return this to where it belongs."

When I pulled it out of the bag and he saw it, I could see tears filling up in his eyes. The

building was so badly damaged that not even a pencil had been recovered. This would be the only remains to the A.T.F. Unit in World Trade Center Number 6.

There was a very, very long silence. I guess I was trying to put myself in his mind to try to tell what he was thinking. I only knew that this was definitely the home for this brass seal. He called in the other agents, and you could see the sadness and grief in each and every one of them. Yet, they were also glad that they actually had something from their office. We must have shook hands about 10 times.

That was a day we were able to accomplish something.

There were other times, too. I was digging near the south tower. We found 20 cases or more of wine that was totally intact. Not one bottle was broken. As we pulled each bottle out of the box, we became more amazed that this wine, amongst all the ruin, the pulverized computers, chairs, twisted beams, melted steel, and ash, remained untouched. I scratched my head in disbelief.

Every time I saw an object to recover, I thought of those wings. And I knew, that finding something, anything, would make someone, somewhere, feel better.

I remember being called to St. Paul's Chapel ASAP. When I arrived I asked what the problem was. Sister Grace had told me the Archbishop of Canterbury was there and he wanted to speak to a recovery worker. They chose me, why I don't know but here I am with the Bishop and he has a few questions for me. He asked me about what my day was from the time I woke till the time I went to sleep. I told him I was woken up at 6:00am, had a cup of tea, 2 Twix bars, for energy, and off I go to the pile. That morning we made a recovery of a victim, female, according to the medical examiner, between 35 to 40 years old. The bishop asked how I felt. I explained to him.

The seal was the only remnant recovered from the ATF agency in Building #6

224

The Archbishop of Canterbury, the Rev. George Cary, holds the highest rank in the Episcopal Church

Honorary Firefighter Mike Bellone explains the recovery process to the Archbishop

225

CHAPTER 27
THE LITTLE CHAPEL
THAT STOOD

Dennis Fisin
Coordinator, St. Paul's Chapel
St. Paul's Episcopal Relief Center

After waking up from a sound sleep and hearing the news that a plane crashed into the WTC towers, I went outside to the nonstop sound of sirens in Midtown Manhattan. Floods of people were moving toward the Uptown direction away from the towers. It was only when I walked to 5th Avenue that I saw the smoke coming from downtown. I made my way past people, in shock, going the opposite direction. People crowded around the front windows of the FAO Schwartz building and watched the television sets. I knew we had a major problem, but what to do, was the question.

Disaster itself is chaos. I wanted to help in some way, but in "chaos" it's always best to go in prepared. Even though there was no way to prepare for this kind of chaos, I knew that the Red Cross and their volunteers would be allowed within the perimeter of the disaster area. I went to Red Cross headquarters at 66th and Amsterdam. Their auditorium was packed with people wanting to help. They were also collecting blood for the victims.

That entire day we waited in the auditorium to get orders on what we should do. Red Cross workers went out to survey the disaster area, and it was 12 hours before they returned to headquarters. Many questions were raised. "What is needed? What is the chain of command?" This was now a national disaster. I knew the National Red Cross would soon be taking over.

Their orders came in around midnight. The Red Cross was briefed on the situation in the city, and 11 shelter operations were set up to deal with the disaster. Questions continued to be addressed. "What bridges are closed? What roadways? What is open?" There were about 25 of us in that room, and we were divided between the shelters. Three of us, a ham operator, myself, and another volunteer, opened up the shelter in the auditorium at Houston and Avenue D.

A day or two later I was walking down the West Side Highway. I came to a checkpoint where no one could go any further toward the site unless they had proper identification. People were coming in from all over and dropping off supplies at those corners because they couldn't take them any further. It was amazing. Neighbors, people from the area, were dropping off anything and everything; boxes of socks, cases of water, food, clothing, and on and on.

At the same time, cars and busses were bringing rescue workers in and out. As rescue workers passed by, people tried to hand them supplies. Water was the most important commodity and it went fast. Just as I was trying to figure out what was going on, a truck full of water pulled up. Due to the overwhelming amount of supplies being dropped off at the three corners, I ended up staying for hours helping with this neighborhood relief effort.

Then it got dark and started to rain. There were only four of us left. Someone had brought in a picnic tent, and we attempted to save the supplies from perishing. We were then informed that the entire checkpoint was moving down a block to the West Side Highway and Canal Street. We realized that if we didn't move to the new area immediately, and set up some type of organization structure, it would be chaos the next day.

Top Row L to R: Judy Young, Julie Bellone, Brian Sheley, Linda Lawrence, Rick Wormwood
Bottom Row L to R: Yvonne Gruel, Susan Bartow, Kim Young,

We went over to survey the new checkpoint area, and, as luck would have it, the owner of a Mobile gas station allowed us to take over his station. He helped us barricade the area. We now had a roof, electricity, and access to the facilities. He even supplied an attendant. Five of us ran relief efforts from that Mobile gas station from September to November. We became one of the main drop-off points for supplies.

As time went by we found ourselves dealing with enormous amounts of supplies. We realized that once we received these supplies, we needed to create a better distribution. St. Paul's Chapel was on our list of possible distribution points because of its strategic location about 100 yards away from Ground Zero.

As we walked into St. Paul's Chapel, my first impression was, "Wow." The marbled floors and dark-wooden pews appeared as though they were standing in time. We had just walked through masses of rubble and mud, and as I looked around me something became quite clear. Nothing was broken within this church. Just across the street, the WTC's acres looked like an atomic bomb had gone off.

Built in 1766, President George Washington had attended worship services at St. Paul's Episcopal Church when New York was still the national's capital. The Presidential Seal still hangs above his pew at St. Paul's. It seemed ironic that this same place had seen the Revolutionary War, and now this.

A small relief operation was already up and running in St. Paul's. We approached a person working in the chapel and asked if they needed supplies. They gave us a list of soda, water, paper goods, paper plates, napkins, clothing, and tee shirts. We went to the warehouse where we kept our supplies. We filled their list and brought it back. Up to now, St. Paul's had depended upon small quantities of donations. We told St. Paul's we'd be back at the end of the week.

Again, St. Paul's had a list for us. This went on for two or three weeks. Rescue efforts had now cleared some of the debris surrounding the area, and things were starting to move around the perimeter. By now it was Thanksgiving, and one of the pastors at the chapel asked my friend and me if we wanted to work for St. Paul's. We said, "Okay."

Nothing much changed, except now we were in the Chapel full time. We still used our same contacts and what we had learned during the previous three months. We split the shifts and had three coordinators on 12-hour shifts. I worked at St. Paul's for a year and a half.

At St. Paul's Chapel we served breakfast, lunch, and dinner to the workers. We were open 24 hours a day, seven days a week. We provided a full-line of drugstore supplies, a full-line of clothing, and practically any supplies the workers needed. We served 5,000 to 6,000 meals a day.

Saint Paul's chapel

Julie Bellone
Volunteer
St. Paul's Relief Center

I live in Seneca Falls in upstate New York, and when I learned about St. Paul's Chapel and their work at Ground Zero, I emailed their website. St. Paul's called, and I was scheduled to volunteer on December 9, 2001. I assembled a group of eight people to go down to volunteer. From our initial entry into the Chapel, I immediately felt God's presence. I could physically feel the warmth and love.

We worked our first 12-hour shift, 8:00 a.m. to 8:00 p.m., and we handed out supplies to the workers such as warm clothes, band-aids, and food. We also spoke to them with casual conversation.

When we returned to Seneca Falls, we continued to help St. Paul's by seeking out supply donations from the central and upstate New York areas to bring back on our next visit. Through a collaboration of supplies from friends, family, and the graciousness of the area businesses, we brought the workers winter hats, gloves, sweatshirts, candy, gum, cough drops, coffee, and more.

Since I and the other volunteers had regular jobs, we worked the weekend shift at St. Paul's on a monthly basis. It was a ten-hour drive there and back, and this usually meant taking Friday or Monday off for traveling.

Hon. Firefighter Mike Bellone with Sister Grace and a firefighter

I met Mike Bellone in January at St. Paul's. He seemed to be a familiar face throughout the day in the Chapel. I had brought Dalmatian dog Beanie Babies down, and I gave him one. He saw it as an expression of friendship, and asked if I had children. I don't, but I mentioned that I have four nieces. Mike provided me with a memento to bring back to each girl and offered photographs and Fire Department patches. From that point on, we struck up a conversation each time he came into the Chapel on my subsequent monthly volunteer trips.

I saw Mike's bravery, dedication, and respect for the deceased, and immediately realized he was a special presence at Ground Zero. The more I saw Mike give this dedication and respect to others, the more I wanted give him the same dedication and respect back.

L to R: Kathy Shelly, Pam Jones, Julie Bellone, Sally Covert, Carah Covert

Bob Barrett
Retired Firefighter, Ladder Co. 20
Fire Department City of New York

For me, St. Paul's was more than a place to find a meal or to get some rest. It gave me a chance to contact my spiritual side. I enjoyed being in the Chapel late at night when there were few distractions. I was alone with my inner feelings, and I could renew my spirit by talking to my God. At this somewhat peaceful or at least quiet time of night, I found that I needed to be in touch with something other than myself. There had to be a reason for all this, and this was the best place to search for it. When I was not in a meditative spiritual state, I read letters that children had written. This, too, helped fuel my spirit and inspired me to go on. The simple words of children are often as soothing as any words written by bards or scholars. I found great inspiration in the simplest expressions of our youth.

I often wondered who was writing these letters. I pictured their age, what they might look like, and how I would ever be able to thank them for all they were doing for me at that moment. I knew that somewhere down the road I would get the chance to thank them.

In most cases, I knew that it would be impossible to find and thank the actual person who had sent me the wonderful letter. I say "me" because at that particular moment, that letter was addressed to me. I knew that even though I didn't know the actual writer, that if I could thank "any" child, I would be speaking to the person who wrote to me.

Reverend Mitties DeChamplain in the cemetery of St. Paul's

I imagined that some of these letters were the result of a well-meaning teacher giving out an assignment. I wanted to let that student know that this letter was being read, that it had meaning, and that it had found someone and touched someone deeply.

It was not a waste of their time to write to us. In fact, what they did was something wonderful. How could I let the children know that the letters and their prayers, and whatever good wishes they felt for us, had such meaning? None of their efforts were wasted. Each child and each letter and each prayer made a difference in the lives of those who came in contact with their efforts.

St. Paul's was also a place of camaraderie. We were all there as a family drawn together by a single noble purpose. We could relate to one another not only in regard to the work that we were doing, but to the effect this trauma was wrecking on us. Sometimes words were unnecessary. A smile, a hug, or a mere wave of the hand would bolster whatever wave of doubt that had come over us.

Reverend Mitties DeChamplain at Ground Zero

This was a place not of strangers, but of brothers and sisters in a tremendous struggle to maintain our faith and humanity. Our physical needs were also taken care of at St. Paul's. We could get something to eat or drink, a change of clothes, minor medical attention, and, of course, whatever sleep we could reach.

I slept in a pew, but sometimes I would just sit there and think. I imagined myself somewhere else, and I was delivered from this spot to another place. Somewhere in my mind I often thought of happy times. Sometimes I thought of when I was a kid in simpler times, times without worries or cares. But I couldn't remain in this peaceful time too long. Something would always happen to bring me back to the present. Usually it was a call that a recovery was at hand or a call for assistance from someone who needed help in one endeavor or another. Times away from Ground Zero were brief and rare.

While I was in St. Paul's, without knowing it, we started to form a relationship with all of the volunteers and workers who supplied us with all of our needs, including conversation. In the middle of the night I would converse with my inner thoughts. During the day, I conversed with people like Dennis Fisin and Diane, Barbara, or Sister Grace.

The pews in St. Paul's Chapel covered with letters of love and hope from children around the world

At St. Paul's, Dennis Fisin was always on the scene. When I saw him I felt secure that, yes, I was in the right place. Feeling secure in the midst of chaos was like sanity in an insane place in time. Little by little we began to acknowledge each other as brothers and sisters and it was comforting to have this family away from home. It was difficult to maintain our normal family life. "Normal" was in a state of suspension to picked up at some other time, somewhere down the road, when sanity was restored. Until then, we had to feed off of each other's strengths. We had to lend each other whatever support we could supply. Sometimes a smile was worth all the frowns of the proceeding hours of work on the Pile.

I often filled my plate with food, not even being hungry, but as I walked down the line of servers who were reaching out with their ladles, it was not so much what they were offering as far as food, but the good will that came from the ladles of their hearts which they dolled out in huge portions. I think the soul was hungrier than the stomach.

At the time, I never really thought about how all of this was being accomplished at St. Paul's. Later on, I realized the amount of work and hours it took to provide us with whatever comforts these volunteers bestowed on us. It took many people many hours and good intentions to sustain the rescue workers over all those months. The volunteers also paid a price in sacrificing whatever normalcy was available in their lives and tried to bring normalcy to us. I respect each and every one of them for they acted in the truest sense of selfless people, giving without reward, and seeking only the common good.

The Gates of St. Paul covered with banners, letters, shirts and flowers of hope and love

Mike Bellone
Honorary Firefighter, Ladder Co. 20
Fire Department City of New York

The second pew was my pew. Not because it was more comfortable, but because it was close to the door and I could easily run out without disturbing anyone. For some reason, it just became the place where, "Mike sleeps."

I remember one morning in October waking up in my pew, opening my eyes, and seeing a rough draft of a poem in front of me. Cards and letters of support were always taped to the pews of St. Paul's. I began reading the letter sideways because I was still lying down.

I said to myself, "Wow, what a great poem sideways. Maybe it's even better if I get up and read it."

When I read it again, I could feel the passion in the person who wrote it. For some reason, that poem struck me right in my heart. It was a poem I had to read over and over again. Someone a half a continent away could actually feel my pain. I found it comforting.

Most of the letters I read were signed but left no address. This letter included a school, a town, and a state. That afternoon when I came back from the hole, I pulled the letter out of my pocket and read it again and again and again.

The pews in St. Paul's Chapel covered with letters and poems from children around the world

I said to myself, "Someday I have to meet this person who wrote what was in my heart."

I was able to find the phone number to the school. I called the school and told the person who answered the phone, "My name is Mike Bellone, and I'm from Ground Zero in New York City. I just read a poem that Dawn Hayford wrote, and I just wanted to thank her for making me feel so good."

The person asked me to hold on and she would get Dawn Hayford out of class. And she did. Dawn and I had a brief conversation. She seemed like such a great kid. I assured Dawn that I would work twice as hard so I could make her proud of her fellow Americans. Then I said, "I hope that someday I'll be able to thank you in person."

Top & Bottom: St. Paul's Chapel covered wall-to-wall. pew-to-pew, aisle-to-aisle
with banners, flags and letters letters from children around the world

Dawn Hayford, Age 16
Valley Christian High School
Oshkosh, Wisconsin

Heroes of America

by Dawn Hayford

What is a hero?
Many will ask.
Who do the young
Look up to?
Those who have
Fought for freedom.
Those who pay the
Ultimate Sacrifice.
Those who strive
For justice and truth.
Those who work
Day and night
In hope of finding
Just one more survivor.
Those who sift
Through the debris and dust.
Those who have
Worked nonstop
In New York and
Washington, D.C.
These are the ones
We all admire.
These are the ones
Our children adore.
They preserve though
Hope seems slim.
They work without
Want for reward.
With them are our
Prayers and tears,
For they are the
Heroes of America.

CHAPTER 28
FATHER AND SON

Chief Jim Riches
Battalion 11
Fire Department City of New York

I was at a funeral when I received a phone call that they found my son's helmet. When they found Jimmy, his helmet was right next to him. His helmet was crushed, but his memory will always be there. On September 11, I spoke to him that morning. His birthday was the next day, the 12th. That's how I knew he was working on the 11th.

That morning I called him up and said, "Are we going out to eat? Are we going out to eat?" You know, go out for his birthday.

He said, "Okay, okay."

That was the last time I spoke to my son.

He was a New York City Police Officer and transferred over to the Fire Department. He was working in Engine 4 that day.

Thousands of firefighters, police officers and city officials line 5th Avenue to honor fallen firefighter Jim Riches, Jr.

I was five minutes away from the site when they found him. We went through the Battery Tunnel, and we were there in minutes. Up on the ramp, Mike Bellone picked me up with his A.T.V. and took me into the north tower. Jimmy Cody showed me the helmet. We were all digging and digging like animals.

My other three sons were with me when Jimmy was placed on the stokes. When he was ready, my sons and other firemen carried him out. I am one of the lucky ones.

They found my son's body. When you lose your son, it's not in the right order. You expect them to bury you. When you have to bury them, that's heart wrenching. I'll never forget. There is no closure. It will always hurt.

Jimmy was always helping people. He always had a smile on his face. He was always laughing, and everyone loved him. He was a bartender. He would get on the bar and have everyone laughing with him. He was a comic, a good kid, and very respectful.

We always remember the old stories about him, and that's how we keep his memory going. He always had those silly superman shirts underneath. We'll never forget this. There's no such thing as closure.

The Riches family begin the Honor Guard for Firefighter Jim Riches, Jr.

Mike Bellone
Honorary Firefighter, Ladder Co. 20
Fire Department City of New York

On March 25th, Jimmy Cody and I were talking about going down to the north tower. Every once in a while, Jimmy Cody and I would set aside some time to look for Chief Riches son, Jimmy Jr.

Chief Jim Riches is one in a million. He's always there for you. He always has something nice to say. He always has a great attitude for someone who carried the burden of not knowing where his son was.

That morning, Jimmy Cody called me on the radio for tools and batteries, but he said it in a way I have never heard him say it. When I got down there, I've never seen him dig the way he digging.

I said, "Are you going to tell me what's going on?"

He said, "We found a helmet."

And he showed it to me.

My eyes filled up, and there were too many men already digging there, so I just started to cut rebar. When I heard that Chief Jim Riches had arrived at the site and was now on the top of the ramp, I drove to pick him up.

Without me saying anything, he said, "Take me to my son."

We drove down the ramp to the north tower, and Cody handed Chief Riches his son's helmet.

Now everyone was digging. We finally found Jimmy's fireman jacket. He was then respectfully placed on the stokes and carried up the ramp. Of all the Honor Guards I've stood in, this one was the most heartfelt. To see the whole family together for the last time was not just an honor, but also something I will remember for the rest of my life.

Thousands of firefighters, police officers and city officials line 5th Avenue to honor fallen firefighter Jim Riches, Jr.

Deputy Chief Jim Riches and his three sons bring his son, Jim Jr., up the ramp in an Honor Guard

The Riches family at the memorial service at St. Patrick's Cathedral

CHAPTER 29
CAPTAIN PATRICK BROWN
LADDER COMPANY 3

Mike Bellone
Honorary Firefighter, Ladder Co. 20
Fire Department City of New York

I was talking to my friend Paul Martinovica from Engine 80, Truck 23. He asked me if I would like to go to Capt. Patty Brown's funeral at St. Patrick's Cathedral. When I arrived, about 10,000 of Capt. Patty Brown's friends and brothers were present to honor him. I looked out over a sea of blue uniforms.

I felt out of place when I first walked through the doors of the Cathedral. I understood that this was a very private, intimate moment for the Fire Department. I did not want to intrude, but when I walked in, a number of firemen said, "Hi, Mike. Glad you could come. Nice to see you."

Right away, they made me feel like I belonged. As I walked down the side of the aisle, another fireman was holding a seat for me. I didn't want to sit. There were so many firemen standing.

They said, "It's okay, please sit down, Mike."

But I stood anyway.

They started with the Eulogy and Members of the Service spoke. The Chief of the Department spoke. Mayor Guiliani spoke. Members of Capt. Patty Brown's Unit got up and spoke. It was probably the first time I was off of the site when I felt it was all right to express my emotions. This was because so many around me were doing the same.

At the end, Capt. Patty Brown's helmet was walked out of the door. Everyone followed behind. When we got outside the streets were lined with thousands of firemen. I could see nothing but blue uniforms up and down 5th Avenue.

Capt. Patty Brown's helmet was placed on the rear of the fire truck, and the procession started to walk down 5th Avenue.

What was so amazing was that 10,000 people all had the same feeling of loss, at the same time, and for the same person. It's an experience I will never forget. I have never before seen such loyalty and admiration for a man that was loved by so many

Capt. Patty Brown was a very unassuming man. I found out during his Eulogy that he was a Silver Star winner in Viet Nam. He had held many degrees. Capt. Patty Brown was probably one of the nicest guys you could talk to. He always lent an ear.

I can never thank Paul enough for letting me experience this with the rest of the Fire Department.

When I left, I headed back down towards Lower Manhattan. I stopped by St. Paul's Chapel and lit a candle. I asked God to please take care of my friend Capt. Patty Brown.

And then I went back into the hole to work.

Captain Patrick Brown

Captain Patrick Brown

CHAPTER 30
FIREFIGHTER LADDER 20

Bob Barrett
Retired Firefighter, Ladder Co. 20
Fire Department City of New York

I was born in 1941 in the Borough of Brooklyn. I come from a family of eight. Unlike most of my friends who had fathers and relatives who were firefighters, no one in my family was in the Fire Department except for a cousin. One day my cousin asked me if I'd like to be a firefighter. We were just discussing his job, and he was looking to recruit people that he knew into the Fire Department. I said, "It sounds like a good idea." My cousin sent the application in and paid the fee.

I had no intention on becoming a firefighter. It was accidental happenstance that led me to become one. I was a telephone repairman at the time. I received a notification in the mail to take the test. I took the test and passed. Then one day a chief from the Fire Department called and asked my wife, "Does your husband want to be a firefighter? He's the only one who hasn't answered."

I called the chief back, went down, and I was sworn in. That was March 30, 1974. I went to the Fire Academy that was located on Roosevelt Island at the time. I took eight weeks of training and was assigned to Ladder 20.

I reported to my firehouse after the graduating ceremony. My parents and my wife accompanied me. It was one of the proudest days of my life. My father was very proud that I had become a firefighter, and this meant a great deal to me. As soon as I walked into the firehouse I knew that this was the beginning of my destiny. I felt like I had just won the lottery, and I never thought differently for the next 28 years.

Ladder 20 was my home away from home. It was an extended family. We worked together, slept together, ate together, and went to parties and picnics. The firefighter standing next to me at a job was looking out for my life, as I was for his. This was the perfect atmosphere to form close and lifelong friendships. Each day we talked to each other not only about fires and how to extinguish them, but also about personal and family problems. We gave each other advice on the remedies we thought would work. We tossed them around at the dinner table, breakfast table, or after work at the local pub over a few beers. The brotherhood we formed with each other is no secret. Everyone knows the camaraderie of firefighters. It can be seen quite readily in the manner in which we stick together. People often comment to me just how different firefighters are in comparison to other occupations.

I feel fortunate to have been a firefighter, and I truly believe it is the job that makes the man and not visa versa. I know that the position I was put in allowed me to become a better person. It was my duty to do good for people. It was not uncommon for people to say, "God Bless you." I basically only saw the good side of my fellow New Yorkers. This left me with a mind filled with beautiful memories I shall treasure my entire life. I wonder had I chosen some other occupation, what kind of person would I have been. For this I am thankful for the choice I made by becoming a firefighter.

Firefighter Bob Barrett

Mrs. Kathy Barrett
Bob Barrett's Wife

On the morning of September 11, Bob took me to work and went home. I was outside my building when I heard the news. I ran in and down the stairs to call Bob.

I told him, "Put on the television! Something terrible happened at the World Trade Center."

I was thinking it was just an accident. I started crying.

I begged Bob, "Please don't go! Bob, please don't go!"

Bob said, "I have to go. I have to."

I didn't see him for 5 days.

I didn't want Bob to be a fireman. I was always proud of him, but I always worried about his safety. I was his wife, and I almost didn't go to his graduation. I was pregnant when he was at the Academy. When he graduated, I told him, "I'm not going to watch you. I'm not going, because I don't want you to do this."

I don't know how I found my way down there. How could I not support him in this? I took the train. I don't know how I found it. But I did. I saw him standing up there. He turned around and saw me in the audience. He gave me a big smile. And that was the point when I had to accept him being a fireman.

Soon after, there was a big fire at the telephone company. Bob had just gotten on the job and now he was hospitalized. I told Bob, "This is not what we want."

I have always supported him. Bob was so happy. This is what he wanted. I had no choice. I had to stick by him.

Bob Barrett

As a firefighter, there are times I remember. One time there was a woman. I told her, "I'm going to have to take you down the fire escape because the stairs are still smoking."

She had two heavy bags with her.

I said, "Do you have to carry those heavy bags?"

She replied, "This is everything that I own."

As I was taking her down, she said, "I have a tendency to faint."

I said, "It's going to be hard for me to get you down if you faint."

She told me, "Pretend I am your mother."

We started to descend the drop ladder of the fire escape, and sure enough she fainted. I was holding onto her and the ladder for about 10 minutes until someone came and saw us on the ladder and then assisted. When I got her to the ground and she woke up, she said to me, "God bless you. You are my son."

That was a great feeling. For in my mind, I was thinking of my own mother and hoped that if she were in the same situation that someone would do the same for her.

But one time, I entered an apartment through a fire escape window and found a wall of flames in front of me. I could hear the voice of a woman calling "Help! Help me!"

I approached the flames and got as close as I could. But there was no way I could get to her.

I whispered to myself, "Miss, I'm sorry. I'm so terribly sorry, but there is no way I can get to you."

In my mind, I surrendered to the fact that she was gone. Later on I found out that the rest of my company had gotten her out through the front door. I felt guilty because I had given up. I felt this was unfair in a way that I had to make this choice. This was something that stayed on my mind for weeks and weeks. Sometimes there are choices to be made, and I did not like that choice. It seemed unfair to me that I was forced to make this kind of decision. It weighed heavily on me until I realized that we are merely humans doing a job that requires super human decisions.

Mrs. Kathy Barrett

During those first few days of 9/11 our daughter was very upset. She was crying and having nightmares. I was having nightmares. When Bobby did come home after those five days, we were sitting on the couch watching the news. We all sat on the couch together and watched what was going on. Then it was announced that they found five firemen alive.

Bob jumped off the couch, threw his arms up in the air, and shouted, "I knew it! I knew Dave was going to get out! I knew Dave would find a way out!"

And then we found out it wasn't Bob's Company. I looked up at Bob's face. I started crying. I felt so bad for him.

Bob and Kathy Barrett

Bob Barrett

During 9/11, Richie Synder and I were assigned as Family Liaisons for the Fire Department. We were to let the families know when their loved ones were found. I had never done that before. I guess in one's life there comes a time when we have to make funeral arrangements for a loved one, but who could foresee making arrangements for so many at one time.

The families asked me to notify them personally when a member of Ladder 20 was recovered. They did not want to hear it from a stranger, not even the Mayor. They wanted someone from the firehouse. Somebody they knew.

Perhaps I'm still wondering why I was not working that day. Maybe I'm a little guilty for still being here. But it is left to me not to waste the life that their death has enriched beyond anything I could have accomplished myself. It is their example, their dedication, their heroism, which will be my guiding light for the rest of my life.

Bob Barrett

I had a dream that I was talking to a priest.

And I said to the priest, "I want to be a good guy.

The priest transformed before me, into Jesus.

And Jesus said, "I can't make you a good guy, you have to leave a trail of good deeds for yourself. But I can grant you a wish."

And I said, "I would like it to be September 10, 2001."

And it was.

I was ecstatic.

In my dream, I went to a tavern and started celebrating. But I soon realized that all of the patrons didn't know about September 11. I immediately knew that I had to warn Ladder 20.

I ran to the firehouse and tried to convince my buddies, that when the alarm came in for the World Trade Center, they shouldn't respond.

They said to me, "Bob, are you crazy? We have to go."

The alarm came in at that moment.

They started to jump on the truck.

I paused.

I asked myself, "Do I go with them?

John P. Burnside
Firefighter, Ladder Co. 20
Fire Department City of New York

We used to call him Johnny Menudo because of his boyish good looks. Johnny was a Minnesota Viking fan. We would tease him mercilessly whenever the NY Giants beat the Vikings. At Johnny's memorial, his sister handed out ribbons for us to wear that bore the purple and gold colors of the Vikings. We all wore the ribbons with pride. John had a twin brother and they were identical. It was so strange to see his brother at John's memorial, not only because of his facial resemblance, but he had all the mannerisms of John. It was a constant reminder of my lost friend.

John used to play the guitar, and he would often practice at the firehouse. I would always enjoy listening to him play some of my favorite tunes.

Little do we know at the time what we might miss in the future. We have to enjoy each moment for what it is. Everything is in constant change, and this particular moment stands by itself as a moment that we shall remember.

Capt. John R. Fischer
Firefighter, Ladder Co. 20
Fire Department City of New York

I worked with John Fischer probably one out of every three or four tours of duty. John was an excellent father, and he was involved with his kids in sports. He coached basketball in his community.

He was an excellent cook, and often cooked meals in the firehouse. He used to make Buffalo wings and Chicken Marsala. He was also a "fireman's boss" in the sense that he never forgot where he came from. He was one of us in spirit and in heart. We always felt that we could talk to John like he was one of the guys, because he was one of the guys.

John always worried about the men who were working with him. His concern was that they would all go home safe to their families after each tour. Perhaps it is ironic that John did not return with his men, but I am sure that John is still leading them through their journey, with a flashlight in his hand, and showing them the way to go.

Members of FDNY Ladder 20

James M. Gray
Firefighter, Ladder Co. 20
Fire Department City of New York

I have the image in my mind of Jimmy Gray's nine-year-old daughter speaking at his memorial. I can remember perhaps two lines.

She said, "Daddy, if I knew you weren't coming home, I would have let you tickle me a little harder."

The rest is a blur. There was no more that needed to be said. We sometimes don't realize how such a little thing can mean so very much, a daddy tickling his little girl.

It is up to us to make sure that we don't forget these little rituals, the little things we do for one another, how important they really are. You can't think, "I love you." You have to say it. You can't say, "You know how much I want to make you happy." You have to do it. I think sometimes we are just lazy and do not realize how much we could accomplish by attending to the little things in life.

Here's a little girl who needs her daddy to be there for the little things. This is what we're all about. I'm sure that if I'm remembered for anything, it will be for something rather simple that will be attached to me by those who knew and cared for me. They will say, "That's just Bob."

Members of FDNY Ladder 20

Sean S. Hanley
Firefighter, Ladder Co. 20
Fire Department City of New York

The first firefighter we recovered from my company was Sean Hanley. He was one of the younger members of Ladder 20. Sean came from a large Irish family.

The day we found Sean, I called his family and said, "I'm coming over."

By the time I got to Sean's house on Staten Island, his whole family was there.

I guess I must of looked like a wreck, because his family ran over to me and said, "Bob, cheer up, you're giving us a blessing. You're bringing our son and our brother home to be buried with dignity and honor and respect."

And I knew from that moment that this would be a mission for me, to bring back to their loved ones as many as I could find.

Robert T. Linnane
Firefighter, Ladder Co. 20
Fire Department City of New York

I only knew Bob for a short period of time, and yet, what I remember most about him was his constant smile. Bob smiled from ear-to-ear, and it was such a good thing to see. It kind of gave you uplift. It is no small thing to be able to smile at the drop of a hat. I found that it rubbed off on me and I soon found myself joining in. It made for a happier, lighter moment during the day. I will miss your smile, Bob. But I'm sure that right now, someone is looking at that smiling face and feeling better.

Robert D. McMahon
Firefighter, Ladder Co. 20
Fire Department City of New York

Bobby McMahon had an 18-month old son, and two months after 9/11 his wife Julie gave birth to another baby boy. This was the real tragedy. Two sons will never know their father. Two sons will never learn to ride a bike or hit a baseball with their father watching them and feeling proud.

The hardest part of being a family liaison was the emotional tugging at my heart to see the kids who lost their fathers and the wives who lost their husbands. It was a tremendous drain on top of all the other trauma of this event. No one can compensate for this loss.

Yet, life must go on. Life is just that precious. We cannot be fathers to the children of our lost brothers, but we can be uncles. We cannot be husbands to their wives, but we can be brothers. We must console one another, for we have all lost a piece of our lives.

We must remember it's not what we've lost, but what we have left that counts. Sometimes it is difficult to remember the happiness we felt with each other. But it is necessary to remember the richness of the lives we have lost and not dwell on that loss alone.

Even in the worst tragedies there is a light at the end of the tunnel, a hope, a lesson to be learned. Three hundred and forty-three firefighters gave their lives along with countless of other rescue workers so that we might enjoy ours. We cannot waste this gift. Life is precious, and it is short.

We must live each day as if it is our last chance at happiness. It is said that each of us leaves a footprint formed by our lives. Let us try to make that footprint a little bigger each day. There is no greater accomplishment than one can make than to help someone in need.

David J. LaForge
Firefighter, Ladder Co. 20
Fire Department New York

How do I speak of my friend at a time like this? First of all, I know I shall miss him dearly. We worked together for the good part of 24 years, and for the majority of those years, Dave was in the front and I was his tiller.

He was a quiet man, so quiet that even when he mumbled or groaned at me for not being quite precise in the tiller, I was forced to strain my ears to hear him. Dave, in the front-end of a fire truck, was like a child opening a Christmas gift. He was a Dale Earnhardt driving in the Daytona 500.

He took quiet joy in his absolute mastery as a chauffeur. The rest of us remained in awe. He was simply put, the best chauffeur I've ever tilled for. There was nothing greater than the two of us responding to an alarm at breakneck speed. One time I remember Dave saying to me after such a run, "This is the greatest pleasure I have in life."

I have always said that firemen are really just "boys." Perhaps a gray hair, a bald spot, or events like September 11th, betray our age, but as firemen, we still remain boys. I guess we were kids. I hope we will never grow up.

My comfort is in my belief and knowing that someday God will gather me, and all of us to Him. I have two requests, prayers if you will. That when He has that 0900 Roll Call, and as He hands out assignments, He will say, "Dave you're in the front, and Bob, you're his tiller."

And in the meantime, Dear Father in Heaven, please take care of the Boys.

"Bravest Painting"
Firefighter Poem

Ladder Company 20
John Burnside, John Fischer, James Gray, Sean Hanley
David LeForge, Robert Linnane, Robert McMahon

CHAPTER 31
SEARCH FOR LADDER 4

Mike Bellone
Honorary Firefighter, Ladder Co. 20
Fire Department City of New York

The rain hasn't stopped. It's been raining all day. Jimmy Cody and I came across what looked like the top of a rear mount ladder truck.

I looked at Jimmy and said, "There's no way we can just pull this truck out, because those guys might still be in there or underneath the truck. We have to dig this out by hand."

I had my Gator that day, and something told me this was going to be a very busy long day and night. The process of digging the truck out took over 24 hours. The truck was approximately 50-60 feet below street level. There was a lot of debris and a lot of rebar steel rods hampering the recovery process. The dirt, or debris was tightly compacted because the fire truck was located below the south ramp. For six months, every time a truck went up or down that ramp, it compacted the debris below.

We were digging inside the truck, and the water was sliding down the side of the ramp. It was like a sea of mud coming down on top of us. There was no clean spot to dig. No matter where you went, it didn't matter. The only thing dry, and not muddy were my armpits.

There were so many rebar steel rods that I must have gone through eight batteries just cutting away at the rods. I had to cut the rebar first before anyone could use rakes, gardening dirt-claws, and shovels. We had to be so careful while going through the debris, but my adrenalin was flowing. I knew this was it. We would find somebody.

I must of made 100 trips up and down the south ramp between tool runs, getting rain gear, and candy bars so that we could keep going without stopping. It just seemed to never end. I had met Timmy Lapinski before on the site and at the Belle Harbor disaster, but this was the day that Timmy and I formed a special bond.

We dug through the day and night. When the fire truck was finally taken out of the hole, we took off what is called the truck ID plate for Ladder 4. We hung the plate on the side of the slurry wall.

As the fire truck was dragged out and taken out of the crypt it lay in, I remember hearing its tires pop. There was no sign of the men.

We found nothing but an empty truck. There were no clothes. There were no jeans, as someone previously published in a book about the World Trade Center. We were there. We dug that truck out with our own hands. Why someone would say something like that and try to bring discredit to some of the greatest guys on the face of the earth is beyond my comprehension.

As the fire truck was hoisted up, I made another trip up the south ramp. The widows of the Ladder 4 men were at the top of the ramp waiting to hear any news of their loved ones.

I saw Bob, and Bob said, "What are we going to do? What are we going to say to the widows?"

As I made another trip down the ramp, I went over to Timmy Lapinski and Jimmy Cody.

I asked them if I could cut off the truck's compartment doors and give each widow a piece of the truck. Timmy and Jimmy both agreed. As we began to cut out the empty compartment doors, we loaded them up in the back of the Gator. I brought the pieces of the truck over to the 10 and 10 firehouse. The widows could now have a small piece of something tangible in remembrance of their husband's enormous act of courage.

Finding Ladder 4 sixty feet below street level

I remember meeting two of the widows. My heart was broken for them because I knew what it was like to lose a loved one. After seeing all of the loss, I felt a special part of this recovery. This one somehow struck me differently. I then made a special note to myself that we had to find these men who had left these young, wonderful wives, no matter what it took, or how long it took. We would find them.

Timmy Lapinski and I loaded up Timmy's van with Ladder 4's ID plate along with pieces of the truck. We brought this over to 48th and 8th Avenue that once housed these Ladder 4 heroes. I dropped it off and went back to the site.

I went over to St. Paul's Chapel. I lit seven candles as a light of hope of finding the men. I walked over to my pew and went to sleep. I remember waking up from a call coming over my radio to go to 10 and 10 firehouse. When I got there, the widows wanted to meet me. We created a special bond that day.

After we found the truck, every other week, the widows went down to 10 and 10 and asked me how the progress was going.

They said, "Maybe some day you'll find our husbands.

Ladder 4's truck ID plate affixed to a wall by F.F. Jim Cody, Hon. F.F. Mike Bellone and an iron worker

Tim Lapinski
Firefighter, Engine Co. 76 Truck Co. 22
Fire Department City of New York

It was pouring rain. I got down there, went by the hobo shed, the west hut, and the chiefs were in there.

I heard them say, "Four truck, edge of ring."

It didn't sound like they had found a member.

I went over to where I thought the truck was. I saw the rig and thought everyone who was working on it was gone. I climbed down, and found Squad 18 digging it out. I was with Russ Reagan, John Speck, Jimmy Cody, and Mike Bellone. We were there until five in the morning.

I helped Mike cut the compartment doors off the rig so that we could give each of the widows a door. This way they could at least have something.

They pulled the truck out of the hole and pulled it 30 yards away. I saw Russ digging through the crew compartment and the only thing we found moveable was the ax and the generator.

There were no guys in the truck. We figured the guys dove under the rig. We found nothing. And I don't care what anybody says, there wasn't one pair of jeans around that rig.

By six in the morning we must have made a 100 trips up the ramp. We found the ID plate. We were having trouble removing it. One of the signs was all ready off, and Russ was trying to pull the other one.

I said to Mike, "Get me a torch."

Digging around Ladder 4 for any firefighters or civilians

Mike got a portable torch, and Mike, myself, and an Ironworker tried to burn the rivets off the plate.

We got the plate off and we put it in the Gator. We needed a place to put everything.

We asked each other, "What are we going to do? Put all the doors and pieces of the truck in the Gator?"

You couldn't even tell the crew cab door was a door. I wiped it with my hand. I put that in there, drove up, got the A.T.V., and got it all in my van.

We were walking up the ramp and a guy comes over to me and says, "I'm the Teamster Super. My flatbed drivers don't come in until 7:30. Where can you put all of this?"

We said, "What about 48th and 8th?"

He said, "I'll put this thing in Gracie Mansion if you want. Put it on top of the ramp by the 10 and 10."

The grappler who was working on it said, "My shift ends in 15 minutes."

We had little time.

I told Mike, "I'd rather have him rake back and scoop so that the grappler operator can see if anything's under there."

Mike went over to the operator and asked if he wouldn't mind staying.

He stayed for another 45 minutes to help us after he was supposed to leave.

Top & Bottom: Pieces of Ladder 4 after being removed from the pit

CHAPTER 32
CHRISTMAS AT GROUND ZERO

Bob Barrett
Retired Firefighter, Ladder Co. 20
Fire Department City of New York

I remember discussing with my wife Kathy if we should have a Christmas tree, whether or not it was appropriate to celebrate. I thought it was appropriate, because I felt that those we love and who have gone away would always be with those they love on Christmas Day.

Christmastime at Ladder 20 was bittersweet. On the one hand, we were glad we were with our families during the holiest time of the year. We were also saddened when we looked upon the faces of the wives and children of those we lost. After all, Christmas is a time to remember all our loved ones, those present, and those who have gone ahead.

Everyone walked around all day hugging and kissing and remembering all the different ways our lives had been touched by one another. If one could bottle the warmth we felt on Christmas Day, the world would be a much better place.

Mike Bellone
Honorary Firefighter, Ladder Co. 20
Fire Department City of New York

To me, Christmas Eve is usually the day I buy last minute Christmas presents for my friends and family. I swore that this year I would give the families of the deceased a different kind of present. One that could not be found in a store, but found in the ruins of the World Trade Center.

On December 24, 2001 I was in the pit when I got a telephone call from my mother in Florida.

She told me, "Dad is gone."

I kept thinking that this sorrowful news should have jolted me. It just didn't.

We would be having Dad's funeral in New York, but I asked Mom if she needed me to come down to Florida. I'd be on the next flight. She said no, she'll be coming up and was working on a way to fly up immediately. She said everything was okay. She couldn't wait to see me. I shouldn't worry about her, and continue doing what I was doing.

All of my life I have given my mother a pretty rough ride. I was always the rebel in my family. She always stuck by me, and my decisions, and always gave me support and was there for me. I knew now I had to be there and wanted to be there for her.

I called my brother Alan and asked him if he was all right since my mother had already called him. Alan said he was fine and that we would all get together when Mom came up in two days, the morning of the 26th.

I went to St. Paul's and lit a candle for my father and said a prayer. I also lit a candle for my mother and my brother and asked God, "Please love them as much as I do."

Signs of Christmas

I went back to the site and I dug in the north tower for approximately eight hours. I didn't tell a soul about my father's death.

I got a call from Frank Silecchia, and Frank said, "Let's meet at "the Bubble", Mayor Guiliani is supposed to serve breakfast."

I could hear Frank laughing in the background.

He said, "Come on, Mike. Take a break, this should be interesting."

When I walked through the Bubble door, I saw Frank. That big heart of gold came tumbling out through his big hug. It felt like we hugged for hours.

The press was there with cameras all over the place waiting for Mayor Guiliani to arrive. I hadn't noticed all the cameras until the moment I spoke to Frank.

I told Frank, "I just lost my Dad.

Signs of Christmas

Like a big grizzly bear, Frank swung out his hand, and said, "Get those cameras out of here."

I was then able to have my private moment.

Frank tried to cheer me up by saying, "Here comes Guiliani, he's going to serve us breakfast. This ought to be a real kick."

I pulled myself together, and Frank and I stood in the food line. The Mayor served Frank

264

first and then he served me breakfast. Frank and I went over to a table to sit down. Mayor Guiliani walked around and wished people a merry Christmas.

I never got a chance to visit with Mayor Guiliani because my radio went off and I was called into the north tower. They needed rebar cutter. I must have been down in the north tower a few hours cutting away and helping in a recovery. When it was over, we stepped back a little. I was leaning against one of the barrier walls and Mayor Guiliani drove by in his SUV. He stopped, got out, and he walked over to me.

He said, "Mike, I'm really sorry about your dad, my condolences."

I said, "Your shoes are getting dirty"

He said, "Don't worry about that. Are you okay?"

I told him, "I'm okay. I really appreciate your stopping, it means a lot to me."

Mayor Guiliani continued to walk along the wall and wished some of the workers a merry Christmas.

Frank came down and said, "You'd better get some sleep, Mike."

I went back to St. Paul's. I lit a candle. That candle was for God, for getting me through the day.

Nicholas Gallo
Michael Bellone's Cousin

Mike's mother and my father were brother and sister. Mike and I grew up in different worlds. Mike grew up on the streets of Brooklyn, and I grew up in the suburbs of Long Island. I had it much easier than Mike. We were always good friends. Sometimes you take it all for granted over the years. Mike's my closest friend. We don't see each other everyday, but he is like my brother.

On 9/11 he called me and told me he had gotten down to the site and was getting involved. He felt it was something that he had to do. He felt it was his calling. I absolutely supported him.

Mike said, "This is where I belong. This is where I need to be."

It fit Mike's strengths. He was really focused. A lot of his family didn't understand what he was going through. Mike did a good job there. He found his place. He had a passion about working at the site and felt he was doing something good for other people. I encouraged him.

I told him, "If you feel right about it, stay with it."

Mike was not an opportunist like some people who were at the site. I don't think he ever stopped to think about the total impact of what he was doing. He was just doing it. It wasn't for glory. He was anonymous. He was just there to do what was right.

Mike didn't see the total picture of what he was doing to help people. What Mike saw was a disaster and that people needed help. That's what made it very special. Mike wasn't concerned about what was going on around him; he was just doing his job.

Mike's father had suffered from Alzheimer's for a long time. Mike's father was a really good man, and it was hard for Mike to see him that way. He was very close with his family and had a hard time dealing with it.

Mike's father passed away on Christmas Eve, December 24, 2001. I saw Mike at the funeral and we spoke quite a bit. Mike was very upset about it. I think he was devastated, and I think it drove him to work harder at Ground Zero.

Signs of Christmas

Signs of Christmas
Frank Silecchia
Concrete/Excavation Specialist

I met Michael Bellone around Thanksgiving time during a church service held beneath the cross. On Christmas Eve Michael was contacted and told that his father had just passed away. I was there to bring Michael comfort through his despair, and I went to his father's wake.

I grew to know Michael while we worked on the site. We were both volunteers, and we both had the same mission: to help others. We became very good friends.

This was very important to me. We are all WTC Veterans, and our friendship went beyond being friends. It is a brotherhood. I love Michael with all my heart, and I assume he feels the same way about me. But keep in mind our experience was in hell. We tried to bring comfort to families by bringing their loved ones home. Our future is still to help and save people. It is something we will never forget.

Honorary F.F. Mike Bellone at Rockerfeller Center with a children's chorus

Signs of Christmas

CHAPTER 33
PATH TRAIN STATION
PORT AUTHORITY TRAIN HUB

January 2001

Mike Bellone
Honorary Firefighter, Ladder Co. 20
Fire Department City of New York

At 126 feet below the street level, smoke and debris had settled for months in the tunnels. I was with Tim Lapinski and Sam Elijah. At the escalator track area we found the PATH Train. It was eight cars long. The first two cars were intact. The building had leaned on it and crushed the train. The train was three feet tall.

125 feet below street level. Tunnel leading to the WTC Subway Station

Some railroad cars were crushed so severely that they were only five feet tall

Tim Lapinski
Firefighter, Engine Co. 76 Truck Co. 22
Fire Department City of New York

Mike and I walked down eight flights of stairs to get to PATH Train M. Then we had to walk about a quarter of a mile of track. We had to take the right tunnel because the left tunnel had collapsed. We followed the wall. There was zero visibility. If your flashlight went out, you'd have to just sit there until someone came to get you. I had four flashlights, two on my helmet and two on my side.

We found escalators and trains. It was a mess. The walls and floor were like wet plaster. We had to climb up the escalator because the stairs were full of debris. We went into the commuter bar and the whole roof had collapsed. Every once in a while we'd hear a noise, like, "Is the tunnel going to collapse on top of us?"

Escalator leading to train station

Mike Bellone

We heard creaks and the sounds from up above us. When a creak occurred, sometimes we could see a line of dust come shooting down through my beam off the light from my helmet. I remember Sam holding onto the back of my shirt and saying, "It's okay if you want to leave now. If you want to leave, it's okay."

Timmy and I had been down there before early on in the recovery, and we knew what to expect. We felt for Sam, but we had to keep going.

We walked through a railway car. We got to the next car and the roof of the car was on the floor. It was completely crushed. And within the commuter bar, even though its roof had collapsed, not one bottle or glass was broken above the bar.

Sam Elijah
Photographer

I ran into Mike Bellone and asked where he was going. He said he was going down to do a search with Timmy in the PATH Train area. I asked if I could come along. Mike called to get permission. Permission was granted to Mike because they trusted what he was doing. The PATH Train is a very local train line that provided service back and forth from New Jersey to Manhattan.

Mike, Timmy and I went down an emergency escape stairwell for the PATH Train station. As we were making our way down the stairs I noticed the poured concrete walls. The heavy concrete walls now had major fissures in them. It reminded me of earthquake faults.

It was very dark. Workmen had strung a few light bulbs in the stairwell, and the light bulbs were spaced so that you could sort of see where you were going. I could see the steps, but dimly. We were in a central stairwell that wound around. We wound our way down about one or two flights of stairs.

When we reached the station level, about the eighth sub-ground level, the stairwell opened up to a series of train tracks. We were now suddenly walking on train tracks. The light was still very dim. We used flashlights and our head lanterns to see. As I kept looking at the walls, I couldn't help but think that before 9/11, those heavy concrete walls were smooth and not filled with major cracks.

The first sensation I had was that everything was slippery. It was as slippery as ice. My feet went out from under me. The floor was like silt, but what I was slipping on had to be more than just a mixture of chemicals and dust. I was struggling to keep my balance, and at the same time maintain the camera equipment around my shoulders and take photographs.

When I looked west toward the New Jersey tunnel, it was totally dark, no lights. It felt weird. I had a mask on, but sometimes it came off. I couldn't define the smell.

Hon. Firefighter Mike Bellone used as scale to determine the distance between the floor and the platform

We headed toward the terminal platforms where people had gotten on and off the trains. As we walked, I was dragging behind Mike and Timmy and occasionally stopping to take photographs. I was using a Mamiya 645 camera. I set my photo lens on infinity. I had the camera preset to shoot into the dark. I used a Profoto Battery Powerpac and a ring light to full power. I had initially taken a light reading with a Sekonic 508 light meter.

It was very quiet most of the time; however, periodically when the grapplers in the trucks worked above us, we heard growling sounds. It felt and sounded like we were in the bowels of the earth.

It was very eerie. We walked along in total silence. It was a silence where you could hear your thoughts. You could feel your body temperature. Your senses turned inward, and then all of a sudden there'd be a loud growling inside the earth.

Through the very dim lighting I could see something that looked like powder trickling down from above. It was like you could almost feel the environment moving, and you were standing still. It tested my resolve.

A few years prior to 9/11 I had taken photographs in King Tut's Tomb. I had eerie feelings about that. It was like being someone's home and taking photographs without getting permission from their spirit. I had a very deep respect for those who had perished in the PATH Train.

My whole approach to taking photos at Ground Zero was not to take a million pictures. Only take photographs of deep meaning to me. I lost a friend on Flight 93. Her name is Wanda Green. I say, "is" because I feel that she is still with me in memory.

272

Firefighter Tim Lapinski and Honorary Firefighter Mike Bellone
coming through turn-styles with the floor ripped and mangled

I photographed very respectfully, selectively, and with introspection. To me, it could only be a black and white scene. To me, I was photographing the colors of the rainbow through grays and silver tones, from the darkest black with no detail, to light grays and white with detail.

I had been taking photographs in complete darkness. When we reached the train station platform, and I was facing west, there was some light. I looked toward the end of the platform and saw an elevator lift. I took a number of photos because I could see what I was photographing.

When I developed the film a couple nights later, I noticed that I had spots on the negative. I used a magnifier and I still saw spots on the photos. I was disappointed, because I thought I hadn't washed the film thoroughly.

I looked at the next frame, and that one didn't have the spots. But then another frame did have the spots again. And so on.

I thought it so strange. It was so sporadic. Spots on one frame, no spots on frames that followed, then spots again. I called Mike and left message, "I have strange spots on the film."

He called me back the next day, and said, "Yeah, I know."

I asked, "What do you mean? How do you know I have spots?"

He said, "Well, I get that all the time with my camera when I take pictures down there."

Apparently Mike was getting the same phenomenon. Octagonal shaped, translucent spots.

Photographically, I've dissected it over and over again I don't have an explanation. It's not dust. Dust would be opaque not translucent.

At the distance the particles appear, the spots would have to be the size of a large rocks or boulders. On the platform there was enough lighting. Certainly we would have seen rocks or boulders floating in the air. I had kept the same aperture, the same I had preset. There was no dust on the lens. I do not have a photographic explanation for the spots.

The next day, I showed a friend the film phenomenon.

He said, "Oh, yeah. I didn't tell you that we had found the remains of those who had died of affixation at that location."

It was a haunting experience for me. I am still haunted by the magnitude of devastation. Eight-inch thick slabs of concrete now the size of pebbles and grains of sand. The crumbled, twisted, office-memorandums strewn throughout the site. There is no way to fathom what those who were unable to escape experienced.

Mike Bellone

About two weeks later I was asked to go down and do an air test in that area. I saw Sam and asked, "Sam I'm going down to the PATH Train do you want to take a walk?"

He gave me a dead stare and said, "Not in this lifetime."

Hon. Firefighter Mike Bellone doing a search in the PATH Train Station

CHAPTER 34
CORTLAND STREET STATION

I remember going into the Cortland St. station, unlike the PATH station, this station was 40 feet higher, though still underground. The amazing part that I saw was the girders bent from the collapse. This train station took the brunt of the collapse compared to the PATH station whereas the girders in the PATH station were not bent. Though both stations had severely collapsed, the Cortland St. station had no victims.

We walked in to the station just below street level . As we walked in, it appeared that the station had been evacuated safely because it was closer to street level. The 18 foot ceiling had collapsed to about 10 feet. There was not a lot of debris above the station so we never felt at risk for further collapse.

Honorary Firefighter, Mike Bellone at Cortland Street Station

Cortland Street Station

Cortland Street Station

Cortland Street Station

Cortland Street Station

CHAPTER 35
SIX-MONTH ANNIVERSARY

March 10, 2001
Mike Bellone
Honorary Firefighter, Ladder Co. 20
Fire Department City of New York

We were watching the CBS special on the six-month anniversary of Ground Zero hosted by Robert DeNiro. We sat in a store a few doors down from the 10 and 10 firehouse on Liberty Street. It was just chiefs, firefighters, some of the construction workers, basically the key players that had been there for a while. I was sitting with Chief Riches and Jimmy Cody.

We watched the show, and after the show was over about midnight, I received a phone call. It was my brother Alan telling me that our mother had passed away.

You could tell in everyone's face that they didn't know what to say.

I said, "Let's get back to work. We have to finish up what we started a few hours ago.

6-Month Anniversary Twin Tower lights

Everyone came over and gave me condolences. At that point I was just numb.

I went over to the west hut where we proceeded to come up with a plan, and we went back to work. After being with these men for six months, a conversation was not needed. Just by looking at each other we had our conversation. Now we could move on and do our work.

I went to St. Paul's Chapel that night. I lit one candle for my mom and one candle for my dad. I knew that the two of them were together, which is where they belong, and where they wanted to be.

I was so wound-up I couldn't even sleep. I just sat in the pew where I normally sleep and reminisced about all the good things my mom and I did together and all the values she installed in me. That's probably why I am who I am today.

That morning we were ready for the six-month anniversary. At 8:47 a.m. they said the First Prayer of the Cross. At 9:05 they said another prayer. And at 10:29 they said a final prayer.

I was with Chaplain Mitties DeChamplain, Chief Ron Werner, Chief Kaletta, retired Lt. George Riley, retired Lt Dennis Oberg, and Eric Joyner, HAZMAT Specialist.

I could feel it in everyone's eyes that they didn't know what to say to me. I knew that they all understood my loss. They knew that I would have to go through it again, what I went through on Christmas.

Memorial Mass in front of the cross at Ground Zero

This time, unlike Christmas, Bob Barrett was away. Jim Cody had to stay on the site. Still, I found myself surrounded by all of my friends and this new family I had met at ground zero. At my father and mother's funerals many of the people from the Fire Department, and many people from Ground Zero and St. Paul's attended both funerals.

Jimmy Cody wanted to come down, but I told him he should stay at Ground Zero because one of us had to stay there. We both couldn't be at the funeral at the same time. My dear friend Chaplain Mitties was with me both times, and said beautiful prayers that I will always remember.

But what stood out in my mind the most was Father Chris Keenan, the new FDNY Chaplin who took Father Mychal Judge's place. He sang the most beautiful song I will never forget. Although I lost both parents within a very, very short amount of time, I gained a large family in even a shorter amount of time.

They can never replace my parents, but they sure come close.

L-R - Hon. Firefighter Mike Bellone, Lt. George Reilly, Chief Warner, HAZMAT Specialist Eric Joyner, Chief Kaletta

Six month anniversary towers of light

CHAPTER 36
MEN OF LADDER 4 FOUND

Capt. David T. Wooley

FF. Joseph J. Angelini Jr.

FF Michael E. Brennan

FF Michael H. Haub

Lt. Michael F. Lynch

Capt. Daniel O'Callaghan

FF Samuel P. Oitice

FF John J. Tipping II

March 12, 2001

Mike Bellone
Honorary Firefighter, Ladder Co. 20
Fire Department City of New York

I knew right away. I could see it in everyone's eyes. "Today" would be a phenomenal day with recoveries. A bunker jacket had been spotted in the south tower.

Chief Rasweiller and Jerry Summerville led us into the south tower ramp, and you could just feel the presence of the men who were there.

Jerry said, "Mike, get as many batteries as you can. Get as many saw blades as you can. Pack your A. T. V. with as many tools as will fit. We're going to need them."

I drove up the ramp and went to the 10 and 10.

I said, "Tommy, I need everything you got. Every battery you can find. Every saw blade you have stashed away back there. We need it now."

Tommy ran frantically throughout the tool room gathering batteries and saw blades and picks and spades. I jammed them into my A.T.V. and headed down the ramp.

I saw Mike LaRosa.

He said, "Mike, if you can start clearing this area out first," and pointed to a section that was full of rebar.

Mike LaRosa
Retired Firefighter, Squad 252
Special Operations HAZMAT
Fire Department City of New York

It was like digging up a cemetery and finding your friends. That particular day was a warm, hot day. It was hard on the men to do the recoveries. Mentally it was exhausting because most of the guys knew the people they were recovering. We found the men of Ladder 4.

Members of Ladder 4 during prayers

Tim Lapinski
Firefighter, Engine Co. 76, Truck Co. 22
Fire Department City of New York

We were digging by hand. Mike Bellone was bringing the tools down in an A.T.V. We constantly needed batteries for the rebar cutter. The rebar was thicker than your thumb and with some of the small rebar cuttings you constantly needed new batteries.

Mike Bellone

I must have gone through 10 batteries. I could feel my arm tightening up because the 18-volt rebar cutter is very heavy. It snaps a rebar in seconds. We had to make it easier for the firefighters to get to the jacket. I wanted to assist them in any way I could.

They were calling for sifters. I drove up and picked up a half a dozen sifters to bring down so we could look for any remains and personal property . . . any and all signs of evidence leading to the men of Ladder 4. We kept sifting through the dirt searching for any other small evidence or property that belonged to the men. I couldn't get emotional. I had to stay focused. There was a lot going on and it was happening fast. It was, "Mike, come and use this sifter. Go over here and use that sifter. Come over here to cut rebar."

I remember when we came across the first member. My heart was racing, the first thing I though of was what my Mother told me: that she prayed and God told her they would be found. I felt how ironic it was that she had just passed away and I was led to the Men of Ladder 4.

Members of Ladder 4 in the Honor Guard

Mike LaRosa

We took a front piece off a fireman's helmet before it disappeared into the bags. Once we lost something to a bag, it was never to be seen again.

Mike Bellone

We kept sifting through the dirt searching for any other small evidence or property that belonged to the men.

I couldn't get emotional. I had to stay focused. There was a lot going on and it was happening fast.

It was, "Mike, come and use this sifter. Go over here and use that sifter. Come over here to cut rebar."

Mike LaRosa

When we found the guys, their company came down to the sight to watch. The members of the company then carried their friends up the ramp. The ramp was lined on both sides with Honor Guard. They were saluted until they were placed into the ambulance and taken away.

Mike Bellone

As items were brought out, the Honor Guard began filing in up on the ramp. I drove up the ramp in my ATV. When I reached the top, the wife of the firefighter whose helmet we found ran over to me and hugged me and we both cried.

After the Honor Guard, Mike LaRosa and I took the front piece from the firefighter's helmet to the medical examiner's hut to try to clean it up before giving it to his wife.

Mike LaRosa

We took all the pieces that had been found over to the medical examiner's hut. We then took the front piece to a De-con (decontamination) to make sure it was safe, so that it wasn't contaminated. It was then taken to the firefighter's wife.

Mike Bellone

That day did not end until 4 in the morning when I went to St Paul's. I lit seven candles, and I thanked God for that gift.

I lay down in my pew, closed my eyes, and just waited for the next day to start. With the passing of my mother the day before, I knew that she couldn't have left yet . . . without leaving me this special gift of assisting in finding the men. It couldn't have been a better gift. She couldn't have left this world without giving me the greatest gift she could imagine.

In memory of Ladder 4 men.

Capt. David T. Wooley

Lt. Michael F. Lynch

Capt. Daniel O'Callaghan

**Firefighter
Joseph J. Angelini Jr.**

**Firefighter
Michael E. Brennan**

**Firefighter
Michael H. Haub**

**Firefighter
Samuel P. Oitice**

**Firefighter
John J. Tipping II**

Members of Ladder 4 in the Honor Guard

Members of Ladder 4 in the Honor Guard

Members of Ladder 4 in the Honor Guard

Firefighter John J. Tipping II led by his father Jack Tipping and brother-in-law Joe Milne

CHAPTER 37
NOAH

Noah Silecchhia
10-years-old/Ground Zero
Frank Silecchia's Son

I was at Ground Zero with my dad for four days. I worked with him and stayed with him because my mom was away. I miss it. I miss being there. But is it wrong to miss it? I haven't talked about this. It feels wrong, because it was such a horrible tragedy. I'm not happy about what happened, but sometimes I feel like I miss it.

But in listening to my dad, and listening to that question, I started to understand that it's not bad if you keep it, the missing it, to yourself. While I was at Ground Zero I was meeting new people who were kind and who respected each other and me. They related to what I was thinking about or feeling during that time. When I was at Ground Zero and talked to someone, I was talking to someone who was feeling the same way I was.

In a way, I guess I'm lucky. I was able to meet all those people and know them. Others who were outside of the fenced area tried to get a glimpse of what was happening on the inside. They couldn't see what I was able to see. Sometimes I could tell that people felt cut off, like they weren't part of it. They were striving to be a part of it. They were trying to look in from the outside, but because I was down in Ground Zero, I witnessed what other children or even older people will never see.

The second time I was at Ground Zero, I watched my dad do some of his work. I watched him and how he reacted when he saw the people he had met at Ground Zero. My dad made a lot of friends down there. While I was there, I was learning some lesson in life.

I learned that even though you don't know somebody for a very long time, that in spending just a little bit of time with them, it makes you realize just how much faster you can get to know people. It can be like you've known that person for years.

It was weird. As time progressed, and I was with my dad more at Ground Zero, I became part of it. Before I knew it, I was sitting in the Bubble, the lunch area for the workers. I sat with volunteer workers, firemen, policemen, PAPD… that's the Port Authority Police Department, and basically everybody in law enforcement or in just regular life. I listened to them talk about how they thought things might get better. They talked about how hard it was for them to deal with so many deceased family members. When they found someone, they tried to figure out "who is this person" or part of a person. They talked about how sorry they felt for the family whose body it belonged to.

On one of the four days I was with my dad, I watched him on Fleet Week when the ships came up the Hudson River. My dad comforted the sailors who were coming back from fighting the war on terrorism. The sailors were feeling sorry for the Ground Zero workers. When I think… really… that the sailors didn't even realize that they were the people going out there and risking their lives for us.

The sailors sat with my dad and talked with him for hours upon end. One sailor gave his dog tags to my dad. My dad was overwhelmed that this person gave him such a monumental remembrance. Another sailor gave my father the medal he won for saving somebody's life in a fire. To me, that person was extraordinarily kind, but, then again, my dad was giving them the same thing by comforting them.

My dad talked about the cross he found. How he had to fight to try to save that cross and keep it at Ground Zero. And now, anybody going to the Ground Zero site can see that cross. My dad worked really hard at saving it so that people could look up at the cross, pray when they see it, and remember their families. If my dad hadn't fought to save that cross, who knows what would have happened to it.

I watched the news and I heard all about the controversies, who discovered what, or who they thought put their name on something they didn't actually find. To me, I get angry and annoyed over it, because I know the truth.

When I watch the news, what I see is that most people are disguised or are shadowed by the real thing. Maybe the news people can't show the whole story, because it can be so sorrowing or make your spirit down. I know that the news people and the anchors have to accumulate a story. Maybe they can't put on the news what people were really going through. Maybe they can't show exactly what happened.

For instance, when I saw Mike Bellone on the news during 9/11, I said, "I know that guy, that's Mike, my dad's friend."

They told Mike's story, but they didn't tell it in its actual entirety. The public didn't know what I knew. They didn't know the real Mike. The public didn't know what was really happening at Ground Zero.

They didn't know that Mike could sleep standing up because he was so tired from finding all of these heartbreaking artifacts.

They didn't know that I didn't see my father for 10 months.

They didn't know how Mike's family felt when they couldn't see him or be with him.

They didn't know that a lot of the time in those 10 months, I cried because I wanted to see my dad. My dad always told me on the phone, or when he came home, that he loved me. He always brought me a present, but a present doesn't make up for a dad.

There are things people can't say, because they don't know the families or the friends of the family. When they look at the workers that were on the news, they can say, "Wow, those people are great workers."

But for whoever is watching, they don't know that these people are fathers or mothers or cousins or sisters. They don't know what the families went through by missing them.

CHAPTER 38
THE CHILDREN

Bob Barrett
Retired Firefighter, Ladder Co. 20
Fire Department City of New York

Mike and I had discussed with one another the need for visiting a school and speaking to the students about 9/11. We wanted to help them with what we had learned. We knew the kids had a million questions about what happened, and we felt that someone who had been there could be helpful in alleviating some of the doubt and fear. I also knew that when I thought about speaking in front of an audience . . . that represented fear to me.

I had never spoken to an audience of more than several people. I wasn't sure if there was something I could actually do, but I knew it was something that had to be done. I asked and prayed to the Holy Spirit to help me formulate my words. That gave me the confidence I needed to speak out about what I had learned.

Mike spoke to his friend, Justina Schiano-Romano. He told her that we would like to come to her school and speak to the kids.

Robert Crawford with the children

Mike Bellone
Honorary Firefighter, Ladder Co. 20
Fire Department City of New York

I stopped by P.S. 226 to see my friend Justina Schiano-Romano. I asked her if she would mind if Bob and I spoke to the kids in her class. She thought it was a great idea. When we spoke to the kids, they had some of the most unassuming questions. It really made me think before I answered.

"Why did God let this happen?"

"How did you feel when it happened?"

"What did we do to them that made them do this to us?"

"Will it happen again and, if it does, do you think it will happen to me?"

Those were the questions that have frequently come up whenever and wherever we speak. After being in Justina's classroom for 20 minutes and answering questions, I asked Justina if it would be possible to speak to the rest of the school.

She discussed it with her principal, Mr. Porter. She said that she would put an assembly together. When the word got out, that we were doing this, Whitney Casey from CBS News and Chris from CBS's 48 Hours, wanted to come down and film what we were doing. When we got to the school that morning, Justina did an excellent job on the assembly. The school Color Guard followed The Star Spangled Banner. Then her Glee Club and her orchestra sang a number of songs. Justina said some moving words, and Mr. Porter followed.

L to R: Honorary F.F. Mike Bellone, F.F John Masera, F.F. Bob Barrett, HAZMAT Specialist Eric Joyner

Bob and I started with questions and answers. We told the kids how important they are to us. Every time we asked a question and we received a correct answer, we rewarded the child with a firefighter patch. This got the students more and more involved with what we were saying and expressing. The questions came pouring out, and you could tell that these children had had these questions on their mind for a long time. When it was over, Bob and I realized how therapeutic it was for us, too. We had to search our hearts for the answers the children needed.

Stephen P. Porter Principal, P.S. 226
Alfred B. De Mason School Brooklyn, NY

Mike Bellone and Bob Barrett were a firsthand experience for the students of Alfred B. De Mason. They were from the Fire Department and had expertise in the area. For the children to see men who were actually involved was so much more meaningful and important than any movie, story, or anything we could have done for the students.

We decided to have a special assembly so that Mike and Bob could come and talk to our students. We notified all the parents that Mike and Bob would be speaking to the second grade classes up to eighth grade. We told the parents their permission was needed and that photographs would be taken.

The teachers sat with their students, and the kids were very excited. The children were intrigued and honored that Mike and Bob came to our school. For the students to be able to talk to these men, ask questions, and to shake their hands, was probably the most single valuable experience for the children that entire year. The children will remember Mike and Bob's visit for the rest of their lives.

Mike and Bob also provided a really positive role model for the students. These are men we had seen on TV and in the newspaper. These are the same men who came to our school to tell our children that they were the most important things in our country. This empowered the kids. It gave them a positive reason to continue in school, to continue to learn, and to follow these role models that were willing to share with us.

Mike and Bob gave us information on the World Trade Center itself. You could have heard a pin drop when they were speaking. There were hundreds of students in that auditorium raising their hands when Mike or Bob asked a question. The kids got excited when they gave the correct answer. Their reward was a Fire Department sticker or a patch. If the answer was right, they received a patch. The teachers came up afterwards and asked Mike and Bob for extra stickers, a sticker for every child.

Mike and Bob were open to any and all questions; "How tall was the World Trade Center? How many floors? How much steel?"

Mike and Bob had samples with them as to what the questions referred. The younger ones wanted to know, "How many floors? How high up? How many feet?" Some of the answers from the younger ones were, "Twenty feet. Eighty feet. A million, five-hundred thousand."

We held two assemblies that day. During the second assembly, CBS wanted to videotape Mike and Bob. During the CBS 48 Hours taping, the students asked some different questions the second time around. They asked about Hiroshima. Mike and Bob told them that Pearl Harbor lost almost the same amount of people, 3,000. Just as with Pearl Harbor, it was a surprise attack here in New York. There were similarities. At Pearl Harbor they raised the American Flag, and at Ground Zero the American Flag was raised.

The children asked if Mike and Bob found anyone alive. They were curious as to why it happened. "What did we do to them that made them do this to us? Why didn't glass cut people? How did Mike and Bob feel? Were you scared? Were you angry? Will it happen again?"

Mike Bellone
Honorary Firefighter, Ladder Co. 20
Fire Department City of New York

One thing that Bob and I tell the children is, "People weren't jumping out of buildings."

We explain to them that the people fell from the towers. They didn't jump. People didn't have time to make a conscious decision on taking their own life. There were too many obstacles; people were scared, injured, lost, frightened or upset. They didn't know which way to go or how to get there. With all that going on, they didn't have time to think about how to take their own life, they were thinking about how to survive.

Kids need to know that jumping is NOT an option. Wait for rescue to come.

The press wasn't there. They were blocks away. One hour and forty minutes passed before the public saw people at the windows. What the press saw were people trying to survive. At 1,400 feet high there is air turbulence. The smoke wasn't rising. It was going side to side because the wind speed was 40 miles per hour or more within the building and the air. There was absolutely no visibility whatsoever; it was dark with no floor in front of them. People were walking and suddenly there was no floor beneath them.

Some of the people who looked as though they were jumping had already expired from the impact of the plane. Some of the bodies were sucked out of the building. This was reported as "jumping." The skin of the building was so hot that people could not hold on anymore. They had to let go and those people fell, they didn't jump.

The World Trade Center towers were made of glass and steel. Had a plane hit the Empire State Building, the plane would not have penetrated the building. Because the towers were made of glass and steel, the large windows created vents for the fire to keep going. When the South Tower started to implode, the outer part of the building banged against the North Tower. Everything in the towers disintegrated.

Bob Barrett
Retired Firefighter, Ladder Co. 20
Fire Department City of New York

After we were done talking at P.S. 226, in seeing the reaction that we received - the hugs, the smiles, and the expressions on their faces - it was as though lights were being turned on. I felt a great deal of satisfaction. This told me that what we were doing was good and important, and I wanted to do more of it. In fact, I wanted to go out and speak to everyone who wanted to hear our message.

Our message is that even in the midst of tragedy there is good that can come out of it. Life is precious and we have to make the most of it. Each child is a special person and is like a jewel that has to be polished and cherished. Children need to know just how important they are. They are our future. They are our meaning to life. Our children are the heroes of tomorrow. The children asked questions that, to me, revealed some of the things that they had been thinking about for a long time. "How did you feel on 9/11? Were you afraid?"

As I thought about the answers, I knew that I had to speak from my heart and answer the questions, not only because they were asked, but also because it was a medicine for me as well as for the children. We needed to make that contact between us. We needed to tell them that two big guys like Mike and myself were scared. We were confused. We were hurt. We had felt all the feelings that the children themselves felt. We were all, big or small, merely human beings. Once we had made a connection between our feelings and theirs, we noticed faces lighting up and smiles of recognition coming from the children.

Basically, there were only variations of the same question, the theme of which could be covered with a handful of answers. It was broken down, over and over again, wherever we traveled, into a search for one's feelings. It is a matter of respect; a matter of love and emotions. These questions had to be answered from the heart. After 90 minutes of speaking, I found it to be quite a draining experience emotionally. I was tired after speaking for any length of time, but it was a good sort of tired. It is like a job well done, where one could lay his head on the pillow at night and feel peaceful.

Firefighter Bob Barrett and Hon. Firefighter Mike Bellone at a library in Wisconsin with the children

Julie Franco Volunteer
St. Paul's Chapel

In March 2002, Mike Bellone started talking about visiting schools in the New York five boroughs, and bounced ideas off me about how to develop and organize a plan to reach out to children.

Friends and family throughout upstate and northern New York had realized the importance of what Mike and Bob had to say about Ground Zero. They also saw, and continue to see, the importance of empowering our children on how to respond during a traumatic situation. Education is a critical component to responding to a critical incident.

In July 2002, I was inspired to assist Mike and Bob in their presentations throughout New York State. This eventually led to visits in other states. Interested parties contacted me with information, and I worked with those involved to set up presentations ranging from one day to one week. This involved presentations in schools, churches, day camps, hospitals, firehouses, and other service organizations.

Because of this need and the importance of educating others, Mike Bellone founded TRAC Team (Trauma Response Assistance for Children).

In witnessing their presentations, and the children's reactions the moment Mike and Bob walked into a classroom, you could see that the children were immediately comfortable in revealing their fears and anxieties. They eagerly raised their hands in order to have their questions answered and to express their emotions.

Mike and Bob very carefully and deliberately address each child. They make each child feel validated and let them know that their questions are important. Mike and Bob also convey the message that the cards, letters, and supplies that were sent to Ground Zero were greatly needed and made a real difference in helping with the relief efforts.

One story in particular is when Mike and Bob learned of a young boy in Buffalo, New York, who baked and sold cookies to raise money for Ladder 24. We then made a surprise visit to the young boy's school. He and his fellow students felt honored by the FDNY. This is just one example of what Mike and Bob will do to help children feel important and to let them know that, no matter how old you are, you can make a difference.

Jay Schnitzer, M.D., PhD
Massachusetts General Hospital
Department of Pediatric Surgery

I met Mike and Bob about a year later, in September of 2002 at MIT in Cambridge. It was a special remembrance day at MIT to honor people from the Boston area who had helped out in New York following 9/11, and to honor all individuals involved for their work during 9/11. Gail Willman and others organized the Remembrance Day, and Mike and Bob were invited as honored and distinguished guests and presenters. I was also invited, because they knew of my work with the NDMS. There were other people on the program as well.

I met Mike and Bob at that event and, as part of that, we arranged for them to visit of the pediatric patients at Massachusetts General Hospital and the Shriner's Burn Hospital. We just clicked and became good friends. I was incredibly impressed and moved by their presentation. I was then really blown away by the way they interacted with the children in the hospital wards.

When I would walk into a hospital room and tell the sick children that Bob and Mike came from New York to visit them, their faces would just light up. And when I became more familiar with their story, and the details on how long they stayed at Ground Zero - how hard they worked, and what they went through - I was just totally in awe. My closing slide, when I give my presentation to various groups, is a "Thank You" slide for the number of people and groups that truly earned thanks on a number of levels. I also mention the heroes of 9/11, and

Mike and Bob are the real thing. They're the real heroes.

Since then we've kept in touch on a regular basis. Mike and Bob have come to Boston several times, to visit the hospitals again and to see the children in the wards. They also speak at area schools, including my daughter's elementary school. When Mike told me about his plans for TRAC Team and related work, I was very enthusiastic and excited. When he asked me, somewhat shyly, whether I would be willing to serve as a board member on TRAC Team, I instantly said, "Yes!" I was honored, surprised, and pleased by the opportunity to be involved with TRAC Team.

Mike and Bob have an enormously important message for children, in terms of emergency and disaster preparedness from an educational standpoint. And equally important, they have a phenomenal ability to pull from the children their fears and concerns, about 9/11 specifically and disasters in general. They talk with the children in such a way that you can watch the children relax and become less anxious and less concerned. Over my career, I've witnessed a lot of clinical reactions between caregivers and pediatric patients with respect to emotional and psychological issues. I can say without hesitation that Mike and Bob have a real gift in terms of how they interact with worried children and how the children respond in such a positive way to that interaction.

I think it's crucial that they have the support to be able to continue their mission of talking to as many children as possible. They have a phenomenal message and a phenomenal ability to communicate it. I also admire their incredibly humble and unassuming attitude, and I refer to them as the real heroes. They refer to themselves as just a couple of regular guys.

Honorary Firefighter Mike Bellone with Boy Scout Troop in South Florida

Nicholas Gallo
Mike Bellone's Cousin

What Mike is trying to do with TRAC Team is to let people understand what really happened at Ground Zero. Sometimes people don't understand the impact of what all took place down there. There are so many who don't know what happened, and Mike is a person who can tell them.

At schools, Mike's able to answer kids' questions. He's sharing what he experienced with a lot of people. He's very good with kids, and they feel comfortable hearing it from him. Mike has a good way of answering. He tells them the truth.

What Mike and Bob are doing with TRAC Team is good. This is something that can't be forgotten. Sometimes people just go on with their lives, and 9/11 is something that needs to be remembered. For Mike personally, this is the best thing that's happened to him. He's trying to give back and share what he knows. Mike didn't plan it, but he walked out of Ground Zero with a lot of experiences. He needs to tell his story.

CHAPTER 39
CUTTING THE LAST BEAM
THE BEGINNING OF THE END
May 28, 2002

Mike Bellone
Honorary Firefighter, Ladder Co. 20
Fire Department City of New York

The Cutting of the Last Beam ceremony was to start at 7 p.m. Bob and I were there all day working, looking for any last minute bone fragment, identification, anything that could be turned in.

Bob and I needed to be alone with the beam. As ridiculous as that sounds, this was our time. In the center of the beam I put my mother and father's name on it in remembrance that, while I worked here the whole time, they were my immediate loss. Bob did the same. We just stood there and watched the beam as it stood tall and proud, and we both knew that it was really over.

We lined up at 7 p.m. and we gathered around the beam as the ironworkers cut the beam down. It was placed on a flatbed tractor-trailer and tucked away for the ceremony on May 30th. We then had a ceremony of our own.

The firemen lined up on the ramp to honor the construction workers and the contractors for all their great work, cooperation, dedication and loyalty. As I remember all those men walking up the ramp, I remember everyone stopping to shake my hand. I must have shook 200 hands that night. The fact that everyone stopped just to say "thanks" to me was probably the best feeling I have ever had in my whole life.

Afterwards, like a bunch of high school kids, we were hugging and kissing and exchanging phone numbers. And unlike high school, to this day, I still speak to all those men with whom I shared a very unique and traumatic experience.

It was a nightmare that you never wanted to dream, but never wanted to end.

Bob Barrett
Retired Firefighter, Ladder Co. 20
Fire Department, City of New York

The hardest part was that it was coming to an end. This had been on our mind. For nine months we were a family and now we didn't want it to end. It was bittersweet. There was nothing left to search, but we didn't want to leave because we didn't find everybody.

We knew we would never forget one another. We went around meeting and greeting and we told each other we'd always remember the work we did at Ground Zero. We promised each other that we would never lose contact. This was an event that had formed an alliance with people from all different backgrounds and walks of life. We had become one. Out of this tragedy we had formed a bond that will never be broken.

Top & Bottom: Preparing to exit after nine months

303

L to R: Honorary Firefighter Mike Bellone and Firefighter Bob Barrett in front of the last beam

L to R: Firefighter Bob Barrett, Mayor Mike Bloomberg, Hon. Firefighter Mike Bellone

L to R: Honorary firefighter Mike Bellone, FDYN Chaplin Chris Keenan, Firefighter Bob Barrett

Closing Ceremony
May 30, 2002

Mike Bellone

It was very hot. The families were coming in by the hundreds. Bob and I stood right behind Mayor Guiliani and Mayor Bloomberg near the west hut. I remember hearing the bagpipers play. I started to feel chills running up and down my body.

I knew it was over, but I still felt it wasn't over yet for me. We only found 189 of the 343 firemen. I felt like I wanted to dig right through the concrete with my bare hands just to find one more person.

The truck drove up the ramp with the last beam as the firemen saluted in the form of an Honor Guard for the last time. As the truck passed and the men on the Honor Guard were ordered to fall out, they followed the truck down West Street. Bob and I joined in that line and walked down West Street. I saw the widow we had given the front piece of her husband's helmet to, and we hugged and we cried, and I told her, "If you ever need a brother, I'm only a phone call away."

I couldn't think of a better person to end that last day with. I walked back to the church. I lit my little candle and I prayed for all those people who we didn't find.

Bob Barrett

On the last day we paid respects to one another and went over all that we had accomplished during the nine-month period. We laughed, we cried, and we deliberated over the whole time period of time. Again, the hardest part was that it was coming to an end, but really, it will never end. All the time we spent down there, will always live on. Even in 10 years, those nine months are somewhere in the back of our minds. Those moments made an impression on us that never be erased.

The Closing of St. Paul's
June 1, 2002

Bob Barrett

On the last day Mike and I stood together at the pulpit in St. Paul's Chapel. Mike delivered the closing speech. He spoke for all of us. We just wanted to acknowledge all those who had done such a significant job during that time period. Everyone had made such a tremendous impact.

St. Paul's, after all, was a rescue for all of us. It was a place where we could find rest, recuperation, and say a prayer. It was a place were we could feel the support from all our fellow American citizens and people all over the world, most of all through the letters from children from schools all over the country.

St. Paul's was a place we went to, to get in touch with not only our God, and ourselves, but to hear from our fellow human beings from around the world. St. Paul's provided us much solace and we were going to miss this wonderful refuge. St. Paul's will remain that special place for all of us for the rest of our lives.

Mike Bellone's Speech

Goodbyes are never easy. All of us would agree that September 11th has changed our lives in many different ways. However, in the aftermath of this great tragedy, during almost nine months of a rescue-turned recovery operation, St. Paul's Chapel reached out and touched us all, providing much needed spiritual and emotional healing.

Volunteers with heavy hearts wore smiling faces and worked tirelessly night and day providing hot food, snacks and drinks during our 12-hour shifts. Cots and blankets were provided so we could get some much needed, though troubled sleep when we were too physically exhausted to go on. And encouraging words and hugs were given when we were too emotionally exhausted to go on.

St. Paul's also provided podiatrists, chiropractors, massage therapists and counselors – all very much needed and very much appreciated.

From the beginning, amidst all the rubble, St. Paul's stood proud and tall and whole as a symbol of hope and as visible proof that miracles can happen; that good can overcome evil, and that God did not abandon us in our hour of need. In His mercy and wisdom, He left St. Paul's Chapel standing, and He's been working through St. Paul's ever since.

How comforting it's been to be able to step inside this Chapel 24-hours a day and light a candle or say a prayer and then walk out again into the dust and rubble feeling somewhat renewed.

What better reminder that God lives in this Chapel as He does in all our hearts. With God all things are possible and He will continue to show us the way as He's done through the efforts of St. Paul's.

He has shown us, through St. Paul's, that we are stronger than the enemy, that we can overcome evil together, and that we can accomplish this through the power of love.

The directors of St. Paul's allowed the walls and pews and even the gate outside to be decorated with banners, cards, and letter of love and support from people all over the country and world. It's been this overwhelming outpouring of love and support that helped heal us during our recovery efforts and encouraged us to keep going on and giving more whenever we thought we had no more to give.

Although our work here is finished, and we've done all that could humanly be done, many of us will still carry the scars of this enormous tragedy and these emotional nine months for many years to come.

But, we'll also be carrying with us the love that we found here in this blessed Chapel. We'll be able to look back on many warm memories of the love shown to us mostly by strangers, and the many friends we made along the way, some even lifelong, but all of them vital and necessary in aiding our efforts.

If New York is to heal, and the country as well, it will be as a people united together in love, the kind of unity and love that was shown to us here in St. Paul's Chapel. St. Paul's set the tone for this healing process. It's up to all of us now to continue it.

Hon. Firefighter Mike Bellone giving his farewell speech

CHAPTER 40
HONOR

Mike Bellone
Honorary Firefighter, Ladder Co. 20
Fire Department City of New York

Throughout the course of my work at Ground Zero and my friendship with Firefighter, Bob Barrett, I spent a great deal of time at the Ladder 20 Firehouse on Lafayette Street. We spent many hours together at Ground Zero, all looking for missing firefighters and civilians. Out of respect for my work and dedication, they bestowed upon me an Honorary Firefighter award in June 2003.

The ceremony took place in the Ladder 20 Firehouse, with Division Commander John Coloe, Captain Weldon and the firefighters of that house. They honored me with an official certificate and Line Card.

This event humbled me and made me feel more connected to the FDNY since this award is rarely given. I worked on the site with the utmost respect for the Department and those who were lost.

Julie Bellone

I received a phone call from Mike and could tell by the tone of his voice that whatever he was about to tell me was very important. He started talking about the men from Ladder 20 and the camaraderie that they had shared since working together at Ground Zero.

He then told me that he was asked to attend a special ceremony at the firehouse though he was not sure quite "what was up." He knew that various FDNY chiefs and firefighters had sent letters of commendation to the FDNY Headquarters though he was not aware of any specific recommendations.

Michael called me immediately after the ceremony and told me that he had received the Honorary Firefighter award and certificate. I couldn't have been more proud of him to be rewarded and recognized for something that meant so much to him. He has cherished this honor to this day.

During 2002, Mike Bellone and Bob Barrett spoke to over 700 schools, organizations, hospitals, emergency services, houses of worship of every denomination, and more, in an effort to teach, educate, and empower our children throughout this great country and world, and to thank them for their prayers and heartfelt support, and to also teach them the importance of preparedness.

Ceremony at Ladder 20, inducting Mike Bellone as an Honorary Firefighter, Ladder 20

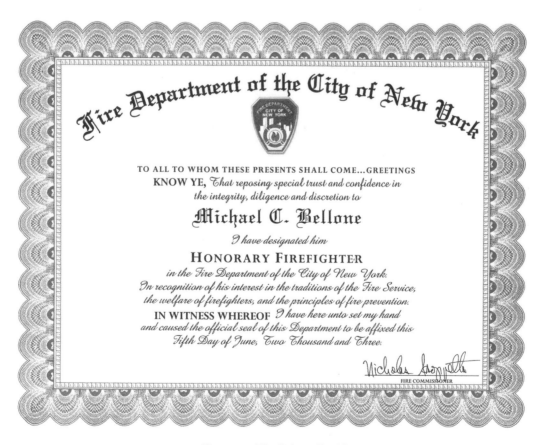

Honorary Firefighter Certificate

Division Commander John Cohloe, Hon. Firefighter Mike Bellone, Firefighter Bob Barrett, Captain Weldon

CHAPTER 41
CONNECTIONS - A NEW FAMILY

Kelly A. Cox
Base Manager Flight Service
Logan Airport
Boston, Massachusetts

I met Mike about a year after 9/11, when one of my staff members – Denise Doherty (a Flight Service Manager) attended a voluntary workshop on Post Traumatic Stress Syndrome as part of her own educational development program and enrollment. While there she met several responders from Ground Zero who learned she worked for American Airlines (AA) in Boston. A few of them told her about this guy, Mike Bellone, who worked at Ground Zero as a volunteer from the first moments of the tragedy up to the last day that the site was open. Mike had told people he wanted to meet some of the American Airlines people from Boston. He felt a particular need and connection since he found the remains of one of our Flight Attendants, Sara Low (AA #11).

Kelly Cox and Hon. Firefighter Mike Bellone

Hon. Firefighter Mike Bellone and Firefighter Bob Barrett

Hon. Firefighter Mike Bellone, Julie Bellone, Firefighter Bob Barrett, Kathy Barrett

Denise came back from her weekend workshop all excited to learned of the many amazing feats of the men and women at Ground Zero, and especially to learn about Mike. She felt a strong connection and desire to talk with him. They had numerous telephone conversations that she shared with me along with a special invitation to come to New York to meet him and his colleagues from TRAC. He told her she could bring whoever she wanted from our group. She extended the invitation to our Flight Service Staff, which included about 20 managers and staff support. As you might expect, the reaction was very mixed. We were so entrenched with the post-9/11 activities; people were in different emotional phases of processing what happened. This was such a shocking and personal situation for us in Boston – we knew all the crew members, and also from AA #77 to hit the Pentagon. This was our airline, our people, our friends, our colleagues … It was our tragedy and loss – so it's not surprising that only a few of us had an interest in going to New York at this time. We were all doing our best to "move on" in our professional and personal lives.

Denise really wanted me to go with her. I honestly didn't feel the need, but wanted to be supportive. I never felt the "pull" to go to Ground Zero – it was too much – my world that day (9/11) was all encompassing to take care of the flight attendants and their families – I needed to keep myself from taking on the enormity of the situation. But Jim Sayer also wanted to go and I felt that was the right thing to do. Jim was one of the three people on the phone with one of our Flight Attendants (AA#11) – Amy Sweeney. Jim, along with two other staff members were able to obtain information from Amy that turned out to be key pieces of info that the FBI and authorities were able to piece together who was involved and what had happened onboard.

Firefighter John Masera, Hon. Firefighter Mike Bellone, Firefighter Bob Barrett

Firefighter Jeff Viola, Captain John Viola

315

So Denise, Jim and I headed to New York in the late afternoon and planned to stay over night and part of the next morning. Mike had all the arrangements for pick up, site visit, hotel, etc. We had no idea what we were embarking on for this visit, other than meeting someone that found one of our flight attendants (Sara) and a man that was amazing to have worked at Ground Zero for nine straight months – everyday! Especially knowing that during this time, he lost his mother and father to illness and still went to work.

Mike and his motorcade escorts picked us up at LaGuardia airport during rush hour and we got into the city in record time. You would have thought we were VIPs – that was how things started. He brought us to the TRAC office downtown and began to show us the artifacts from Ground Zero. It was very emotional – he had a piece of our airplane (AA Flight 11). To actually see and touch the fuselage was very overwhelming for us. It made things real. He also showed us other items and told us about their group, and especially him and Bob Barrett, going out to schools and talking to children about what happened as a way for them to heal.

HAZMAT Specialist Eric Joyner

The TRAC group then took us over to the Intrepid and we were part of a private reception that evening onboard. He introduced us around and we met so many incredible individuals. Each of their stories was more powerful and inspiring than what we can ever understand in terms of the scope, size and reach of what happened on 9/11. We later had dinner at the Holiday Inn on Wall Street (Mike knew the staff well), and had an earlier start the next morning to go to Ground Zero.

At this point Ground Zero was closed to the public, but Mike was able to secure access. It was a pleasant sunny day (not a lot different from 9/11) and we stood on this hallowed ground without saying very much to each other. We each had to take in what was happening – a very personal process. We saw the names of our crew members and the thousands of others that perished that day. Again, the enormity takes over. It's more than what a human mind can comprehend or absorb. My heart was heavy and hurt for the loss of so many lives and the loved ones left behind. Then a white butterfly flew by us, as if to say, "It's okay – we are okay. Life is here and the positive spirit will prevail." That was such a powerful moment.

We also went to St. Paul's Chapel, where Mike and the recovery workers sleep and ate. He showed us the pew he slept on. What strikes me most was when we were outside the chapel and read the timeline of events; it showed when the first plane hit (our plane) and up to the rest of that day with the United plane, tower collapse etc. What stood out was the fact that this historical day started much later for New York than it did for me and us in Boston. My timeline, our timeline, was much earlier – it started when the crew checked in for their flight. Our event timeline was when the plane took off and shortly thereafter when two of our flight attendants, Amy Sweeney and Betty Ong, called into our office and System Operation Control (SOC) to inform us about the high jacking and stabbing of our first class flight attendants, Karen Martin and Bobbi Arestegui, and an unnamed business class passenger.

HAZMAT Specialist Eric Joyner and Firefighter Lou Chinel

It was hard for me to grasp anything more than what we dealt with in Boston. But coming to New York, in spite of my personal hesitation, ended up being a wonderful experience. It made me (and us) think beyond just our piece of the tragedy. It was much larger – we actually knew that all along – but it made me accept it that way. Somehow that was helpful and an important piece of my own process of recovery.

So we spent a whirlwind 24 hours with Mike in New York and the four of us made a pact to stay in touch. How could we not? In some way, I knew we also helped Mike. He needed to have that connection with people that knew Sara, and we did. =Mike gave us a copy of his book and came to Boston some months later with Bob to visit the kids at the Shiners' Burn Hospital. They would make field trips to the hospital, as well as visit schools around the country to tell their story about 9/11. Bob and Mike didn't know each other before 9/11, but became best friends during those nine months at Ground Zero. As Bob tells the story, he lost his best friend (another firefighter) that day, but made his new best friend – Mike.

It still amazes me to think about what Mike, Bob and thousands of others did that day in trying to rescue and recovery the thousands of victims. I don't know how they did it, day after day. I have tremendous respect and admiration for what so many people did in a time of need.

Hon. Firefighter Mike Bellone, HAZMAT Specialist Eric Joyner and Firefighter Jimmy Cody

Mike, Denise, Jim and I stayed in touch and become true friends. Yes, we have a mutual bond due to the circumstances – but more importantly we now have a real friendship – a care and concern for each other.

Denise and I were able to visit Mike and Julie at the New York State Fair one year and later at their wedding a couple of years ago. What an honor and privilege to share in their journey and how they were connected at St. Paul's Chapel. Over the course of these ten years, I have gained an even greater appreciation, love and respect for Mike and Julie in all that they do to keep the message of hope alive. In spite of his worsening illness – he continues to reach out to help others and Julie is there every step of the way in supporting him.

He now is driving his special 9/11 fire truck around to various events and even drove to

D.C. for a special dedication at the Pentagon last year. He always invites me and I was able to join him in New York for the 2009 remembrance. That was another amazing moment. It was a rainy, cold day and we actually got stuck in the tunnel before the bell rang at 8:46am(?). But once we did arrive into town, I was able to get out and through the private family entrance after I introduced myself to the security supervisor. In the sea of thousands, I was able to stand there for a few minutes listening to names being called out. Then for some reason I looked to my right and there was Mr. Low and Allison (Sara's sister). The three of us just looked at each other and then hugged. Sara's name was about to be called and we stood silent. Then I left them to be with their thoughts.

Pepper Burruss and Hon. Firefighter Mike Bellone

Just earlier at St. Paul's Chapel, I was walking around inside and sitting still to say a prayer and saw on the table of photos – Sara and then Karen. I felt their spirit, their presence. Especially Sara – perhaps she was trying to say to us (her family and me) that she's okay now and that's why she brought us together at that moment in time. Her spirit, her energy, her smiling face that touched so many was there in strong force that day. When I got back into the truck – I had to tell Mike what just happened. We both had tears in our eyes. There have been so many moments like this since we have met. There are no words that adequately explain them – and we don't need to – we just both know. It's an unspoken acknowledgement of how and why we are connected. It just is.

Denise, Jim and I have also had these moments of clarity and spirit. This was often at odds with others in our office, sadly. What I have learned, among many things, is that if you are a spiritual person, self evolved and open – there are endless possibilities of how energy and spirit can appear. This has been proved time and time again. I feel blessed to know this and welcome this into my life. I have been provided everything I need when I simply allow myself to experience what will happen naturally. Allow me to share with you why I was where I was on 9/11 and why I was placed there. There are no accidents, no coincidences – only reasons to explain how fate brings us together.

Mike's positive strength, in spite of his declining health, is what keeps me focused on remembering 9/11. It's painful to relive the moments, but we should never forget, not one of us. It would be disrespectful. That's why I don't call 9/11 any year an anniversary – that sounds like a celebration, although I know the real definition means "to turn the yearly return of the date of some event". I prefer "remembrance" to anniversary. It needs to stand alone – 9/11 Remembrance. I find it more fitting.

Joe Adonalfi, David Clayton Thomas (of Blood, Sweat & Tears) and Firefighter Bob Barrett

Likewise, all the events that have shaped my involvement up to this point, including the accidents and incidents are "remembrances" on those calendar dates. Most importantly, I always remember the people we lost, we knew; the families, the friends, the colleagues, the spirit and contributions of each one – that's what I remember, as well as all the care and concern of all the helpers that were there to lend support. I thank you for all you did and continue to do. Mike I thank you!

HFF Michael Bellone
Ladder 20
New York City Fire Department

I received a phone call one afternoon from Denise Doherty telling me her story pertaining to September 11, 2001. It lasted about 2 hours and after our conversation I felt we were friends for years. I invited her to New York City to experience and see first hand how devastating our world was. We immediately bonded and became more than friends -- we were family. Today I stay in contact with Denise and John, but Kelly and I have a much tighter bond, a more emotional relationship. We are now family. I was able to learn so much from her that I began getting in touch with some of my feelings and emotions. Through this event, though tragic with excessive carnage and devastation, I was able to find three people that changed my life: Julie Bellone, Jim Cody and Kelly Cox. It is true what they say, "For every negative, there is a positive."

Hon. Firefighter Mike Bellone and Firefighter Michael LaRosa

Bob Barrett
Retired Firefighter, Ladder Co. 20
Fire Department City of New York

I think the number one effect it may have had on us as firefighters is the loss of the feeling of invulnerability. Prior to 9/11, the New York Fire Department was known for its aggressive, interior attacks on fires. We equally awaited fires with almost a lack of respect for the dangers we faced. I think this made us stand out from other departments around the world. That day, our warranty ran out. We no longer felt invincible. We now knew that the next fire could be our last.

It's not that firefighters didn't die at prior fires. It's not that we didn't care. We just felt so confident at what we were doing. We didn't think that anything could happen to us. No one ever believed they would die. Now the difference is that the possibility of death is so much more real to us than it was before. The question is, is this a good thing or a bad thing? Do we lose some of the luster from our reputation? Does it affect the way we do our jobs? Or does it bring us closer, in knowing that we are not the supermen we thought we were. I hope the latter is the case.

L to R - Julie Bellone, Frank Silliccia, Judy Young, Linda Lawrence

When I used to go to a fire, my adrenaline was pumping. I was looking ahead for what I could see. As soon as the building came into view, I was looking for smoke and signs of fire. I was already planning what I was going to do, what my actions were going to be once I approached the building. Never once would I let any doubt about the outcome of the fire come into my mind. Now I think that would be impossible. Some part of me, as I approach the building, would be remembering what could happen to my fellow firefighters and me. Even though people got hurt, never did we believe, as we were going to a particular fire, that there would be a loss of one of us. We just thought we were that good.

This confidence was instilled by older firefighters who passed it on to the younger guys. As for myself, when I first came on, one of the seniors would tell me about the fires they went to and the precarious situations they had escaped. They passed on their feeling of invulnerability to me. But after 9/11, what guarantees could I pass on to one of the other firefighters? There are none. So where do we go from here? I know, for myself, I would still maintain the same bravado, even in the face of all that has happened, because I believe it is necessary to function as a firefighter on an everyday basis. Doubt creates more chance for injuries than zeal.

At this time in my life, I think I'm able to look back and realize how fortunate I have been; great parents, great wife, great family, great country. What could I possibly complain about? Even in the midst of 9/11, I thank God for the life I have been given. Nothing can ever cause me to take that statement back. I have been rewarded beyond that which I deserve.

Chief Dave Dean, Firefighter Louie Lupo, Honorary F.F. Mike Bellone, Firefighter Bob Barrett, F.F. Phil Doleshal

HFF Mike Bellone
Ladder 20
New York City Fire Department

FF Bob Barrett taught me the meaning of life. We traveled around the country together speaking about September 11 and his whole heart was dedicated to his message of hope, happiness and the will to live. He felt strongly about firefighters and other rescue workers giving their lives so we can enjoy ours.

Capt. John S. Viola
Ladder 15, Engine 4
Fire Department, City of New York

It is hard to believe that ten years have passed since that horrible day. I retired as a Captain in 2003. My son Jeff has since followed me into the FDNY being sworn in in June of 2006 and upon graduation from the FDNY Fire Academy was assigned to Engine 332 in East New York Brooklyn.

Robert Crawford and Jan Snyder

The very same Firehouse I was promoted out of in 1996. From my experience as a recipient of so much goodwill following the attacks on the World Trade Center, I knew I needed to find a way of returning all of the support we witnessed. I was lucky enough to find a group called HEART 911. A group of Firefighters, Police Officers, Construction Workers and Family members, all who had a direct relation to Sept 11. Heart 911 was created by retired Port Authority Police Lt. Bill Keegan. Our mission is to respond anywhere a disaster has occurred. I now serve on the Executive Board and I am the Project Manager for all of our responses both here in the U.S. as well as abroad. In the past several years we have responded to such disasters as hurricane Katrina in New Orleans, the Texas and Nashville floods, Haiti (nine times), we helped rebuild an old shuttered fire house in Brooklyn N.Y. (used to serve firefighters and there families in there time of need) and in 2009 we built a complete home in New Jersey for a severely wounded Marine returning home from Iraq.

Heart 911 has allowed me to continue serving people in need, and at the same time helped others, as well as myself, to heal.

HFF Michael Bellone
Ladder 20
New York City Fire Department

Captain John Viola is a man of many talents. He traveled around the world to help out in disasters in every measure of devastation. He continues to respond through the organization Heart 911. I am proud to know John and honored to be his friend.

Honorary Firefighter Mike Bellone, Sister Grace, Don

Kenny Escoffery
Firefighter, Engine Co. 20
Fire Department City of New York

It's a healing process, with time. Time is helping to heal. Before, even though firemen died, you didn't think that it would happen to you. This number brought it so close to home.

Everyone who's a fireman lost a father, a brother, a son, or a best friend that day. Everybody was hit. Ah, man, that night was so rough. John Burnside's mother kept calling. I was on the watch.

She said, "Be honest with me. Is my son okay?" I didn't know what to say.

It's like you can't close it, because you don't have a body. It's like they all vanished. I keep thinking that I'll see them coming around the corner or sitting at the kitchen table. That is the day most of us try to forget. But we will never forget. People talk about the survivors. The survivor guilt is real. I went through it. I tried not to think about it. Sometimes you wish you were dead. You're glad you're alive, but sometimes you wish you had died with your brothers.

The first year was tough. It was like one long continuous week, and the next thing I knew it was a year. It was one long day.

One incident after another kept George and I from going up further in the North Tower. If we had been in the rear of the tower when it came down, we wouldn't have made it. We actually had the other building to protect us. As big as that building was, you wouldn't believe how narrow the staircase was. One line of people tried to come down, and one line of firefighters tried to work their way up.

Hon. Firefighter Mike Bellone, Meaghan Bellone, Solange "Hollywood" Schawlbe

Bob Humphrey
Firefighter, Engine Co. 4
Fire Department City of New York

The first time I took my 11-year-old son to my firehouse to see what I do was the Sunday before September 11, 2001. It really made me think. What would I have done if my son had been with me that day? What if he had gone on the run? Once you're there, you're there.

It's something that I think about. Every once in a while we take kids to the firehouse to see how their fathers work. Now, I would never do that. The firehouse is so close to where it happened. I wonder what I would have done with my son and what might have happened.

Ralph Shakarian
Laborer

It's so ironic that people have blamed God. They blame people, and they blame each other for what happened. But I want to know, to this day... who is this god of theirs who commanded them to do this horrible thing? The terrorists say they're doing it for God.

I guess I will never know the answer. I have only one wish. I wish that whoever did this, or whoever was the mastermind of this, would come and see what he did with his own eyes. Whoever is responsible should see the damage he caused. Maybe then he would show some remorse. Maybe he would ask himself, "What the hell did I do!"

Linda Lawrence, Kathy Sheley, Rhonda Villamia, Julie Bellone, Sister Grace, Honorary Firefighter Mike Bellone

But life goes on, and there isn't a day that I wake up that I don't have a smile on my face. I thank God that I'm healthy. I have two good kids and I look forward to raising them. I went on with my life, and I hope this never happens to my worst enemy.

Eric Joyner
HAZMAT Specialist

I am still working as a HAZMAT specialist, still an associate for TRAC Team and still suffer the physical and emotional pain ten years later. My Ground Zero Family is now front and center of my life and I feel a better person for it. I heard about the effect Ground Zero has had on many people. I never thought I was one. I lost many Ground Zero Family over the years and expect to lose many more. I hope I can deal with it them as I deal with it now.

HFF Mike Bellone
Ladder 20
New York City Fire Department

Eric has been working very hard, maybe too hard and needs to slow down. He won't admit his physical illness to Ground Zero but has been hospitalized many times and recently had hip replacement surgery. We talk from time to time and he still is as emotional today as he was ten years ago. He is still very active in TRAC Team and does other volunteer events. He still, after all he has been through, has the ability to make all of us laugh with his boyish charm and humor.

Firefighter Mike LaRosa and Firefighter Tom Fenech

Dave Dean
Assistant Chief
Hartland Fire Department Hartland, Wisconsin

On September 11, 2001 our Hartland, Wisconsin fire station was shocked by what was happening in New York City. We immediately started plans to charter a bus to take a group of firefighters from this area to the site. As we gained more information, we were surprised to learn that within a couple of days they already had enough help. They advised us to hang tight, wait for a couple of weeks, and then come. We sent letters and cards of support.

The group from the Hartland Fire Station included Heather Burzlaff, Phil Doleshal, Josh Dibb, and myself. When we arrived in New York we immediately wanted to go to the site. Upon arriving at Station 10 and 10, and as we were standing outside, a great big burly man drove up on an ATV. He was there to get dry socks. He greeted us, explained what was going on at the site, and offered to help us get an assignment.

As he was changing his socks we carried on a conversation. He asked where I was from. When the name Grande Cheese came up, I told him Grande Cheese was only 10 miles north of my hometown. From that moment on, I felt like I had known Mike Bellone for a long time.

You wouldn't know that half of Mike is heart. The caring and compassion he showed us was phenomenal. We were there to help them, and he was helping us.

He gave us a tour of the site and told us where we could pitch in. We spent two days there. We helped hand out supplies to the workers. It gave us great satisfaction just making that small contribution. As the day closed, we were going to be leaving the following day, and Mike said, "Make sure you stop and see me before you leave."

Chief Dave Dean (center)

We met Bob Barrett on the second day. I immediately hit it off with Bob, and he gave us each a hug and thanked us for coming all the way from Wisconsin. They were appreciative of all our work. I gave Mike my business card, and thought I had made a really neat contact and good friend. I was hoping our meeting each other wouldn't end. I invited Mike and Bob to Wisconsin for some relaxation whenever they had an opportunity.

Mike said, "What I'm thinking is that, out of all the millions of people in New York, I meet someone who knows Grande Cheese."

I made a special bond with Mike and Bob and, since that first day I met them at Ground Zero, it feels like I've known them forever.

I didn't hear anything from Mike or Bob for about six months after I met them, which is totally understandable. Then one day I got a call from Mike. He and I picked right up from the day we last spoke at Ground Zero. Mike and Bob wanted to come and talk to our Fire Department and meet some of the people who had sent cards and letters.

Honorary Firefighter Mike Bellone and Pepper Burruss

Mike Bellone
Honorary Firefighter, Ladder Co. 20
Fire Department City of New York

On a very cold day in February, I had just come out of the hole. I was soaking wet. A guy was standing out front of the 10 and 10.

He said, "Hey, do you think you can do me a favor? Can you get me into the 10 and 10? I'm a fireman from out-of-state."

I said, "Come on in."

He offered to lend me a hand and then proceeded to help me take off my wet, muddy gear. We got into a conversation, and he told me he was a firefighter from Hartland.
I asked, "Where is that?"

He replied, "Wisconsin."

I said, "The only thing I know about Wisconsin is Grande Cheese and the Green Bay Packers."

Amazingly, he came back with, "I know Grande Cheese."

Stunned, I looked at him and said, "Of the 300 million people in this country, I have to meet someone who knows Grande Cheese? I used to know someone who worked there," not thinking that anyone would have heard of that company.

For the short time we spent together, Dave Dean, Chief of the Hartland, Wisconsin Fire Department, and I had a special bond between us. We said we would keep in touch and, as time went by, we spoke over the phone. Eventually, Bob and I planned a trip out to Dave's native land of Wisconsin to speak to the children, visit his firehouse, and also see some of the places he had told me about.

Bob and I arrived at Wisconsin's Mitchell airport and were greeted by Chief Dave Dean and Members of the Hartland Fire Department. I was looking forward to talking to the children in Hartland because it had gone so well at New York's P.S. 226 and some of the other local schools.

Bob and I gave our presentation to the chorus of Arrowhead High School who, in turn, sang patriotic and spiritual songs. Their performance was equal to that of a symphony at Carnegie Hall. Bob and I were astonished by their huge hearts, and so far away from Ground Zero. I didn't think that could be topped, but then Dave continued. He took us on a trip north to Green Bay.

On the way up Dave told us that he sometimes sells his milk to Grande Cheese. He thought we should stop in and say hello.

When we arrived at Grande Cheese, we met Nancy Witkowski. We sat in her office and we explained what we did. The longer we spoke to her, the more she felt we should be talking to everyone at Grande Cheese.

Bob and I began our presentation in their conference room with approximately 25 Grande Cheese associates. Towards the end, the owners of Grande Cheese asked us to wait, because they were on their way from a meeting and wanted to meet us.

We went outside on the front lawn of Grande Cheese and took a photo with all the associates. We shook hands and hugged after presenting them with some artifacts from Ground Zero.

Grande Cheese had been affected by 9/11 because they had associates in New York who were affected. Grande Cheese had raised money for the widows and children of the FDNY. My heart will always have room for the Grande Cheese Company.

It seems that no matter where Bob and I go, there is always a connection with whomever we meet. We continued up to Green Bay, and we had a police escort into Lambeau Field - home of the Green Bay Packers. They escorted us onto the field, and we watched the game from the Packers' bench. We formed a special friendship with trainer Pepper Burriss, who then became a lifelong, dear friend.

After the game we headed back south to Hartland. We passed a farm named "Pam and Butch's Farm." Pam and Butch had huge American flags on their silos.
I said, "Dave, we have to stop. I have to say hello to these wonderful American people."

When we pulled up in front, Pam came up and greeted us with a warm hello and a mid-western smile that could light up America. We told her we were from New York City and we were part of the recovery team at Ground Zero. She said that her son had just returned from New York and had sung in the choir at St. Paul's Chapel on Easter, which Bob and I had attended. We all looked at each other, and once again said, "No matter where we go, there is some kind of connection between us."

Pam let us milk her cows, and she showed us her whole milking process. The connection got even greater. Pam sells her milk to Grande Cheese. After a heartfelt goodbye and exchanging numbers, we promised to keep in touch.

We continued south to Hartland. Ten minutes into the trip, we passed a town hall with loads of cars in the parking lot.

I said, "Hey, let's stop and see what's going on here."

As I walked into the lobby, I spoke to a gentleman and said, "I'm from New York and I was curious as to what was going on."

He said, "This is a wedding."

I said, "Wow, I'd just like to give my congratulations, and I'll be on my way."

He said, "Okay, I have to find the groom; he's with some of his firefighter buddies."

As it turned out, the groom was a firefighter. Not knowing who we were, the groom told us, "My one wish is to meet someone who was a part of the recovery from Ground Zero."
God works in mysterious ways. The groom received his wish on his wedding day.
The groom pulled up a table, grabbed some chairs, and said, "You guys do not need an invitation to my wedding."

We gave everyone posters and firemen patches. We danced and celebrated and thanked everyone individually for the support and prayers sent to Ground Zero.
They wouldn't let us leave, as hard as we tried. When we did leave and got back into the car, they tried to put tape over my mouth, because they said, "If you keep stopping at everyplace you see, you'll never get back to Hartland.

The amazing part of this story is: 2,000 miles away, we were in four different places in the State of Wisconsin. In each place we went to, we found a definite connection to Ground Zero. Bob and I knew then that we had to go to every state. This is part of our mission.

Nicholas Gallo and Honorary Firefighter Mike Bellone

Nicholas Gallo
Michael Bellone's Cousin

Mike lost both of his parents, within three months of each other, while making recoveries at Ground Zero. Their deaths greatly affected all of us. Having them pass so quickly was a shock to us.

Working at Ground Zero and losing both parents was a defining moment in Mike's life. I think it scared the hell out of him. But fear never stopped my cousin Mike from doing anything. Mike is a survivor. He was able to bring this trait of strength to the site, and it was needed. They needed people like Mike who could stay with it and not panic. He is also a compassionate person, and he spent a lot of time comforting people at Ground Zero.

HFF Mike Bellone
Ladder 20
New York City Fire Department

My cousin Nicky is my lifeline to my family. He always stuck by me through good times and bad with no reservation or judgment. I love my cousin Nick and of all the relatives in my family. He holds a special place in my heart.

Firefighter Bob Barrett, Chief Dave Dean, Hon. Firefighter Mike Bellone

Vincent LaTerra
Labor Foreman
Bovis Lend Lease

Going through all that we did at Ground Zero - myself, Nunzio Sr., Nunzio Jr., Mario, Felix, and Dean - we grew so close to each other that we wanted to have something to share between us as we went forward in life. Being that I was the "mentor" in the group, they came to me.

The iron cross, found in Building 6 at Ground Zero, meant a lot to us. Each of us decided to have the same replica of that iron cross tattooed on our arms. Like the cross that still stands on the site today, this is a remembrance for ourselves of what we went through together.

As the cleanup of Ground Zero concluded, I had something I had to do before I could leave. On the last beam that was recovered from Ground Zero, I wrote Carl Asaro's name on it. My friend, and firefighter, Carl Asaro was never found.

Lt. Claudio Fernandez
New York City Highway Patrol

On September 11th, I personally worked the next 36 hours straight through. When I was finally able to go home, I kissed my daughter and my wife. My wife had been very scared for me, and she was probably the only sane person I had seen in that 36 hours.

In the months to come, the outpouring of support and resources was unfathomable. It was extraordinary to say the least. On one occasion, civilians surprised us by having organized up to 40 truck escorts loaded with supplies. These civilians deserve so much recognition for their efforts in support of the work we were doing.

Civilian volunteers at Pier 40 felt compelled to give their love and support to all the first responders. How they did this was by simply asking us what we needed, and it was done. The food they brought to us made long days go by a little better. The batteries and flashlights they supplied allowed us to continue our recovery efforts.

There were approximately 10-16 steady volunteers at Pier 40. In some circumstances they actually quit their jobs to make helping the recovery effort their new undertaking in life. Some of the wonderful volunteers at Pier 40 included Diane Buhler, Deborah Vitale, Margie Edwards, and Angie Mericle Newman.

The last week of July of 2003, Angela Mericle Newman died from an automobile accident. At Pier 40, Angie radiated an energy that touched everyone. She was always so uplifting and provided a lot of support. We're going to miss her. She was a true American hero.

When I came home from Ground Zero, my daughter was walking. My wife Pamela was intuitive enough to have videotaped Ashley Nicole's first step and her initial walk from the kitchen to the living room. This is priceless to me; something I will never physically experience but the videotape allows me to see it. My wife recorded many other events, and I'm grateful to both of them. I love them both very much.

Sister Grace and Honorary Firefighter Mike Bellone

Pepper Burruss
Head Athletic Trainer
Green Bay Packers
(New York Resident 1954-1992)
(New York Jets Assistant Athletic Trainer 1977-1992)

The date, "9-11" elicits a myriad of memories, images and emotions. Time has a way of easing the pain of such a day and one wonders if "we will never forget" is possible. Certainly the legendary photos and videos of the day of infamy and months of clean up will serve to remind us all (and teach future generations) of what transpired during that time. I feel a kinship to that time, not by personal loss, but by birth right in New York State, many visits to "The Towers" and now dear friendships with those who toiled at Ground Zero.

Although I did not suffer personal loss that day, I had several friends and business associates who did and I still ache for them as the anniversary dates roll by.

My connection to "9-11" has been cemented by friendships with NYFD/NYPD members and associates I either knew before, or came to know after, that fateful day.

One special bond that fate would arrange when we met during his post 9-11 touring of Wisconsin, was Mike Bellone. Mike has allowed me (and my family) to grow closer to those days, weeks and months through his visits, recollections and especially his book that has grown worn and tattered over the years in my office. NYFD visitors have gifted me several mementos from their service and they are amongst the most cherished and storied in my possession.

Appreciation or history is important to me and as they say " if we do not learn from it, we are doomed to repeat it." I appreciate Mike, and others, who have served to preserve and share those days for they have done well to help us say, "We will never forget."

Jan Snyder
Met Life Insurance Representative

I first met Michael Bellone and the TRAC Team in the fall of 2005, at the Olympia Resort in Oconomowoc, Wisconsin, while I was eating dinner. I was sitting a couple of tables away (the restaurant wasn't busy). Mike and I struck up a conversation. He was in the area holding power point presentations about the events of 9-11 at the local schools. I was very interested in what he was doing and he offered to show me the presentation right there. It took about an hour, and anyone who came into the restaurant became part of our discussion.

It was a very emotional presentation, and anyone who watched it didn't have a dry eye. That was the start of great ongoing friendship. I immediately asked him how I could get him to come to my area to do his presentations. His response was, "Just ask". He spent an entire week with me the next year giving his power point presentation to all the schools in Williams County, Ohio. We did three presentations a day and I couldn't help but cry at each one. The kids at the schools were incredible; all ages were silent and respectful. They were so interested in what Mike had to say that he didn't even have to use a microphone. I was very impressed with Mike and his team. They watched the kids in each auditorium, and if they found one that seemed to be more emotional than the rest they would reach out to them and ask what their story was. One girl had an aunt killed in the towers, so they counseled her right there. They took all kinds of questions and helped ease the kid's fears about the possibility of something like this happening to them. It was a very scary time for children.

Since that time I wanted to do more so I joined Mike's team and have done many volunteer projects with him. It has been exciting and rewarding and has taken me places that I never would have gone and met people that I never would have had the opportunity to meet otherwise. People are still dying today from the effects of 9-11, and we, as American citizens, need to be aware of what really happened. Mike has done a wonderful job informing people about the true events of September 11th. More recently he has been branching out and helping in many other disaster situations, helping people cope. I will always be thankful to Mike for allowing me to be a part of his team. Thanks, Mike.

HFF Mike Bellone
Ladder 20
New York City Fire Department

Pepper Burruss has been a good friend and like a brother to me. He is part of my Ground Zero Family. Although he is miles away, it is patriots like Pepper who answer the call to help when needed. He's a good listener who gets it done and he is as crazy as me. That's why I love him. On a personal note, congratulations to Pepper and the Green Bay Packers for winning Super Bowl XLV, February 6, 2011. You guys are World Champs on and off the field.

Solange "Hollywood" Schwalbe
Office of Strategic Services
Award winning Sound Editor

My dog. Yes my little Whippet, Tallac, saved me from taking all of my migraine medicine really slow so I wouldn't throw-up. I trusted no one to take care of him. So instead I called my doctor that night and he had me in Crisis Counseling the next morning. Soon after that I started taking medication to help me cope. Is this all Ground Zero-based? Ask any doctor. What would they know? How could they know? This is unprecedented. No one knows.

In 2004 I got a teaching gig in the film industry. Right after I got that job, I got my first feature film job since before 9/11. It was called "Taxi" with Queen Latifah. Since then, in spite of the economy, I have been able to continue working as a sound editor and I still teach.

I will never forget. I wear my colors to work at Sony Studios every Friday. I wear my WTC Cross proudly every day. I got the WTC Cross tattoo on my left shoulder. I will never get over it. I will live and breathe Ground Zero until the day I die. I will worship my GZ Family unconditionally.

What would you have done?

I am still living my book.

If I were to write today, it would be incomplete.

HFF Mike Bellone
Ladder 20
New York City Fire Department

With all my illnesses, whether they be physical or emotional, I would do it again and twice on Sunday. If I had to, the scales would tip to the positive. Frank Capra described it right, "It's a wonderful life".

Noah Silliccia

Michael Bellone
HFF Ladder 20
City of New York Fire Department

The first night I met Hollywood I realized she was special. When I found out she was a sound editor for major motion pictures, I associated myself with her feelings and emotions and knew I was not alone for feeling the need to be at Ground Zero every day. Hollywood would talk to me and would open feelings and emotions like Jim Cody, Bob Barrett, John Masera and the rest of my Ground Zero family. She was now one of us permanently. With her quick one-liners, sassy personality and west coast accent and attitude, she was a diamond in the rough. On a personal note, congratulations on winning an Emmy for the HBO series John Adams and Academy Award for Black Hawk Down, for your expertise in sound editing.

Noah Silecchia
10-years-old
Frank Silecchia's Son

On the first day of the first anniversary of Ground Zero, I saw a lady behind me. She had either lost her husband, family member, or friend. She just cried.

I wanted to say something to her, but I didn't know her. I didn't know how she felt inside, and I didn't know if I should talk to her. I wasn't sure if I had been at Ground Zero long enough to really understand how everybody was feeling.

But when I think about it, when I was there and walked around in the debris, and saw more of the reasons why these people were so sad, I began to realize how they did feel inside. I also remembered, even more, how lucky I was because my mother was working two blocks away when it happened. If the towers had fallen sideways, they would have crashed into my Mom's building. My Mom may not be here today.

For everything I saw and learned from the experience of being at Ground Zero, I don't think I would really want somebody to witness what I saw because of the saddening things. But I do think that children, at some point in their lives, really should learn the lesson I learned during the time I was there.

Whether it's in a happy way or sad, the lesson is this: we should all know what happened at Ground Zero and never forget.

David Dean
Assistant Fire Chief
Hartland, Wisconsin

As I have moments to sit and think back of the events of 9-11, I often tear up and think of the tragedy that was brought to our great nation's shores, not only on September 11, but every day since. My heart aches daily as I think back to my first visit to Ground Zero, the "angel's hole" as I like to refer to the site. Not since December 7, 1941 had America witnessed such destruction and loss of life. Safeguards were in place, drills were practiced, but did we not learn enough from Pearl Harbor. Attempts had been made before on US soil and were not as successful. Were we ready? Did we do enough to prepare? Will this happen again? I think of these questions daily, and wonder about the future and what is in store for us as a community, country and nation.

Hon. Firefighter Mike Bellone and Greg Saunders

Firefighter Bob Barrett, Hon. Firefighter Mike Bellone, Jim Cody

I have been involved in the fire service for the past 23 years, serving as Assistant Chief for the past 11, and continue to learn on a daily basis. Training is continuous and ever changing. The world events have changed the way we prepare for mass casualty incidents and the way we run our everyday operations at the fire station. The trainings increase in hopes of being able to protect life and property.

There is no doubt. Not a day goes by without me thinking of the brave men and women I met on my first visit to "angel's hole." Handing out socks to the workers out of Fire Station 10-10, directly across the street from the site. The station was being used as a storage area for supplies. I had Firefighter Heather Burzlaff, Firefighter Phil Doleshal, and Firefighter Josh Dibb along to share the experience. The people I met were simply amazing; the work went on around the clock. Emotions were high as the hopes of finding people alive were discussed openly. The inspiration and support was so uplifting it helped me to become a better person in life, love, happiness and my professional career. Portions of happiness and time spent with family, friends and loved ones is so precious, every minute is so valuable and appreciated.

We have a shrine dedicated to the 343 firefighters who lost their lives that day. We are able to look at it daily to remind us of our brothers and sisters who died doing what they love. I often gaze at the photos and wonder how I would have reacted and how I will react when the ball is in my court. I am sure we have not seen the end to attacks on America's soil, but I do believe we will continue to do our duties as a nation to protect life and property to the best of our ability.

I have days of bitterness and being angry. Most days I am agitated at the events that took place on September 11, from the World Trade Center, to the Pentagon, to the open field in Somerset County, Pennsylvania. The song "Where Were You When the World Stopped

Turning", by Alan Jackson sums up my feelings. "I will never forget" where I was as the events unfolded.

I think of the thousands and thousands of people we are losing every day, not only our great nation's armed forces but the men and women who worked "angels hole" who continue to lose their lives to sickness and disease that the wreckage placed upon them, from the countless hours they put in cleaning up the site.

My second and third trip to New York was an honor as I met more and more families that were left behind. I was able to escort a widow to a remembrance ceremony and enjoyed my visit and can't help but give them my love and support. Many people cope with tragedy and loss in different ways. I like to talk about it and work on educating the people around me on the events that have taken place. I have not been back to New York since 2002, but will look forward to shedding tears and sharing stories with the many great people I have met when I do. I can only hope the next visit will not be to help with a terrorist attack. Do I think it will happen again? I am afraid so. It bothers me daily, wondering what and where it will be. I tell my children Samantha and DJ to live life for today, laugh, love and cherish the time.

Every day I look up at the flag with respect and honor for our country and what it represents. I thank the people who have given the ultimate sacrifice and those who are protecting our freedoms today. My heart goes out to the families who have lost brothers, sisters, parents, sons, daughters, grandparents, aunts and uncles all in the name of freedom.

I thank God everyday for our great country; we are like no other. Fly the flag and be thankful for what we have.

Julie Bellone
Ground Zero Volunteer

Looking back on the past ten years, I am proud of my determination, community service and resilience to support those affected by the events of 9-11-01. Thanks to the support of family and friends, a different life has transformed before me; one that was unimaginable. I have learned that the good people of this country far outweigh the bad people of the world. Patriotism is hidden in all of us and expressed in many different ways.

The most significant event of the past ten years has been meeting and building a life with Michael. Who knew a "country girl" from Northern New York and a born and bred "city boy" would connect on such a level and through such tragedy? We have taught each other many lessons (not just how to use a lawn mower and how to drive in NYC). Mike is one of the most determined people I know, with an undying dedication to complete strangers that have touched his heart. He is an Oak Tree of life that will stand and take the storm, though also be able to shade and protect those he loves. I am a truly fortunate person to have participated in and experienced the events of the rescue and recovery effort. Along with Mike, I have promised to Never Forget those lost and those who continue to die as a result of physical and mental illness related to 9-11. I hope to be an inspiration to adults and children by encouraging them to become involved in serving others in their struggles.

Look up and not down

look forward and not back

look out and not in

and lend a hand.

—E. E. Hale

CHAPTER 42
FINDING DAWN

Dave Dean
Assistant Chief
Hartland Fire Department
Hartland, Wisconsin

Mike and Bob had told me about Dawn Hayford's poem. They wondered if I could help them arrange to meet her personally. I went to work with my contacts, and I put the details in order.

It worked out wonderfully. When Mike and Bob revisited Wisconsin, we went to Dawn's school in Oshkosh, Wisconsin. Mike and Bob gave an hour-long presentation on what it meant to them to have U.S. citizen support, as well as Dawn's beautiful poem, to help them through the Ground Zero recovery effort. Dawn then read her poem. There wasn't a dry eye in auditorium.

The kids were so quiet and attentive during the their presentation. It was an eerie silence. The children's mouths were closed, and their ears were open.

Mike and Bob said, "You can ask any questions you want, because we are here to help you deal with the situation."

It made the children feel very important. Mike and Bob also gave the kids a lesson being good student, being good citizens and following through with their dreams. The kids and the staff were so grateful. They didn't want Mike and Bob to leave. Unfortunately we did have to leave because we had other appointments.

After realizing the response from the kids and the school, Mike and Bob continued making presentations to about 14 other places. As word spread that Mike and Bob were visiting Wisconsin and speaking about Ground Zero and the effects it had on people's lives, the phones rang off the hook. Families were calling the local media to find out where Mike and Bob were speaking next.

Mike and Bob have the wonderful ability to ease the pain and suffering of all school-aged children from kindergarten to seniors in college who may be having difficulties in dealing with the aftermath of 9/11. After experiencing Mike and Bob's presentation, you leave feeling reassured and have a more positive outlook on life.

Mike Bellone
Honorary Firefighter, Ladder Co. 20
Fire Department City of New York

A couple of months later we were asked to return to Wisconsin because of the overwhelming number of requests. We met up with our friend Dave Dean of the Hartland Fire Department. We were excited, because finally we were going to Oshkosh, Wisconsin to meet 16-year-old Dawn Hayford. When Dawn's school found out that Bob and I were actually coming, they were prepared as was the rest of Oshkosh.

No matter how many times you insist that you're just an ordinary guy, they still try to make you feel like a giant. Bob and I arrived at the school almost a year after my phone call to Dawn, which felt like yesterday.

Bob and I got up and spoke to the school, to the parents, and to the teachers of Valley Christian High School. We explained to the kids that it wasn't just Dawn and her efforts, but that it was the team effort. We explained that we not only got letters from Dawn, but letters from schools across the country.

You could see in their faces that they understood what we were talking about, which made it even more special. We read the poem. Dawn introduced herself to us for the first time. We gave each other a big hug.

We brought Dawn some gifts from Ground Zero. It was not a gift from Mike to Dawn, but a gift from New York City to Wisconsin for all their support and letters and cards and banners and prayers that helped us get through 257 days of recovery work.

I was so glad Dawn was excited, because this was not just a lesson for her or the students, but it's a lesson for everyone that no matter how small an act you do, it reflects back to the size of your heart. And that's what makes us true Americans.

Hon. Firefighter Mike Bellone, Firefighter Bob Barrett, Dawn Hayford

Firefighter Bob Barrett, Dawn Hayford, Hon. Firefighter Mike Bellone

CHAPTER 43
RETURN TO P.S. 226
ALFRED B. DE MASON SCHOOL

Mike and Bob revisit P.S 226 in Brooklyn, New York

L to R - Justina Schiano-Romano, Gail Swanson, Stephen P. Porter

The students ask questions:

Student: Why would the terrorists do something like that?

Mike B: They don't like the fact that we have freedom. We have the freedom to choose our own friends and the freedom to go to school. We like our freedom. They don't agree with that. The only way they can get our attention is to do something like that.

Mike B: If you have questions, let's get them out. That's why we're here. When we keep our spirit together, no one can beat us.

Student: The cross that was found at Ground Zero, do you think it was a "sign from God"?

Mike B: That cross is exactly the way it fell. It is what you see.

Student: Do you think they're going to move it? I want it to stay there.

Mike B: We want it to stay there, too. They have plans to keep it there, somehow.

Bob B: I know God was there. Even through the tragedy, we were blessed. God was in our hearts. He gave us good weather to work in. He gave us good people to work with. In nine months of working there, there were no major injuries. God works with us through other people.

Student: If they build another Trade Center will it happen again?

Hon. Firefighter Mike Bellone and Firefighter Bob Barrett in the classroom

Mike B: We've learned what to correct now and how to better prepare. Our technology is advanced. We're on alert. The chances of them penetrating our country are much less.

Student: Do you know my stepfather? He was there. He was a firefighter.

Mike B: I'm sure I do. We were there together.

Student: Why are they trying to kill people?

Mike B: They want to attack those who are free. They don't want people to be free.

Bob B: Remember that the best thing in life is to help someone who needs our help and not to hurt people.

Strategizing the message

Student: Why do people make fun of NASA, the word?

Mike B: NASA is an agency of our government. Does anybody know what happened on January 16, 2003?

Student: The shuttle?

Mike B: Which shuttle? Can you name the five shuttles? The Atlantis, Discovery, the Challenger of 1986, the Endeavor, and the Columbia. Does anyone know what happened to the Columbia? (The students don't know.) Does anybody know what happened? It exploded on February 1, 2003. Does anybody know why? It's because on lift-off the external rods came loose and broke the tiles. Does anybody know what a tile is?

Bob B: Mike and I went into the space shuttle before it went up. We sat in it. It gets to 2,000 degrees without getting hot. It 's like leaving something on a hot stove but it doesn't get hot.

Mike B: We went down to Nagadoshis, Texas. Something happened with America. We came from New York to lend our expertise. That is why this country is so great. We're all one country. No matter what coast, no matter what happens, anywhere we're going to respond, like the Columbia, amongst all that tragedy, lots of good things came out of it. No one else was hurt or seriously injured by falling debris. Tens of thousands of shuttle parts in an over 13,000 square foot area didn't hurt anybody on the ground. We met a lot of new faces and made a lot of new

350

friends. What happens sooner or later when your leave this school, out of any negative experience can always come the positive.

Bob B: One of the lessons we learned is that there is nothing better than to help one another. Maybe you'll decide to go into public service. You can decide what you want to do at any age.

Mike B: We received letters from schools across the country. The letters you sent us kept us going. They helped us to do our jobs.

Bob B: We needed that support at the time.

Mike B: It's the same for the troops in Iraq. It makes a difference. It makes them feel good for that moment. It's not the size of the act. It's the size of the heart. Any act that you give from your heart will make a difference.

Student: Did they feel anything?

Bob B: It exploded immediately. We don't think they felt anything. They were probably not even aware of what was happening.

Student: Where you scared when 9/11 happened?

Mike B: I was scared to death. I ran into Bob. Then I had someone to be scared with. I'm so grateful that I ran into him.

Bob B: When you make a new good friend, you fill your heart up again. My best friend died, but I made a new friend with Mike.

Student: Did you ever find the bodies of the astronauts?

Mike B: Yes, all seven of them were found.

Student: Are they going to leave the cross up?

Mike B: They plan to find a special place for it.

Teacher: How did your families feel during 9/11?

Bob B: They were nervous and upset. My wife didn't want me there. She was crying. She didn't want me to go at all, but she understood that I had to do what I had to do. To me, my wife was a hero. She knew all the firefighters and their families. We felt like parents worrying about our children. A good man always has a good woman behind him. She is my hero.

Mike B: My daughters wailed and wanted me to come home. But then they understood. Between Bob and myself, we found 400 people.

Teacher: I thank you for finding my cousin. That gave us closure. He was on the 107th floor.

CHAPTER 44
TRAC TEAM

TRAC Team

Bob Barrett and I were sitting in a pew at St. Paul's Chapel reading some of the cards and letters displayed on the pews and the walls. "Dear firefighter, I'm sorry the bad people blew up your big buildings. Maybe when you get new ones you should hide it so no one can blow it up." These children sounded so sincere and so emotional that I asked Bob who is looking out for the children. That's when we met Joy Carol. Joy was a spiritual healer and someone you can talk to. She had experience in working for many organizations and heard conversations between me and Bob. She told us we should do something and help guide us. First you need a name so I came up with TRAC (Trauma Response Assistance for Children team). I wanted the word team because working at Ground Zero, we all worked in teams. Joy and Julie Bellone began researching and helped us to receive our non-profit status and put all our paper work in order. After all that, TRAC Team was born.

9/11 Healing Field

Brooklyn, New York
September 7-12, 2007

F.F. Richie Snyder with members of the motorcycle club NYC
Fire Riders who put up 3,000 flags in the Brooklyn Healing Field

TRAC Team at Slidell, LA, for Hurricane Katrina

Firefighter Bob Barrett and Hon. Firefighter Mike Bellone with the Sheriff and Mayor
and Girl Scouts of Nachadochis, Texas, in the recovery of the Space Shuttle Columbia

The TRAC Team Mission Statement

TRAC Team, Inc. is an integrated program of response, preparedness, education and training that supports, protects and empowers children, their families and their communities to deal with critical incidents such as natural disasters, violence, trauma and terrorism. The TRAC Team believes that, especially during difficult times, children have the right to feel confident that their concerns and needs will be addressed. Our children are valuable and effective participating members in the mitigation of critical incidents, and that their decisions and actions related to critical incidents can make a difference. The TRAC Team assists children in their development to become healthy and responsible citizens for our future.

Brooklyn Healing Field

The Program

The National Institute of Mental Health recently reported that research indicates that the manner in which parents, significant adults and communities respond to a critical incident strongly influences a child's ability to recover from it. Parents, teachers, emergency workers and health professionals can help children to be prepared for critical incidents and to recover from such incidents through training and education. Appropriate and timely interventions that protect children from the trauma of critical incidents and support and assist them if they have suffered from such incidents are extremely important in helping children to cope.

Firefighter Bob Barrett, Joy Carol and Hon. Firefighter Mike Bellone

Isabella, Kate and Ian Di Pietro

Building on the already successful work of the TRAC Team with children in schools, day camps, hospitals and universities following 9/11, it is proposed that this work be extended to include all critical incidents in relationship to response, preparedness, training and education. Targeted groups will include schools, camps, hospitals, emergency workers, churches and synagogues, clubs, community groups, medical schools and nursing schools, libraries, Parent Teacher Associations, universities and colleges, prisons.

Five Star Bank Customer Appreciation Day ~ Mike Scaglion, Greg Sarra, members of the branch, Hon. Firefighter Mike Bellone, Julie Bellone, Eric Joyner, Doug Ewell

TRAC Team has traveled to over 20 states, 40 major cities and hundreds of counties, towns and villages in the United States and Canada. They have spoken to hundreds of thousands of children and adults with a moving and stirring PowerPoint presentation and an exhibit with tools and remnants reflecting the September 11 tragedy. The TRAC Team organization has never asked, demanded or requested any funds or donations. If any funds or donations were received, it was clearly made under the discretion of the donator to provide and to help with traveling expenses. TRAC Team has thousands of testimonials attributed to their well-received presentations and thousands upon thousands of letters from children around the country and around the world of thanks and prayer for their message of hope, love, peace and courage. We received hundreds of letters of children joining Fire, Police, Civil Service, and military agencies from the impact we instilled on the children turned adults. Not only is TRAC Team and their associates proud of their accomplishment, but they continue today, ten years later, helping children and adults cope with today's issues, challenges and decisions in life. "God Bless the Children".

Nicholas Gallo
Mike Bellone's Cousin

What Mike is trying to do with TRAC Team is to let people understand what really happened at Ground Zero. Sometimes people don't understand the impact of what all took place down there. There are so many who don't know what happened, and Mike is a person who can tell them.

Captain Liam Flaherty and members of the FDNY Pipe & Drum Corps on Medal Day 2010 in Queens, NY with the 9/11 Memorial Quilt

At schools, Mike's able to answer kids' questions. He's sharing what he experienced with a lot of people. He's very good with kids, and they feel comfortable hearing it from him. Mike has a good way of answering. He tells them the truth.

What Mike and Bob are doing with TRAC Team is good. This is something that can't be forgotten . Sometimes people just go on with their lives, and 9/11 is something that needs to be remembered. For Mike personally, this is the best thing that's happened to him. He's trying to give back and share what he knows. Mike didn't plan it, but walked out of Ground Zero with a lot of experience. He needs to tell his story.

Julie and Mike Bellone at Waterloo Healing Field

F.F. Bob Barrett, Joy Carol, Honorary F.F. Mike Bellone

The 9/11 Memorial Truck backs into its original parking space from 1980 at Ladder 36, Manhattan NY

Hon. Firefighter Mike Bellone and ABC News Anchorman Charles Gibson,
learning to drive the 9/11 Memorial Truck

TRAC Team Members L to R - Carmine Gallo, Jan Snyder, Robert Crawford, Hon. Firefighter Mike Bellone

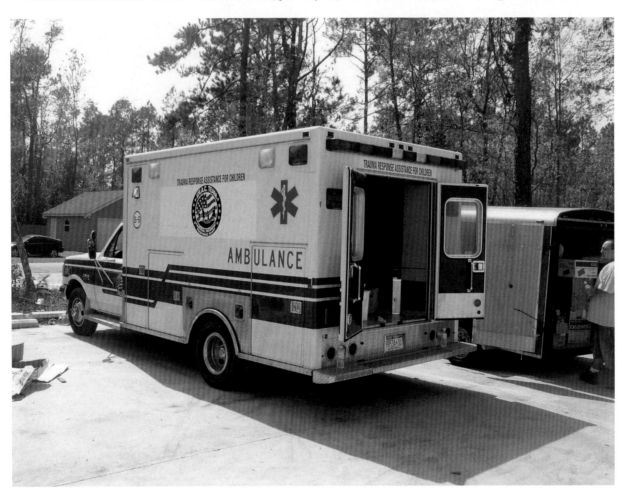

TRAC Team Response Unit #3 dropping supplies for Hurricane Katrina victims

Memorial Truck assisting in raising the flag for a WTC beam ceremony at Arlington, VA

TRAC Team donating a van filled with clothes and supplies to the Tullis family
who lost everything in Hurricane Katrina, Slidell, LA

Hon. Firefighter Mike Bellone recovering a piece of the space shuttle in the debris field

Firefighter Bob Barrett and Hon. firefighter Mike Bellone after finding a
circuit board from the debris field of the Columbia space shuttle disaster

Firefighter Bob Barrett and Honorary firefighter Mike Bellone

CHAPTER 45
DETOX AND CHELATION

Mike Bellone
Honorary Firefighter, Ladder Co. 20
Fire Department City of New York

Immediately after the working at ground Zero, I went to the Medical Network of Long Island to be tested for toxins in my system. My tests show my body has high contents of the following elements: Mercury from florescent lights, diesel fuel, jet fuel from airplanes, Freon from coolant systems, Cadmium from batteries, Nickel, Methane, Benzene, Lead, Ink from toner cartridges, Bleach and Ammonia from cleaning fluids and many more that I cannot pronounce including human remains.

The counts were based on 1-10, one being the lowest, and 10 being the highest and critical. Most of my scores were 10-12 with a few 8's and 9's. There were 65% the toxins in that were a 12. They had to create a new number for me because my body toxic count was so high. I started chelation treatment and did it for a year. I began to realize the chelation treatment was not helping. Many workers were seeing improvement and some were not. Everyone had different exposure at different times and that attributed to the many different ways everyone responded to the treatment.

I then went to the New York Rescue Workers Detoxification Project on Fulton St. in lower actor Manhattan. This was the Scientology project chiefly organized and funded by actor Tom Cruise for the responders. This purification program, designed by L. Ron Hubbard, is designed to purify the body, ridding it of toxins. With its intense daily regimen, there would have to be a total commitment on my part to this procedure, otherwise it would be a waste of our time as well as theirs. This procedure took 4-6 hours a day and committed to 31 days. You could not miss a day. It was very convenient because they had day and night sessions. Bob Barret and I made this commitment together and started our 31 day treatment.

You start with your vitals, they test you to make sure are fit to do this procedure. Next they give you a natural supplement that tasted real nasty, and a lot of niacin. Then you walk on the treadmill for about 20 minutes till your body is red like a lobster, which was a natural , expected reaction from niacin. When we finished walking, Bob and I would get 2-3 gallons of water and step into a sauna box. As we would sit, sweat and we keep drinking. If we began to overheat, there was a shower available for you to cool off. But you must go back to the sauna to sweat more and continue replenishing by drinking lots of water to flush out the toxins in our body.

White towels were wrapped around my legs, arms and on my back. After my session, the towels would have colors on them from the different toxins that were coming out of my pores. Bob and I completed this commitment and this absolutely made a difference.

God bless these doctors and people that responded to the responders who were in physical pain and suffering. This is what America is all about!

CHAPTER 46
TRYING TO MOVE ON

Mike Bellone
Honorary Firefighter, Ladder Co. 20
Fire Department City of New York

Working down at Ground Zero I made not only new acquaintances, new friends and a new family, but a new life. The negative/positive theory works but sometimes the scales are not tipped the way the way you want them to be. Meeting Julie Franco has helped and has saved me from drowning into a deep depression and helped me to see the light. My relationship with my children is great and it gets better every day. My oldest daughter, Meaghan, graduated college, has a good job, has a wonderful personality, and has a great disposition on life. My daughter Maura has wits, poise and is very athletic. She looks and acts like my mother. That is a great thing. My son Patrick is passionate, smart and loves to explore. He is a risk taker like his sisters, and this is part of their high spirit as they respect the gift of life. As for Julie Franco, well we became close friends and later led to a relationship. Our relationship was a little complicated dealing with my health and financial difficulties, but the best part was spending time with the children.

Second from the left: Michael W. Festo with firefighters from Australia

We met December 9, 2001 at St. Paul's chapel where she volunteered and I slept there a few hours a night. Five years later in the pew that I slept on December 9, 2006 I asked the whole church, filled with friends and mostly strangers, if I could use this moment to say something. With her mom present and her sister listening on an open cell phone I asked Julie to marry me and to spend the rest of her life with me. She is now Mrs. Julie Bellone.

Andrew Macchio at Brooklyn Healing Field

There is a negative side to my family. In the past 9 years we have lost 1,040 rescue, recovery and Ground Zero workers due to injuries sustained while working there. Every week there is another brother or sister that we lose and not all injuries are physical. I don't know the exact figures but the amount of self-inflicted wounds is heart wrenching. For many Ground Zero workers, the September 11 tragedy ended in June 2002 when the work on recovery and excavation ended. For me, and I can speak for the hundreds and hundreds of Ground Zero personnel, the Ground Zero event never ended. In nine years I have been to at least 500 funerals and memorials for our fallen families. The heartache never ends. It is emotionally draining. I lost my very close, dear friend Michael Festo, who drove tractor trailers of food and clothing for the Red Cross to Ground Zero. I've lost family, East Meadow Long Island Commissioner Jimmy Martino, my first cousin EMT Joann La Cari and my dear friend from the department of sanitation (the singing sanitation man) Andrew Macchio. Andrew sang at most of my events and had a heart and spirit bigger than the planet. Some were much harder to let go. F.F. Michael Francis La Rosa and I worked together almost everyday. We were very close and talked often. His Fire House Squad 252 never found any of their members lost on September 11. Michael was a very dedicated and loyal fire fighter as well as a husband and dad. The biggest loss to this day, seven years later, is FF John Masera from Engine 331 in Queens. This broke my heart and left me devastated. John was a member of the ATV unit and he and I partnered together often. John and I talked almost every day. I loved John Masera, he was my brother. I was in Florida when Jimmy Cody called me and told me John was in the hospital and not doing well. I flew up and went to see John with Julie and I held his hand and talked to him like always. He died the next day and that left a big hole in my heart. I miss the hundreds and hundreds of Ground Zero Family that have passed on, but the sad and scary part is that this is just the beginning. God bless their souls.

L to R: John Masera, HAZMAT Specialist Eric Joyner, Firefighter Steve Society

L to R: Honorary Firefighter Mike Bellone, Firefighter John Masera, Firefighter Bob Barrett

Andrew Macchio singing the National Anthem at the Brooklyn Healing Field

Bob Barrett
Retired Firefighter, Ladder Co. 20
Fire Department City of New York

Trying to Move On" and "Closure" present problems to those who were closely affected by the 9-11 attacks. We can no more close the book on Ground Zero than we can stop breathing, nor should we. 343 Firefighters, 23 Police Officers, 37 Port Authority Officers, 6 EMS Responders and the many rescue workers sacrificed their lives so that we can enjoy ours. Who would want to waste the gift they have given to us. They have taught us just how precious life is. We shall never close the book on 9-11, but rather turn to the page that remembers how noble and valiant they acted. We can only move on if we carry their memory with us, as for Mike and myself "closure" is not an option. We will never forget.

CHAPTER 47
RESILIENCE

Mike Bellone
Honorary Firefighter, Ladder Co. 20
Fire Department City of New York

As I reflect back on the past 10 years, I see a life filled with, grief, laughter, tears, love and sheer determination to carry on in the name of those lost. I have crossed paths with many people expressing different beliefs and attitudes about the events of 9-11, though have always stayed true to my promise to honor the victims and "Never Forget".

There have been times of struggle when I close my eyes at night and see flashbacks of the scenes at Ground Zero that no person should have to face. Something as simple as seeing a chandelier or a certain chair at an unrelated event will trigger the emotion, the smells and sounds of Ground Zero. I have resolved myself to the fact that these reactions will not cease though with consistent counseling my hope is that the profound effect on my emotions and mental state will lessen. I am working now with my 5th counselor and feel that I have finally connected with a person who is helping me recover. There is a definite "line in the sand" that I will not discuss certain topics with my wife and family and there are also certain topics I have yet to breach with my counselor. On the other hand I still do have a handful of close comrades that I feel I can call at anytime to discuss any memory with, because we all went through it together and they just "know."

L to R - Patrick, Meaghan, Michael and Maura Bellone

L to R: Meaghan, Maura, Julie, Patrick and Michael Bellone

Maggie and Moka Bellone

Aside from the physical and mental health aspects, there have been times of personal trial as well. For example, an incident in 2005: I had been travelling with TRAC Team for over three years offering presentations and an artifact display to various communities across the United States when I received a call from the FDNY headquarters requesting my presence at an inquiry. They were challenging the legitimacy of my non-profit status, accusing me of impersonating a firefighter and alleging my possession of stolen property. It was devastating to me that the department heads would question my motives and accuse me of capitalizing on the very event that has so deeply changed my life. This was an unnecessary embarrassment and attack not only on me, but also on my family and those who have graciously volunteered their time with TRAC Team. As the Department discovered, my non-profit status was verified in good standing with the federal government and New York State Attorney General, my Honorary Firefighter Certificate is legitimate, and the property I possessed was acknowledge by the FDNY counseling unit. My understanding is that this has either stemmed from jealousy of a very few, though apparently influential members of the FDNY and/or my outspoken views on certain misreported events such as the government's original denial of finding the black boxes of the airplanes. It has taken a deep toll on me, given the hard work and dedication that I VOLUNTARILY showed while at Ground Zero recovering their department members.

Julie and Michael Bellone

I have personally purchased and restored a 1981 Seagrave ladder truck and designed this into a moving memorial to the 343 firefighters lost on 9-11. I do not charge for appearances at parades and special events though request the opportunity to offer memorial T-shirts for donations to help offset the cost of fuel and maintenance on the truck. Some have seen this as exploitive of 9-11, though I see it as keeping my promise of keeping the memory alive and it is by no means a profitable venture.

As I look to the future my focus will soon shift to Mike Bellone, the family man, while attempting to place Mike Bellone, the Ground Zero guy, in the back seat. I vow to NEVER FORGET those victims, though my remembrance will take place in a more personal and subdued manner.

In closing, I would also ask that we Never Forget those who assisted in the recovery that have died since 9-11-01 and are sick and dying at this time. This includes close personal friends as well as those I never met, despite our arduous work, to complete the recovery process. I very much appreciate the support of my fellow patriots, friends and especially my family as this chapter in my life takes a new direction.

Bob Barrett
Retired Firefighter, Ladder Co. 20
Fire Department City of New York

Approaching the 10th Anniversary of 9/11, my thoughts go out to the victims of Ground Zero. Mothers and fathers who lost sons and daughters. Husbands and wives who lost their spouses. But the saddest seems, to me, to be the children who lost parents. It's like losing the steering wheel in a car or the helm of a ship. Thinking about the influence my mom and dad had on me. If my mom had handle bars, I would have been a bicycle. How does one survive without that love, advice, and guidance? We can only pray that they have the love of family to guide them through the right path. Love always wins. I send mine to them each night in my prayers. May each and every one of us do the same. Father, take care of them. They deserve no less.

We will never forget—those of us who have so far survived. Till we meet again, remain in awe of all that you sacrificed.

The Barret Family: L to R – Bob, Tommy, Kathy, Sandy, Simone, Kari, Ryan, Olivia